THE six essays which appear in this book were first published separately in the series of University of Minnesota Pamphlets on American Writers and, together with the other pamphlets in the series, are intended as introductions to authors who have helped to shape American culture over the years of our colonial and national existence. The editors of the pamphlet series are Leonard Unger and George T. Wright. Many pamphlets, in addition to the six represented here, are available, and others are scheduled for publication by the University of Minnesota Press.

SIX CLASSIC AMERICAN
WRITERS ⚙ *An Introduction*

edited by SHERMAN PAUL

UNIVERSITY OF MINNESOTA PRESS · MINNEAPOLIS

PUBLISHED IN GREAT BRITAIN, INDIA, AND PAKISTAN BY THE OXFORD UNIVERSITY PRESS, LONDON, BOMBAY, AND KARACHI, AND IN CANADA BY THE COPP CLARK PUBLISHING CO. LIMITED, TORONTO

3 3771

Contents

SIX CLASSIC AMERICAN WRITERS

SHERMAN PAUL

Introduction

THE life span of the writers brought together in this volume is almost two centuries. Franklin was born in 1706; Whitman died in 1892. During that time, the epic events of our history occurred: the creation, in rebellion and war, of a nation from diverse seacoast colonies; the exploration and exploitation of the West, its settlement and closing frontier; the fratricidal War of the States; the conquest of an agrarian-mercantile society by industrialism, urbanism, and finance capitalism; the diversification of immigration; and the centralization of a corporate-collective life. During that time the democratic vistas that had been opened by the statesmanship of Franklin's generation and that Whitman still proclaimed in 1871, in his famous essay, were, on his own testimony, considerably foreclosed. Yet during that time, our literature, so closely identified from the days of revolution and independence with national pride and destiny and chosen by Whitman as a saving spiritual force, came of age. Literature itself, during those centuries, became an acceptable calling; and our literary wealth, contributed to by many writers as different in their ways as those presented here, was sufficient to constitute a tradition — a tradition or store that subsequent generations, come to criticism, in varying degrees found "usable."

The notion of a usable past was first advanced and applied in repudiating much of that tradition by Van Wyck Brooks in *America's Coming-of-Age* (1915). His work, and that of his generation of critics, reminds us of the inevitable, ongoing cultural process by which a selective tradition is determined. We do not use all of our past, just those portions we find useful — or relevant, to employ the vibrant word of our time. Like James Harvey Robinson, the proponent of a "new" history, we stand in the present looking back to the past down the perspective of our need, and we judge the past by conferring our attention on it. This is right, having the sanction of vital interest.

But for any given moment in history this intensely focused seeing cancels much of the past that an awareness of selective tradition-making should make us grateful for having readily available, like the seldom used books of a library. In Brooks's first account of our usable past only Whitman, of the writers under consideration here, was found worthy. As his associate Lewis Mumford said, "one might remove Longfellow without changing a single possibility of American life; had Whitman died in the cradle, however, the possibilities of American life would have been definitely impoverished." The test for inclusion is stringent, defined by the belief of a particular generation in what Croly had called "the promise of American life" and in the writer's essential role in its fulfillment. Not art so much as artistic or creative personality is the test demanded by this generation in search of exemplary men and creative life styles. Yet, as Brooks realized later when pressed by other needs and historical occasions, he had excluded too much, or perhaps defined usefulness (a dangerous category to apply to art) too narrowly. He eventually learned that before one can select *a* tradition he must have *tradition* in all its fullness. For the past also becomes usable when we understand it fully and turn to it in itself as an object of concern, as an essential legacy or ground, valuing it because in this way, beyond the pressure of immediate event, it may become more richly ours and, in Whitman's phrase, "filter and fibre" our being.

Of course it is convenient, especially in the presence of such diverse writers, to determine worth by means of a single touchstone. This seems to be a critical alternative to the inclusiveness of literary history or the generosity of an "American Pantheon" (the phrase is the title of Newton Arvin's collection of essays on nineteenth-century American authors). There is often an engaging incisiveness in the limited approach, as critics like Vernon Parrington and Paul Elmer More demonstrate in their treatment of these writers in *Main Currents in American Thought* and *Shelburne Essays on American Literature* (the title of a recent collection of More's substantial work on American writers). Parrington's populist-democratic Jeffersonian perspective, for example, provides the measure of the following appraisals: Franklin ("Yet considered in the light of social revolutions, what other figure in eighteenth-century Europe or America is so dramatically significant?"); Irving ("An incorrigible *flâneur*, Irving's business in life was to loaf and invite the picturesque"); Emerson ("A free soul, he was the flowering of two centuries of spiritual aspiration"); Thoreau ("one of the great names in American literature," "the severest critic of the lower economics that frustrate the dreams of human freedom"); Whitman ("the most deeply religious soul that American literature knows, the friend and lover of all the world, the poet of the democratic ideal to which, presumably, America was dedicated," "a great figure, the greatest assuredly in our literature"). Parrington dislikes Irving's Tory sensibility and Longfellow's aloofness from politics ("he was not made for battle"); he approves in Franklin the self-made democrat and triumphant man of affairs, in Emerson the transcendental critic of politics, in Thoreau the transcendental economist, in Whitman the active Enlightenment faith.

More's touchstone is ethical rather than political. He treats writers as texts in a preachment of New Humanist doctrine, and this doctrine provides the moral test of their character. His fundamental critical concern is to distinguish between what he considers the lower and the higher planes of imagination. He finds the former in Franklin's service to the present and to the utilitarian and in Longfellow's sentimentality (and presumably that of Irving, whom he does not consider); he finds the latter in the spiritual reach of Emerson, Thoreau, and Whitman. To merit More's approval a writer must have a profound sense of "dualism, or duplicity in human nature" and be an initiate of the "mysteries of experience." Thus, though Franklin is warmly appreciated as the possessor of "an intellect enormously energetic," he is not accorded a place in literature. Having used his remarkable literary skills to "practical rather than literary ends," he showed a "real deficiency in his character," the lack of "the deeper qualities of the imagination" that More, in contrast, found in Jonathan Edwards. Franklin's bagatelles are praised ("They show what was lost to pure literature") but not the *Autobiography* ("a document in petty prudence and economy"). Longfellow, a genuine man of letters, is said to lack "the inward check" and to have "imported into Cambridge the sentimental note that runs through German letters." Yet More exonerates him — praises his art and character ("the sweetest . . . that ever revealed itself in rhymes") — because he "represents a beautiful society now passed away and almost forgotten." Parrington said that after Longfellow, there was Charles Eliot Norton, and then sterility; but More, spiritual child of New England, remains faithful to Brahmin culture: "One need not be a New Englander, or a Harvard man, to join heartily in honouring the poet who represents the highest and most homogeneous culture this country has yet produced . . . it is wholesome for us to read and praise Longfellow."

Emerson, for More, is "the outstanding figure of American letters" — and a dangerous one. His expansive romanticism, checked in his own case by "ancestral inheritance" (a Puritan character and calling) has, in Emersonianism, "wrought in our religion, our politics, and our literature a perilous dizziness of the brain." More's patience with Emersonianism is short, for its optimism is too "jaunty" and "facile" and as much to be scorned as Alcott, "that dilapidated Platonist," in whose person More attacks his own admittedly beloved master. Emerson's philosophy, with its "vanishing dualism," is "fatally easy," a philosophy (as we still sometimes hear) for youth. Its spiritual openness and restlessness disturb him.

Thoreau, whom More emulated by withdrawing to the woods of Shelburne, New Hampshire (the *Shelburne Essays* thus pay tribute to Thoreau and Emerson), is considered "the greatest by far of our writers on Nature," the only one, it seems, who managed to avoid the pitfalls of scientific curiosity and pantheism. Possessing the "old tradition of wonder," interested chiefly in the "moral significance of Nature," and steadied by the sturdy, manly, stoic virtues of the New England tradition, Thoreau, in More's account, is perhaps the writer who best achieved the difficult reconciliations occasioned by the incubus of romanticism. Whitman, to be sure, did not: The *Leaves of Grass* represents the "dithyrambic annunciation of the wedding of Romantic individualism with sentimental democracy . . ." Yet More is both open and generous toward Whitman, somewhat in the way he is with Franklin, attracted, apparently, by men wholly different from himself. His study of the poet is mediated by his reading of Traubel's *With Walt Whitman in Camden* and Whitman's own *Specimen Days* — by appreciation of the old poet to whom time has brought "only sweetness and breadth" and whose sympathy, finally, made him face without fear the "invisible world" his spirit had penetrated. Since Whitman has a temperament "richer" than Emerson's (he was not a New Englander — but that is only part of the story) and a "more striking . . . verbal felicity," More sees no reason why we should "hesitate to accept him."

These appraisals have considerable merit and are not to be discounted so much as amended by our current way of estimating worth. Parrington is not interested in appraising a writer's art, and neither is More, though he is sensitive to it and sometimes writes about it, as in the case of Longfellow's sonnets, in order to win an otherwise withheld approval. For neither critic is art the touchstone it is for most of the critics represented in this volume — critics, in this way, representative of our time. We have turned away from doctrinal or extrinsic approaches to literature; it is partly because of the work of Brooks, Parrington, More, and others of their persuasions that critics now attend more closely to matters intrinsic to literature. Yet their views, like those of Brooks, Parrington, and

More, have the limitations of all views and need the rounding, the recollection of others.

Theodore Hornberger, for example, no longer has the problem More faced in writing about Franklin. More said: "There is a certain embarrassment in dealing with Franklin as a man of letters, for the simple reason that he was never, in the strict sense of the word, concerned with letters at all." More managed to accommodate this problem, which was compounded by a conflict of principles and admiration, by noting that Franklin's "life is almost literature." But, for Hornberger, Franklin is pre-eminently a man of letters, and, accordingly, he attends most to Franklin's life in literature. His distance from Parrington and More can be seen in the indifferent way he raises the very issues that prompted their judgments: "If the advancement of science and the resolution of political differences are of major importance, he was [a great writer]. If the exploration of the depths of human psychology is the primary purpose of literature, he was not." What matters to him is that Franklin is still read.

By these standards both Irving and Longfellow, the most popular writers of their times, are ruled out of consideration. Yet Lewis Leary and Edward Hirsh find other reasons for renewing our interest in them. Leary declares his point of view at the start: "Few writers have successfully stretched a small talent farther than Washington Irving." Small talent, perhaps, but significant literary accomplishment. For this successful man of letters — the first in America — was, as Leary shows, the literary pioneer who gave us the sentimental sketch book of European travel, a comic folklore, models of romantic history and of the literature of the frontier. It does not especially matter to Leary that "somber critics," asking much, find little in Irving. He willingly accepts the very notion of literature that accounts for both Irving's popularity and his importance in cultural history — that literature has the office of pleasing as well as improving, and that by pleasing it may improve (prompt, as Irving said, "a benevolent view of human nature"). Leary's own "agreeable" essay is a fitting introduction to an "amiable" writer. Longfellow, however, presents other difficulties, for

although he owed Irving much and, like him, contributed largely
to "a usable national past," he has not been respected as a writer
by several generations of critics. His sentiment, of course, is not
amiable — it is of the heart but not hearty — and his melancholy
is of a more troubling strain than Irving's, while his faith, which
made him the "uncrowned poet laureate" of America, is Victorian,
genteel, morally naive, shallowly optimistic. Hirsh reminds us of
this but also, and more conspicuously, of his accomplished art, his
resources as a poet, his (the pun is appropriate) "versatility."

Again, in Josephine Miles's essay on Emerson and Richard
Chase's on Whitman, the writer is central. That Emerson was a
"man of wisdom" is Miles's point of departure and settles all those
problems of Emersonianism that disturbed More. She is interested
in Emerson's writing, his "traits of style" and "his individual uses
of tradition." When she says that ideas cannot be treated apart
from their presentation — "his presentation of them gives them
their special identifiable character" — she does not dismiss Emerson's ideas but insists on a stylistic way of discovering, testing, and
placing them. Her essay, a tour de force of criticism and an original contribution to Emerson scholarship, demonstrates, by inspect-
ing vocabulary, syntax, tone, theme, and form, the profound unity
of Emerson's thought.

Richard Chase follows a similar course in considering Whitman. He accepts Whitman's greatness — others may agree "reluctantly or grudgingly" or scorn and neglect him — and sets out to define more exactly the qualities of his art, an art whose subject, he
says, is "the plight and destiny of the self." By means of representative poems, he traces the poet's development (the development of a
self full of "contradictions" and readily adopting "poses") and
establishes his view of Whitman as a comic and elegiac poet. It is
"the poet as poet" who counts, who, according to Chase, is the
"real Walt Whitman" and not, as in Brooks's view, "the poet as
prophet and promulger of a program."

Only Leon Edel is little concerned with writing. His treatment
of Thoreau is biographical and psychological, and is intended to
rectify or replace the more accepting and popular images of the

bachelor of nature. His Thoreau is mother-dominated and eccentric, a "fragile Narcissus" all of whose work is self-concerned — so
concerned because it was necessary for him to hold together "the
parcel of vain strivings" he once (early) declared himself to be.
According to Edel, this explains the lack of spontaneity in his
writing, his incapability of large effort as a writer, his want of a
style, and the various measures he took to moderate and control
his "deep obsessions." Thoreau, we are told, was not a "born
writer" nor a man of consistent principle; he was a child, gestur-
ing, calling attention to himself, and whatever genius he had was
"crooked" and egotistical. Of all the assessments in this volume,
Edel's is the most damaging. It does not recognize such claims as
More's or Parrington's, or those of contemporary critics who have
turned, finally and fruitfully, to the writing. It builds on the work
of Emerson, Lowell, and Stevenson, Thoreau's first detractors.

　　These essays, by their very treatment, show us the stability of
their subject-authors' reputations and indicate those who are still
vitally a part of our imagination. Irving, without apology or reassessment, is accepted; his place in American literature is settled.
This is pretty much the case with Franklin, although John Lynen's
recent study (in *The Design of the Present*) will increase his stature
as a writer. It is not quite the case with Longfellow. None of these
writers figures significantly in the literary discussions of our time;
none engages us as do Emerson, Thoreau, and Whitman (writers
who have recently been associated, respectively, with Paul Good-
man, Gary Snyder, and Allen Ginsberg). We see this in the free
and tonic way in which Josephine Miles treats Emerson, in her
"laborious but joyful understanding"; in the equally free but dis-
paraging treatment of Thoreau by Leon Edel; and in the still contentious figure of Whitman, contentious yet "the spokesman for
the tendencies of his country," that Richard Chase presents to us.

　　Another assessment might be made by gathering the authors'
own judgments of each other. Emerson, for example, complained
that he could not find his heavenly bread in Longfellow — a judgment that might be connected with his further observation: "If
Socrates were here, we could go and talk with him; but Longfel-

low we cannot go and talk with. There is a palace, and servants, and a row of bottles of different colored wines, and wine glasses, and fine coats." This may remind us that even within the radius of twenty-five miles there were wide differences in conceptions of the literary vocation and in ways of following it, and that Longfellow served Brahmin society in ways other than the Socratean. It may remind us, too, of some of the things that these writers, taken together, contribute to our understanding of literary history.

In Parrington's and More's judgments, the one founded in Enlightenment secularism, the other in Calvinist theology, American literature comments on itself. Franklin's view of literature is no more utilitarian than More's, or the Puritans', from which Franklin partly acquired it, but it served secular ends. That it did reflects radical social change. The literature of sentiment, of pleasure in Irving and anodyne in Longfellow, reflects an equally radical social change, as does the exploratory literature of the self in Emerson, Thoreau, and Whitman, a literature that united for new ends the spiritual and sentimental uses of art. From Franklin to Whitman, literature may be said to follow the course of self in its relations with society: it records the disintegration of Puritan society and the emergence of one more "brotherly" (open, democratic, and commercial), the self's subsequent release in feeling, and, finally, the self's aggrandizement as a divinely creative power, capable of intuiting truth, of imagining "higher societies" (the phrase is Thoreau's), and of disclosing "democratic vistas" — a self not content with "making it" but "being it." (In discounting the public Whitman, Chase fails to see the connection between the self's demands and the poet's utopian programs.) To some extent these changes may be associated with places — with Boston and Philadelphia, with New York (the Knickerbockers) and Cambridge, with Concord and Long Island, Brooklyn, Manhattan, and Washington. And with characters: Franklin's Poor Richard and the "Franklin" of the *Autobiography*, Irving's Ichabod Crane and Rip Van Winkle, Longfellow's Evangeline, and the personae of Emerson's *Essays*, Thoreau's *Walden*, and Whitman's *Leaves of Grass*. (Of these works, only the *Autobiography* may need explanation. For it is not a tradesman's book to be explained away by saying that it does not do justice to Franklin. Robert Sayre shows, in *The Examined Self*, that its autobiographical art makes it one of the telling books of its age, and John Lynen claims that it is Franklin's greatest work because in it, among other things, he created a great fictional character.)

This literature, moreover, always reflects the complex relationship of America and Europe, a relationship that was formulated by Irving's time in terms of nature versus civilization. Irving longed for the ruined castle and wrote out the difficulties truancy to Europe created for him in "Rip Van Winkle," a fable of national identity. But the story of Rip, the American as irresponsible child-man in love with pleasure, also concerns resistance to change, and this accounted for its tremendous popularity throughout the nineteenth century, when civilization was replacing nature, the very ground of the American faith in a "new world." The writers treated here speak for that earlier America. They show us some of the tasks of its emerging literature: to provide a national identity and a native past, to explore the relation of Old and New, tradition and freedom, and to be a *new* literature.

And the writers treated here also speak for an America still pastoral. In reading them (and in reading about them) we may remember what Lionel Trilling says about the value of knowing another, an alien culture. For this early culture, though ours, is other — another culture not only to take refuge in but to measure contemporary culture by. Consider Paul Shepard's urgent question in *Man in the Landscape*: "What will happen to a people without a pastoral ethos?" To remember or, more likely, to acquire a (the) sense of the pastoral may be one of the high uses our time asks of literature. These writers give that salutary pleasure.

THEODORE HORNBERGER

Benjamin Franklin

NOTHING goes by luck in composition," Thoreau remarked in his journal in 1841. "It allows of no tricks. The best you can write will be the best you are. Every sentence is the result of a long probation. The author's character is read from title-page to end."

The Comte de Buffon is supposed to have meant much the same thing by his statement that the style is the man, and the concept is held in general esteem. It presents some difficulties, however, when applied to Benjamin Franklin, a man whose character remains mysterious and whose voluminous writings are full of what he himself regarded as tricks of his trade.

Many readers may indeed be surprised to find Franklin discussed in a volume devoted to American authors. His fame rests less upon authorship than upon other things. Printer, scientist, statesman, and promoter of schools, libraries, hospitals, insurance companies, savings banks, and the post office, he would be conspicuous among American notables if he had never written a line.

Nevertheless, when in 1771 he began to compose his widely read autobiography, he put "My writing" at the head of the topics to be treated and proceeded to give careful attention to his experience in mastering English composition, which he thought had

contributed greatly to his success in the various roles he had been
called upon to play. He unquestionably fancied himself as a writer,
and it is no more than fair to take him at his word.

Anyone who admires Franklin is likely to wish occasionally
that he had written rather less than he did. Two pieces in particular — and they happen to be his best known works — have provided
much ammunition to his detractors and are likely to diminish his
stature even among his friends.

The first is *The Way to Wealth*, originally the preface to *Poor
Richard's Almanac* for 1758. It strung together into a connected
narrative the pithy sayings relating to industry, frugality, and prudence from twenty-four earlier issues of Franklin's almanac, adding
some new ones for good measure. Later separately published, *The
Way to Wealth* is known in more than 150 editions, many of them
translations into languages other than English. To its enormous
audience Franklin and Poor Richard were indistinguishable, and
hence arose the widespread impression that Franklin's basic faith
was that "God helps them that help themselves" and his gospel
that of acquisitiveness:

> Get what you can, and what you get hold;
> 'Tis the Stone that will turn all your lead into gold.

Those who think of Franklin as materialistic, cautious, and pru-
dent to a fault can feel with some justice that like David Harum,
the shrewd protagonist of Edward N. Westcott's novel of 1898,
Franklin read the Golden Rule as "Do unto the other feller the
way he'd like to do unto you an' do it fust."

One can argue that *The Way to Wealth* does not fairly represent either Poor Richard or his creator, but no such excuse can be
offered for the worldliness of the *Autobiography*. In it Franklin
candidly undertook to explain how he had risen in the world and
his explanation is not a wholly pretty story. Advancement, he implied, is a matter of keeping an eye on the main chance. It requires
calculation and may even mean using one's friends, flattering one's
superiors, and suppressing one's opinions if they seem likely to offend influential people. The good life, according to the *Autobi-*

ography, is not the pursuit of simple saintliness or spiritual serenity but the attainment of economic independence and social position. The aura of finagling and of elasticity of conviction which surrounds the *Autobiography* offends many sensitive readers and is the justification for the castigation of Franklin by such critics as D. H. Lawrence. In his *Studies in Classic American Literature* Lawrence referred to Franklin as "snuff-coloured" and as wishing to confine the "dark vast forest" of the soul of man in a barbed-wire paddock, there to grow "potatoes or Chicagoes." The judgment is severe, but not a gross misrepresentation of Franklin as he explained himself in the *Autobiography*.

Neither his most popular writings nor his detractors, however, have utterly destroyed Franklin as a national hero. He was lionized during his lifetime and visitors still toss pennies on his grave in Christ Church Burying Ground in Philadelphia. How can this be, if his ideals were so pint-sized and mundane?

One answer is that the masses are always worldly in their aspirations and, since like appeals to like, commonplace people create commonplace heroes. Another is that the crowd is readily captured by showmanship, a quality which Franklin possessed as richly as any man of his time. A third answer, and perhaps the best one, is that no man really understands himself, Franklin not excepted. His practice did not always follow his precepts and he often acted upon rasher impulses and nobler principles than those which he publicly avowed. Many discrepancies between theory and practice can be demonstrated in his life and, as will appear, in his writing as well. He was not as uncomplicated a man as he thought he was, nor was his literary style as simple as he believed it to be.

His life can be quickly disposed of, since it is in its main outlines common knowledge.

The son of a candlemaker, he was born in Boston in 1706. After meager schooling he was apprenticed, at the age of twelve, to an older brother who was a printer. Five years later he ran away from home. Following some disillusioning adventures, including an eighteen-month residence in London, he settled in Philadelphia in

1726 and proceeded to make a modest fortune. By 1748 he was financially independent and freed himself from business to turn his abundant energy to science and public affairs. Within a few years he was internationally famous as the author of *Experiments and Observations on Electricity* (1751), a book which assured him a warm welcome when his political activities took him back to England in 1757. At this point the *Autobiography* ends.

Twenty-five of the remaining years of his life were spent in Europe. He was in London first (1757–62) as a representative of the Pennsylvania elected assembly and again (1764–75) as semiofficial ambassador of most of the British American colonies during the series of disputes about taxation which culminated in the Revolution. Finally (1776–85) he was in Paris, where he helped to secure desperately needed naval and military assistance for the armed struggle for independence and to negotiate the peace treaty which recognized the sovereignty of the United States. Suffering from a painful stone in the bladder, he returned at seventy-nine to Philadelphia, where he died in 1790, soon after taking part in the convention which drafted the Constitution. Of this long period of distinguished public service the *Autobiography* says almost nothing.

Europe first knew Franklin as a scientist, and remembered him as the man who rashly flew a kite in a thunderstorm to prove that lightning is an electrical phenomenon. To this dramatic picture others were added as his later life unfolded. One was that of the mild-mannered colonial agent, facing the House of Commons at the height of the Stamp Act crisis to answer 174 questions from friends and critics of the colonies with such directness as to astonish the House and enchant large sections of the British public. Another was of an old man in a fur cap and spectacles, who among the powdered wigs of Paris seemed the incarnation of the simple virtues of the New World, so that when he and Voltaire met at the Academy of Sciences the audience was not satisfied until the two *philosophes* hugged one another and exchanged kisses on both cheeks. Snuff-colored as his ideals may have been, the eighteenth century adored him. "He snatched the lightning from the sky and the scepter from tyrants," Turgot the economist proclaimed in a famous epigram. He was more renowned, wrote his envious compatriot, John Adams, than Leibniz, Sir Isaac Newton, Frederick the Great, or Voltaire, and "more beloved and esteemed than any or all of them."

Franklin, then, was something more than "Poor Richard, the Boy Who Made Good," as Dixon Wecter labeled him in *The Hero in America*. The books on Franklin the "amazing" and the "many-sided" are not wholly in the wrong, nor are the biographers who have called him "the first civilized American," "the apostle of modern times," and, as Carl Van Doren happily phrased it, "a harmonious human multitude." For versatility, wide-ranging intellectual curiosity, and political acumen, Benjamin Franklin has had few peers. His *Autobiography* does him far less than justice.

With his writing as with his life one must begin with the *Autobiography*, but with the awareness that it does not tell the whole story. When he began to write it he was a man of sixty-five, generalizing about English composition as he was generalizing about worldly success, and interpreting his early experience in terms of maturity and mellowed memories.

By his own account Franklin was a precocious, bookish child, and his family naturally thought that he might become an ornament to the ministry, then the most honored profession in the Boston Puritan community. At eight, therefore, he was sent to Latin grammar school as a first step toward Harvard College and a Congregational pulpit. His father, however, thinking of the expense of a college education and the size of ministerial salaries, soon had a change of heart. After less than a year's exposure to Latin syntax he was withdrawn and enrolled in a private school which advertised, in the *Boston News-Letter*, instruction in "Writing, Cyphering, Treble Violin, Flute, Spinet, &c. Also English and French Quilting, Imbroidery, Florishing, Plain Work, Marking in several sorts of Stitches and several other works." In this evidently busy and coeducational establishment, he mastered penmanship but little else, failing, he recalled, in arithmetic. This took a year or so; at the age of ten his schooldays were over.

Home study was another matter. He could not remember when he learned to read, but at an early age was devouring what few books his father had accumulated. Among them were a number of works of theological controversy; he regretted later that more suitable material was not at hand when he was so eager for knowledge. He remembered three other books: Plutarch's *Lives*, Defoe's *Essay on Projects*, and Cotton Mather's *Essays to Do Good*. The time spent on Plutarch was not, he thought, wasted, and it may have had something to do with his lifelong taste for history and his delight in the delineation of character. From Defoe and Mather he derived, he said, a turn of thought which influenced some of the chief events of his later life, by which he no doubt meant his use of some of their ideas on education and mutual association for "good works." His first systematic purchases out of his spending money were works by John Bunyan. "Honest John," he wrote, "was the first that I know of who mix'd Narration & Dialogue, a Method of Writing very engaging to the Reader, who in the most interesting Parts finds himself as it were brought into the Company, & present at the Discourse. De foe in his Cruso, his Moll Flanders, Religious Courtship, Family Instructor, & other Pieces, has imitated it with Success. And Richardson has done the same in his Pamela, &c." Like Bunyan, Franklin was to make effective use of dialogue and allegory.

More books became available in his brother's print shop. The office stock was supplemented by loans from a friendly merchant. At night and early in the morning and whenever on Sunday he could get out of going to church, Franklin read and studied.

In 1718 he ventured into print with a topical ballad about a shipwreck, which sold well enough to make any twelve-year-old vain. Another on Blackbeard the pirate followed; then his father discouraged him "by ridiculing my Performances, and telling me Verse-makers were always Beggars; so I escap'd being a Poet, most probably a very bad one." Thereafter he showed only a mild interest in poetry. He composed verses occasionally, but "approv'd the amusing one's Self with Poetry now & then, so far as to improve one's Language, but no farther."

The father's influence on his son's prose was rather happier.

Among the boy's friends was another booklover, John Collins, with whom he was fond of arguing — a liking for argument, Franklin believed, had been one result of reading theological works. He and Collins debated the mental capacities of women and whether or not girls should be educated. Franklin, already on the side of the ladies, felt himself overpowered, not so much by Collins' logic as by his fluency. To present his own case effectively he wrote out his arguments in the form of letters and exchanged them with his friend. His father found this correspondence, made a point of discussing it, and observed that though Benjamin with his print-shop training had an advantage in spelling and punctuation he "fell far short in elegance of Expression, in Method and in Perspicuity, of which he convinc'd me by several Instances. I saw the Justice of his Remarks, & thence grew more attentive to the *Manner* in Writing, and determin'd to endeavour at Improvement." Franklin never deviated from his father's standards: elegance, in the sense of ingenious simplicity; method, or careful organization; and perspicuity, or complete clarity.

To improve his style Franklin adopted a device which other would-be writers have found effective. He undertook to imitate the writing then most fashionable and admired, that of *The Spectator.* "I took some of the Papers," he tells us,

& making short Hints of the Sentiment in each Sentence, laid them by a few Days, and then without looking at the Book, try'd to compleat the Papers again, by expressing each hinted Sentiment at length & as fully as it had been express'd before, in any suitable Words, that should come to hand.

Then I compar'd my Spectator with the Original, discover'd some of my Faults & corrected them. But I found I wanted a Stock of Words or a Readiness in recollecting & using them, which I thought I should have acquir'd before that time, if I had gone on making Verses, since the continual Occasion for Words of the same Import but of different Length, to suit the Measure, or of different Sound for the Rhyme, would have laid me under a constant Necessity of searching for Variety, and also have tended to fix that Variety in my Mind, & make me Master of it. Therefore I took some of the Tales & turn'd them into Verse: And after a time, when I had pretty well forgotten the Prose, turn'd them back again. I also sometimes jumbled my Collections of Hints into Confusion, and after some Weeks, endeavour'd to reduce them into the best Order, before I began to form the full Sentences, & compleat the Paper. This was to teach me Method in the Arrangement of Thoughts. By comparing my work afterwards with the original, I discover'd many faults and amended them; but I sometimes had the Pleasure of Fancying that in certain Particulars of small Import, I had been lucky enough to improve the Method or the Language and this encourag'd me to think I might possibly in time come to be a tolerable English Writer, of which I was extreamly ambitious.

Those who cherish originality or believe in "inspiration" are sure to scorn Franklin's imitative methods. Fresh perception and wide reading are perhaps more valuable in the long run than laborious exercises such as his. On the other hand, there are few better ways of building a vocabulary and mastering the elements of logical organization. Compared to learning ten new words a day or outlining modern essays, Franklin's technique stands up well, and in his own case undoubtedly produced the results he sought.

To a modern eye the prose of Addison and Steele and the expository writing of Defoe seem overly contrived. They rely upon numerous parallelisms and contrasts, upon balance, antithesis, and climax. All good prose shows careful pruning, but eighteenth-century prose writers, like eighteenth-century gardeners, were fond of the espalier method, patiently laboring to achieve a careful and instantly impressive structure rather than simply to cut out the dead wood and to increase the productiveness of the bearing branches. Some of Franklin's early prose was espaliered, but working against that tendency were other influences: his father's standards, the example of the Puritan sermon which he never mentions but to which he was exposed at an impressionable age, and his newspaper experience, which encouraged both conciseness and a conservatism about language.

His early fondness for contradiction, shared with his friend Collins, seemed to him later a bad habit. He claimed to have abandoned it after encountering the Socratic method of disputation, in which a point of view is established by a sequence of leading questions rather than by direct argument. His curiosity led him to

Xenophon's *Memorabilia*; in emulation of Socrates he dropped "abrupt Contradiction, and positive Argumentation, and put on the humble Enquirer & Doubter." Finding the pose safe and successful, "I took a Delight in it, practis'd it continually & grew very artful & expert in drawing People even of superior Knowledge into Concessions the Consequences of which they did not foresee, entangling them in Difficulties out of which they could not extricate themselves, and so obtaining Victories that neither my self nor my Cause always deserved." This device, more useful in face-to-face oral discourse than in writing, became a part of his bag of tricks. As will appear, he often sought to assume the mask or persona of the humble inquirer and, keenly aware of the importance of his audience in determining his strategy, led his readers into unwary concessions.

As Franklin realized, the Socratic method contains an element of sophistry, in that there is some intentional deception. He said that he gradually gave it up, "retaining only the Habit of expressing my self in Terms of modest Diffidence, never using when I advance any thing that may possibly be disputed, the Words, *Certainly, undoubtedly*, or any others that give the Air of Positiveness to an Opinion; but rather say, *I conceive, or I apprehend* a Thing to be so and so, *It appears to me, or I should think it so and so for such & such Reasons*, or *I imagine* it to be so, or *it is so if I am not mistaken*. This Habit I believe has been of great Advantage to me, when I have had occasion to inculcate my Opinions & persuade Men into Measures that I have been from time to time engag'd in promoting. And as the chief Ends of Conversation are to *inform*, or to be *informed*, to *please* or to *persuade*, I wish wellmeaning sensible Men would not lessen their Power of doing Good by a Positive assuming Manner that seldom fails to disgust, tends to create Opposition, and to defeat every one of those Purposes for which Speech was given us, to wit, giving or receiving Information, or Pleasure." As a politician Franklin was remarkably faithful to this theory of oral discourse, of which the practicality is self-evident to anyone who has ever attended a public meeting or legislative assembly.

He also applied the strategy of the humble inquirer to writing. Good writing, he observed, "ought to have a tendency to benefit the reader, by improving his virtue or his knowledge. . . . an ill man may write an ill thing well; that is, having an ill design, he may use the properest style and arguments (considering who are to be readers) to attain his ends. In this sense, that is best wrote, which is best adapted for obtaining the end of the writer." He who would write to please good judges, Franklin said in 1733, should attend to three things: "That his Performance be *smooth, clear*, and *short*: For the contrary Qualities are apt to offend, either the Ear, the Understanding, or the Patience." The audience, then, was always uppermost with Franklin the writer as well as the speaker.

His training and his theory, in short, gave Franklin some confidence in tricks. An examination of his writings will show how he used them and will also demonstrate, I hope, that he wrote with more variety, color, temper, and whimsey than he himself realized.

Aside from his ballads, neither of which has been certainly identified, Franklin's earliest literary efforts were the Silence Dogood papers, a series of fourteen essays printed in 1722 in the *New England Courant*, his brother's newspaper. The *Courant* had invited its readers to contribute suitable compositions. "I was excited," Franklin tells us, "to try my Hand among them. But being still a Boy, & suspecting that my Brother would object to printing any Thing of mine in his Paper if he knew it to be mine, I contriv'd to disguise my Hand, & writing an anonymous Paper I put it at Night under the Door of the Printing House." He was then sixteen.

The imitation of *The Spectator* is direct and immediate, as Elizabeth C. Cook has neatly shown. "I have observed," Addison began, "that a reader seldom peruses a book with pleasure till he knows whether the writer of it be a black or a fair man, of a mild or choleric disposition, married or a bachelor, with other particulars of the like nature, that conduce very much to the right understanding of an author." Franklin's second sentence was: "And since it is observed, that the Generality of People, now a days, are unwilling either to commend or dispraise what they read, until they are in some measure informed who or what the Author of it is, whether he be *poor* or *rich, old* or *young,* a *Scollar* or a *Leather Apron Man,* &c. and give their Opinion of the Performance, according to the Knowledge which they have of the Author's Circumstances, it may not be amiss to begin with a short Account of my past Life and present Condition, that the Reader may not be at a Loss to judge whether or no my Lucubrations are worth his reading." The idiom the boy so much admired is slightly localized by such invention as "Leather Apron Man," and conciseness is not yet a passion.

Franklin also shows himself a devotee of Addison and Steele in his persona and in his perception of his audience. Silence Dogood tells us that she was born en route from London to New England. "My Entrance into this troublesome World was attended with the Death of my Father, a Misfortune, which tho' I was not then capable of knowing, I shall never be able to forget; for as he, poor Man, stood upon the Deck rejoycing at my Birth, a merciless Wave entred the Ship, and in one Moment carry'd him beyond Reprieve. Thus was the *first* Day which I saw, the *last* that was seen by my Father; and thus was my disconsolate Mother at once made both a *Parent* and a *Widow.*" (One can still feel the pride of the boy who polished off that last sentence, with its antithesis and ingeniously paradoxical climax.) Silence bears some resemblances to her creator. Her education was informal, picked up in the library of a bachelor country minister to whom she was bound at an early age, and who saw that she learned needlework, writing, and arithmetic before he at length married her. Their seven years of "conjugal Love and mutual Endearments" ended with his death, and left her with two likely girls, a boy, and her native common sense. She now enjoys the conversation of an honest neighbor, Rusticus, and an "ingenious" clergyman who boards with her, "and by whose Assistance I intend now and then to beautify my Writings with a Sentence or two in the learned Languages, which will not only be fashionable, and pleasing to those who do not understand it, but will likewise be very ornamental." (Franklin's flair for irony thus appears at the very beginning of his writing life.) Silence has, she admits, a "natural Inclination to observe and reprove the Faults of others," and in her third communication she reveals her calculation of her audience. "I am very sensible," she says, "that it is impossible for me, or indeed any *one* Writer to please *all* Readers at once. Various Persons have different Sentiments; and that which is pleasant and delightful to one, gives another a Disgust. He that would (in this Way of Writing) please all, is under a Necessity to make his Themes almost as numerous as his Letters. He must one while be merry and diverting, then more solid and serious; one while sharp and satyrical, then (to mollify that) be sober and religious; at *one* Time let the Subject be Politicks, then let the next Theme be Love. Thus will every one, one Time or another, find some thing agreeable to his own Fancy, and in his Turn be delighted."

For all his theory, Franklin was not yet a skillful writer. The Dogood papers lack plan, fail to sustain the point of view of the persona, and indeed permit that creation to fade gradually into limbo. Of the fourteen essays, the best are a dream allegory on education at Harvard College (No. 4) and a satire on the New England funeral elegy, with a hilarious recipe for writing one (No. 7). These two essays are the first revelation of Franklin the rebel, whose real feelings break through the mask. They attracted attention of a kind which in his more cautious moments Franklin sought to avoid. He gives as one of his reasons for leaving Boston "that I had already made myself a little obnoxious to the governing Party." The pose of the bland inquirer did not go well with satire.

Nor did the delight in logic and contradiction die as early a death as an unwary reading of the *Autobiography* may lead one to think. In 1725, working in Palmer's printing shop in London, Franklin helped set in type an edition of William Wollaston's *The Religion of Nature Delineated*. Finding himself questioning some of Wollaston's arguments, he wrote and had printed a brief, closely reasoned essay, the gist of which is that God is all-wise, all-good, and all-powerful, and that therefore neither evil nor free will actually exist. Whatever is, is right, Franklin asserted, and the principle which governs human behavior is not the ill-founded distinction between virtue and vice but the inexorable balancing out of pleasure and pain. In other words, *A Dissertation on Liberty and Neces-*

sity, Pleasure and Pain reduces moral conduct to a matter of sound judgment, in which religious considerations are conspicuously absent. He tells us that his employer found the principles of his pamphlet "abominable," and he himself decided quickly that they were at the least injudicious. He destroyed most of the hundred copies that were printed and fifty years later told his friend Benjamin Vaughan that his views had changed.

The *Dissertation* is the only elaborate example of formal syllogistic reasoning among Franklin's works of persuasion. Its content and method go back to his early reading in theology, most probably to Samuel Clarke's Boyle Lecture sermons on the attributes of God (1704–5). That reading, said Franklin, "wrought an Effect on me quite contrary to what was intended by them: For the Arguments of the Deists which were quoted to be refuted, appeared to me much Stronger than the Refutations. In short I soon became a thorough Deist." A Deist he remained, writing to Ezra Stiles only five weeks before he died in terms parallel to those in the *Autobiography* and to the classic statement of Deistic principles in Lord Herbert of Cherbury's *De Veritate* (1624): "Here is my creed. I believe in one God, the creator of the universe. That he governs it by his Providence. That he ought to be worshipped. That the most acceptable service we render to him is doing good to his other children. That the soul of man is immortal, and will be treated with justice in another life respecting its conduct in this. These I take to be the fundamental points in all sound religion, and I regard them as you do in whatever sect I meet with them." Reason, not the Bible, was Franklin's standard for religious faith.

Franklin's exploration of the processes of persuasion was continued in two other early works: *A Modest Enquiry into the Nature and Necessity of a Paper-Currency* (1729) and *Poor Richard's Almanac*, of which the first issue was that for 1733. Both were intimately connected with his main concern in the decade after his final settlement in Philadelphia in 1726 — to establish himself in his trade as a printer.

A Modest Enquiry appeared in the same year in which he acquired his newspaper, the *Pennsylvania Gazette*. His first venture into the realm of economic theory, it resembles neither the Addisonian essay nor the theological polemic, although it is a carefully structured argument. I suggest that its model was the Puritan sermon. No Biblical text heads it, to be sure, but in place of that authority is a truism to which no reader was likely to object: to carry on trade requires a "certain proportionate quantity of money . . . more than which would be of no advantage in trade, and less, if much less, exceedingly detrimental to it."

From this Franklin draws four axioms, roughly parallel to the "doctrines" which the Puritan preacher customarily derived from his text: (1) great scarcity of money means high interest rates; (2) great scarcity of money reduces prices; (3) great scarcity of money discourages the settlement of workmen and leads to the exodus of those already in the country; and (4) great scarcity of money, in such a country as America, leads to greater consumption of imported goods. Plentiful money of course produces exactly the opposite effects: low interest, good prices, encouragement of settlement and of home production.

What persons, he then asks, will be for or against the emission of a large additional amount of paper currency? Opposing it, he replies, in a passage with many emotional overtones, will be money-lenders, land speculators, lawyers, and the dependents of these classes. "On the other Hand, those who are Lovers of Trade, and delight to see Manufactures encouraged, will be for having a large Addition to our Currency." Furthermore, Franklin asserts, plenty of money will make land values rise, and will be to the advantage of England; a currency issue, therefore, will not be against the interest of either the proprietors (the Penn family) or the homeland.

He next turns to the question of whether or not the issue of more currency would lead to depreciation of its value. This demanded his consideration of the nature and value of money in general. To such theoretical discussion, in which he anticipates at some points Adam Smith's *The Wealth of Nations*, he devotes about half his entire space. A number of possible objections are then disposed of and the essay concludes with a paragraph in the persona of the humble inquirer, who had previously been conspicuously absent.

"As this Essay is wrote and published in Haste, and the Subject in itself intricate, I hope I shall be censured with Candour, if, for want of Time carefully to revise what I have written, in some Places I should appear to have express'd my self too obscurely, and in others am liable to Objections I did not foresee."

Despite its final gesture of humility, *A Modest Enquiry* is basically an appeal to the self-interest of the masses, in which their prejudices against moneylenders, speculators, and lawyers were skillfully brought to bear upon a political issue. The piece was Franklin's first real success in persuasion. It was, he said, "well receiv'd by the common People in general; but the Rich Men dislik'd it; for it increas'd and strengthen'd the Clamour for more Money; and they happening to have no Writers among them that were able to answer it, their Opposition slacken'd, & the Point was carried by a Majority in the House. My Friends there, who conceiv'd I had been of some Service, thought fit to reward me, by employing me in printing the Money, a very profitable Jobb, and a great Help to me. This was another Advantage gain'd by my being able to write." The next year, one may add, he was appointed public printer of the province and his business success was thereafter never in doubt.

His decision to publish an almanac was natural for a young printer. Almost everyone needed an almanac. It was a calendar, a record of historical anniversaries, a guide to the times of the rising and setting of the sun and of the phases of the moon. Farming and medical practice were still widely governed by folk belief in the influence of the heavenly bodies. Firewood, to burn well, had presumably to be cut while the moon was waxing, fruit gathered for the winter when it was on the wane. Horoscopes were cast to settle the proper moment to swallow medicine or wean babies. Moreover, since the aspect of the heavens varied with the latitude and longitude, it was not much use to have an almanac unless it was locally prepared. The almanac, consequently, had been a staple moneymaker since the invention of printing and there were dozens in America, beginning with one for 1639 which is believed to have been the second imprint of the pioneer press at Cambridge.

In 1732 seven almanacs, one of them in German, were being

printed in Philadelphia. The most successful was probably the *American Almanac*, begun by Daniel Leeds in 1686 and continued in Franklin's time by Leeds's son Titan. Despite this competition *Poor Richard's Almanac* was immediately successful. Three printings of the first issue were needed, and by the middle 1760's nearly 10,000 copies were being printed annually.

Franklin's triumph owed much to his creation of another persona: Richard Saunders, Philomath (i.e., astrologer). Richard confesses in his first preface that he is "excessive poor" and his wife "excessive proud." She cannot bear "to sit spinning in her Shift of Tow, while I do nothing but gaze at the Stars, and has threatned more than once to burn all my Books and Rattling-Traps (as she calls my Instruments) if I do not make some profitable Use of them for the Good of my Family. The Printer has offer'd me some considerable share of the Profits, and I have thus begun to comply with my Dame's Desire." The purchaser of his almanac, concludes Poor Richard, will get a useful utensil and also perform an act of charity.

A seventeenth-century English astrologer and almanac-maker had been named Richard Saunders and a popular eighteenth-century London almanac was called *Poor Robin's*. Poor Richard, nevertheless, is an imaginative although short-lived creation. At first he is an improvident and henpecked dreamer, not unlike Rip Van Winkle except for his interest in extracting pennies from the public. Within a few years he turns moralist, and in *The Way to Wealth* he is little more than a handy reference for the venerable Father Abraham, who inserts "as Poor Richard says" now and then to punctuate his sermon on the homely virtues. John F. Ross has suggested that like some later American comic creations Poor Richard gradually faded as his creator assumed the role of philosopher and oracle. The persona, in short, was neither developed nor long maintained.

The first few issues of Franklin's almanac are even more remarkable for his experiment with the hoax, a form of joke wherein he pushed the strategy of extracting unconscious concessions from an unsuspecting reader to its limit. A number of his finest pieces are hoaxes, presenting absurdities with such a poker-faced manner that even ordinarily perceptive readers were taken in. The classic example is his "Proposed New Version of the Bible," an ironic paraphrase of Job 1:6–11, which no less a reader than Matthew Arnold interpreted as a lapse of Franklin's customary good sense, failing to recognize it as an attack on the English king and his ministers.

The hoax which launched *Poor Richard's Almanac* was borrowed directly from Jonathan Swift, who in 1707–8 had attacked the pretensions of a London astrologer, John Partridge, in a series of papers purportedly written by Isaac Bickerstaff. Franklin adopted Swift's strategy and many of his details. Poor Richard asserts, in the preface which has been quoted, that he would have issued an almanac many years earlier had he not been "overpowered" by regard for Titan Leeds. This obstacle, he observes, is "soon to be removed, since inexorable Death, who was never known to respect Merit, has already prepared the mortal Dart, the fatal Sister has already extended her destroying Shears, and that ingenious Man must soon be taken from us." Leeds will die, predicts Poor Richard, on October 17, 1733. By Leeds's own calculation, "he will survive till the 26th of the same Month. . . . Which of us is most exact, a little Time will now determine."

Leeds, like John Partridge, saw nothing funny in this macabre joke, and wrote the next year of the folly and ignorance of Poor Richard, who had not only lied about the date of his rival's death but had also perpetrated "another gross Falsehood in his said Almanack, viz. — *That by my own Calculation, I shall survive until the 26th of the said month* (October) which is as untrue as the former." To this Poor Richard replied, as Bickerstaff had to Partridge: "I convince him in his own Words, that he is dead . . . for in his Preface to his Almanack for 1734, he says, '*Saunders adds . . . that by my own Calculation I shall survive until the 26th of the said Month October 1733, which is as untrue as the former.*' Now if it be, as Leeds says, *untrue* and a *gross Falshood* that he surviv'd till the 26th of October 1733, then it is certainly *true* that he died *before* that Time . . . anything he may say to the contrary notwithstanding." In dealing with a satirist it is well to look to the precision of one's language.

Its opening gambit, however, is not what made *Poor Richard's Almanac* a continuing success. Its popularity grew along with Franklin's ingenuity in filling the spaces above, below, and beside his tables of dates and astronomical data with more readable material than his competitors could find. Little of it was original, but not much was borrowed without artful revision to make it more attractive to his audience. Perhaps the transformation of the dreamy astrologer into the moralist was determined by his largely rural audience, which honored hard work and saving more than jokes or sophisticated wit. At any rate, the "sayings" of Poor Richard eventually came close to being gospel to the country folk, and they still find a market in such little books as *Ben Franklin's Wit and Wisdom*.

Robert Newcomb, who has made the most extensive of the many studies of their origins, finds two major types of sources. In the early issues of his almanac, Franklin tended to rely on such collections of proverbs as James Howell's *Lexicon Tetraglotton* (1659) and Thomas Fuller's *Gnomologia* (1732). These were not all in a moral vein; as Van Doren has said, Poor Richard's early period was distinctly "gamy." As time went on, however, Franklin turned more often to literary and moralistic aphorisms, which he found in books such as Fuller's *Introductio ad Prudentiam* (1727), Charles Palmer's *Collection of Select Aphorisms and Maxims* (1748), Lord Halifax's *Thoughts and Reflections* (1750), and Samuel Richardson's appendix to *Clarissa* (1751). Other sources were *Wits Recreation* (1654) by John Mennes and James Smith and an anonymous *Collection of Epigrams* (1735–37). For short poems he plundered John Gay's *Fables* (1727–38), Edward Young's *Universal Passion* (1725–28), Pope's *Essay on Man* (1733), and James Savage's *Public Spirit* (1747). Rabelais, Francis Bacon, La Rochefoucauld, John Ray, John Dryden, Matthew Prior, and George Lillo he knew at first or second hand. He was an expert in the literature of the concise and succinct statement. All his life, in fact, he loved to quote proverbial and well-turned phrases. On one occasion he wrote of his own life as an epigram which, although some of its lines were barely tolerable, he hoped to conclude with a bright point.

Franklin's revisions of his borrowed materials, particularly the prose, were sometimes extensive. His admiration for conciseness was perhaps the determining factor, but he experimented with metaphor, occasional rhyme, and of course the familiar rhetorical devices, particularly balance and climax. Van Doren and Charles W. Meister give many examples, of which a few must suffice here.

Franklin's skill in compression is well illustrated by "Fish and visitors smell in three days," thought to derive from John Ray's "Fresh fish and new come guests smell, by that they are three days old." His sharpening of metaphor may be seen in "Neither a fortress nor a maid will hold out long after they begin to parley," from a Scottish proverb, "A listening damsel and a speaking castle shall never end with honor," and by "Time is an herb that cures all diseases," from Lillo's "Time and reflection cure all ills." His fondness for balance may explain the transformation of Fuller's "The fox is grey before he's good" into "Many foxes grow gray, but few grow good." The mastery of climax, or anticlimax, is evident in "Let thy maidservant be faithful, strong, and homely" and "None preaches better than the ant, and she says nothing."

In one extended borrowing, noted by Van Doren, Franklin deliberately Americanized his material. At the end of *Pantagruel* Rabelais has a book on prognostications, with a chapter on eclipses. This year, he says, "Saturn will be retrograde, Venus direct, Mercury as unfix'd as quicksilver. . . . For this reason the crabs will go side-long, and the rope-makers backward . . . bacon will run away from pease in lent; the belly will waddle before; the a—— will sit down first; there won't be a bean left in a twelfth-cake, nor an ace in a flush; the dice won't run as you wish, tho' you cog them, and the chance that you desire will seldom come; brutes shall speak in several places . . . and there will be above twenty and seven irregular verbs made this year, if Priscian doesn't hold them in." In the almanac for 1739 Franklin reworks the passage as follows: "During the first visible Eclipse *Saturn* is retrograde: For which Reason the Crabs will go sidelong, and the Ropemakers backward. The Belly will wag before, and the A—— shall sit down first. *Mercury* will have his share in these Affairs, and so confound the Speech

of People, that when a *Pensilvanian* would say PANTHER he shall say
PAINTER. When a New Yorker thinks to say (THIS) he shall say
(DISS) and the People in *New England* and *Cape-May* will not be
able to say (COW) for their Lives, but will be forc'd to say (KEOW)
by a certain involuntary Twist in the Root of their Tongues. No
Connecticut-Man nor *Marylander* will be able to open his Mouth
this Year, but (SIR) shall be the first or last Syllable he pronounces,
and sometimes both. Brutes shall speak in many Places, and there
will be above seven and twenty irregular Verbs made this Year, if
Grammar don't interpose." Franklin is not at his best here, but his
eye is obviously on his audience and his ear attuned to the vernacu-
lar, as it was in many of Poor Richard's more successful borrowings.

By the time he was thirty, Franklin had a prospering printing
house, a successful newspaper, and a popular almanac. He had too
active a mind, however, to be content with business. Temperamentally disposed toward the improvement of the society of which he
was a part, he looked at the world about him with a critical but optimistic eye. His disappointments and his failures he was able to
write off quickly, turning to new projects with undiminished enthusiasm. Apathy he appears never to have experienced, and only
rarely was he cynical. These qualities, which account for much of
his personal charm, appear consistently in the writings of his middle years. For convenience they may be treated under three
themes — promotion, science, and politics.

Because he thought a newspaper should be informative and
entertaining rather than an instrument for influencing public opinion, he rarely used the *Pennsylvania Gazette* for promotion. His
early schemes, such as that which resulted in the first American sub-
scription library, were urged by word of mouth, and indeed he always seems to have done some talking before resorting to print. For
a larger audience, however, he turned to the broadside and pamphlet, the customary promotion devices of his day. The most important of his promotional tracts is probably *Proposals Relating to
the Education of Youth in Pensilvania* (1749). The scheme it proposed had been in his mind for at least six years, and for once he

laid some groundwork for it by reprinting in the *Gazette* a letter from the younger Pliny to Tacitus on the subject of education. His pamphlet, a month later, did not get Franklin what he wanted, but it remains a thought-provoking example of his literary strategy.

What he wanted was an academy with a curriculum better adapted to the needs of Pennsylvania youth than that of the traditional Latin grammar school. He hoped to get it by obtaining the financial support of wealthy citizens, most of whom were conservatives and saw little wrong with the central place of Latin and Greek in the training of young gentlemen. Franklin, who a quarter century earlier had satirized the classical tradition at Harvard College, was convinced that it was time for reform, for a new emphasis upon training in English and in practical subjects.

His preface is therefore designed to conciliate a possibly hostile audience. Some public-spirited gentlemen have already approved the plan; he now puts it into print in order "to obtain the Sentiments and Advice of Men of Learning, Understanding, and Experience in these Matters." With their help it can perhaps be carried into execution. If so, they will have "the hearty Concurrence and Assistance of many who are Wellwishers to their Country." Those who incline "to favour the Design with their Advice, either as to the Parts of Learning to be taught, the Order of Study, the Method of Teaching, the Oeconomy of the School, or any other Matter of Importance to the Success of the Undertaking, are desired to communicate their Sentiments as soon as may be, by Letter directed to *B. Franklin,* Printer, in *Philadelphia.*"

The pose of the humble seeker of advice is belied, however, by the pamphlet itself. Before he begins Franklin lists the authors to be quoted: "The famous *Milton,*" "the great Mr. *Locke,*" "the ingenious Mr. *Hutcheson*" (actually David Fordyce), "the learned Mr. *Obadiah Walker,*" "the much admired Mons. *Rollin,*" and "the learned and ingenious Dr. *George Turnbull.*" The steel hand beneath the velvet glove is clear: only a vain and provincial Philadelphian will oppose such champions. Then comes the scheme, in which the only concession to the classicists in the actual text is that the rector of the academy should be "learn'd in the Languages and

Sciences," a combination which at that date would have required something of a paragon. The crux of the argument (which in differing forms is still with us) lies in seven brief paragraphs:

As to their STUDIES, it would be well if they could be taught *every Thing* that is useful, and *every Thing* that is ornamental: But Art is long, and their Time is short. It is therefore propos'd that they learn those Things that are likely to be *most useful* and *most ornamental*. Regard being had to the several Professions for which they are intended.

All should be taught to write a *fair Hand*, and swift, as that is useful to All. And with it may be learnt something of *Drawing*, by Imitation of Prints, and some of the first Principles of Perspective.

Arithmetick, Accounts, and some of the first Principles of *Geometry* and *Astronomy*.

The *English* Language might be taught by Grammar; in which some of our best Writers, as *Tillotson, Addison, Pope, Algernoon Sidney, Cato's Letters*, &c., should be Classicks; the *Stiles* principally to be cultivated, being the *clear* and the *concise*. Reading should also be taught, and pronouncing, properly, distinctly, emphatically; not with an even Tone, which *under-does*, nor a theatrical, which *over-does* Nature.

To form their Stile they should be put on Writing Letters to each other, making Abstracts of what they read; or writing the same Things, in their own Words; telling or writing Stories lately read, in their own Expressions. All to be revis'd and corrected by the Tutor, who should give his Reasons, and explain the Force and Import of Words, &c.

To form their Pronunciation, they may be put on making Declamations, repeating Speeches, delivering Orations, &c., the Tutor assisting at the Rehearsals, teaching, advising, correcting their Accent, &c.

Here, in little more than 250 words, is the summation of Franklin's conviction, obviously based upon his own experience and making use of some of the learning processes which he himself had found profitable. That he knew it to be unpopular with his audience is clear from the elaborate support of it by authority. For these 250-odd words he provided more than 3000 words of footnotes, largely direct quotations, with the great Mr. Locke most prominent among those who had argued for training youth in their native language.

The academy was formed, and later a college, with some provisions for instruction such as Franklin wanted. He himself chose the first provost, the Reverend William Smith, a man well disposed toward the sciences. Smith, however, compromised with the classicists and later became Franklin's bitter political enemy. The pose of the humble inquirer and the marshaling of authorities both failed. Franklin did not take that defeat philosophically, and in 1789, the year before his death, charged in his "Observations Relative to the Intentions of the Original Founders of the Academy in Philadelphia" that the English program had been injudiciously starved while favors were showered upon the Latin part. There is in mankind, he said, "an unaccountable prejudice in favor of ancient customs and habitudes, which inclines to a continuance of them after the circumstances, which formerly made them useful, cease to exist." He illustrated the point by a characteristic story of how hats, once generally worn, had been replaced by wigs and umbrellas. Yet, because of fashion, men still carried them under their arms, "though the utility of such a mode . . . is by no means apparent, and it is attended not only with some expense, but with a degree of constant trouble."

The writing which made Franklin world-famous was of course that related to science. Although he was interested in natural phenomena throughout his life, his chief contributions to the knowledge of electricity were made between 1746 and 1752. The subject was fashionable from 1745, when articles on it by William Watson appeared in the *Philosophical Transactions* of the Royal Society of London. Franklin heard some lecture-demonstrations, read Watson's papers, and when a few pieces of apparatus were sent to the Library Company he and some of his friends began to explore electrical phenomena. Their discoveries were reported by Franklin in letters to Peter Collinson, a Quaker merchant of London, who read some of them before the Royal Society and arranged for others to be printed in the *Gentleman's Magazine*. Collinson was also responsible in part for the publication of a collection, *Experiments and Observations on Electricity*, in 1751. Before 1769 four additional English editions, with new letters, had been printed. French translations appeared in 1752 and 1756, a German one in 1758, and an Italian in 1774.

Science brought into play all of Franklin's best qualities as a writer. It demanded clarity and conciseness. The persona of the humble inquirer fitted perfectly, for in science there is little respect for dogmatism. Yet there was room for imagination, since from the phenomena observed hypotheses had to be constructed, and for persuasion, because those hypotheses had to be supported. For once the writer and his audience were in complete accord. Franklin's literary skill is attested by the general acceptance of some of the terms he invented — *positive, negative, battery,* and *conductor.* His passion for doing good was satisfied, moreover, in his invention of the lightning rod for protecting property from one of the more destructive forces of the natural world.

Many letters in the *Experiments and Observations* are models of reporting and evaluating scientific investigation. The best, perhaps, and certainly the most famous, is the paper proposing the grounded lightning rod (the general theory had been previously stated) and the experimental demonstration of the hypothesis of the identity of electricity and lightning. To illustrate requires a long quotation, but no better example of Franklin's clarity or of the high order of his scientific imagination can readily be found.

After some remarks on the nature of the electrical fluid or element, Franklin notes that the charge in an electrified body can be drawn off by the point of a pin from a foot's distance, while if the head of the pin is the attracting agent it must be moved to within a few inches of the electrified body before a charge is drawn off. Points apparently draw off the electrical atmosphere more readily than blunt bodies do; "as in the plucking the hairs from the horse's tail, a degree of strength insufficient to pull away a handful at once, could yet easily strip it hair by hair; so a blunt body presented cannot draw off a number of particles at once; but a pointed one, with no greater force, takes them away easily, particle by particle." Franklin is not sure of the true reasons for this phenomenon, but it is not of much importance, he says, "to know the manner in which nature exercises her laws; 'tis enough if we know the laws them-

selves. 'Tis of real use to know, that china left in the air unsup-
ported will fall and break; but *how* it comes to fall, and *why* it
breaks, are matters of speculation. 'Tis a pleasure indeed to know
them, but we can preserve our china without it." He goes on:

Thus in the present case, to know this power of points, may
possibly be of some use to mankind, tho' we should never be able to
explain it. The following experiments . . . show this power. I
have a large prime conductor made of several thin sheets of Fuller's
pasteboard form'd into a tube, near 10 feet long and a foot diame-
ter. It is covered with *Dutch* emboss'd paper, almost totally gilt.
This large metallic surface supports a much greater electrical atmosphere than a rod of iron of 50 times the weight would do. It is
suspended by silk lines, and when charg'd will strike at near two
inches distance, a pretty hard stroke so as to make ones knuckle ach.
Let a person standing on the floor present the point of a needle, at
12 or more inches distance from it, and while the needle is so presented, the conductor cannot be charged, the point drawing off the
fire as fast as it is thrown on by the electrical globe. Let it be
charged, and then present the point at the same distance, and it will
suddenly be discharged. In the dark you may see a light on the
point, when the experiment is made. And if the person holding the
point stands upon wax, he will be electrified by receiving the fire at
that distance. Attempt to draw off the electricity with a blunt body,
as a bolt of iron round at the end and smooth (a silversmith's iron
punch, inch-thick, is what I use) and you must bring it within the
distance of three inches before you can do it, and then it is done
with a stroke and crack. As the pasteboard tube hangs loose on silk
lines, when you approach it with the punch iron, it likewise will
move towards the punch, being attracted while it is charged; but if
at the same instant a point be presented as before, it retires again,
for the point discharges it. Take a pair of large brass scales, of two or
more feet beam, the cords of the scales being silk. Suspend the beam
by a packthread from the cieling, so that the bottom of the scales
may be about a foot from the floor: the scales will move round in a
circle by the untwisting of the packthread. Set the iron punch on
the end upon the floor, in such a place as that the scales may pass
over it in making their circle: Then electrify one scale by applying
the wire of a charged phial to it. As they move round, you see that
scale draw nigher to the floor, and dip more when it comes over the
punch; and if that be placed at a proper distance, the scale will
snap and discharge its fire into it. But if a needle be stuck on the
end of the punch, its point upwards, the scale, instead of draw-

ing nigh to the punch and snapping, discharges its fire silently, through the point, and rises higher from the punch. Nay, even if the needle be placed upon the floor, near the punch, its point upwards, the end of the punch, tho' so much higher than the needle, will not attract the scale and receive its fire, for the needle will get it and convey it away, before it comes nigh enough for the punch to act. And this is constantly observable in these experiments, that the greater quantity of electricity on the pasteboard tube, the farther it strikes or discharges its fire, and the point likewise will draw it off at a still greater distance.

Now if the fire of electricity and that of lightning be the same . . . this pasteboard tube and these scales may represent electrified clouds. If a tube of only 10 feet long will strike and discharge its fire on the punch at two or three inches distance, an electrified cloud of perhaps 10,000 acres may strike and discharge on the earth at a proportionably greater distance. The horizontal motion of the scales over the floor, may represent the motion of the clouds over the earth; and the erect iron punch a hill or high building; and then we see how electrified clouds passing over hills or high buildings at too great a height to strike, may be attracted lower till within their striking distance. And lastly, if a needle fix'd on the punch with its point upright, or even on the floor, below the punch, will draw the fire from the scale silently at a much greater than the striking distance, and so prevent its descending towards the punch; or if in its course it would have come nigh enough to strike, yet being first deprived of its fire it cannot, and the punch is thereby secured from the stroke. I say, if these things are so, may not the knowledge of this power of points be of use to mankind, in preserving houses, churches, ships &c. from the stroke of lightning, by directing us to fix on the highest parts of those edifices, upright rods of iron, made sharp as a needle, and gilt to prevent rusting, and from the foot of these rods a wire down the outside of the building into the ground; or down round one of the shrouds of a ship and down her side till it reaches the water? Would not these pointed rods probably draw the electrical fire silently out of a cloud before it came nigh enough to strike, and thereby secure us from the most sudden and terrible mischief?

To determine the question, whether the clouds that contain lightning are electrified or not, I would propose an experiment to be try'd where it may be done conveniently. On the top of some high tower or steeple, place a kind of sentry-box . . . big enough to contain a man and an electrical stand. From the middle of the stand let an iron rod rise and pass bending out of the door, and then upright 20 or 30 feet, pointed very sharp at the end. If the electrical stand be kept clean and dry, a man standing on it when such clouds are passing low, might be electrified and afford sparks, the rod drawing fire to him from a cloud. If any danger to the man should be apprehended (tho' I think there would be none) let him stand on the floor of his box, and now and then bring near to the rod, the loop of a wire that has one end fastened to the leads, he holding it by a wax handle; so the sparks, if the rod is electrified, will strike from the rod to the wire, and not affect him.

Franklin constructs his hypothesis, with its usefulness firmly in mind, from careful observation of experiments with simple apparatus easily obtainable by anyone. His description is clear and factual, although the analogies of the horse's tail and the falling china are valuable aids to understanding. His conclusions are the earliest written suggestions of their kind, and they quickly came to fruition. Lightning rods were erected and found to work, and on May 13, 1752, Thomas-François Dalibard reported to the Academy of Sciences in Paris on his successful performance of the proposed experiment with a tall pointed rod and an electrical stand. "En suivant la route que M. Franklin nous a tracée," he began, "j'ai obtenu une satisfaction complète." With that sentence the triumph of Franklin the natural philosopher was assured. It was to be some weeks before he was to fly his famous kite, in a simpler but much more dangerous experiment.

Franklin's first skirmish with power politics on the international level, where the ravages of war as a means of settling conflicts of interest are an ever-present risk, came at about the same time that he was beginning his exploration of electricity, in 1747. England had been at war with Spain since 1739 and with France since 1740, which meant that the British colonies had enemies to the south in the Spanish Main and to the north in French Canada. To the west, moreover, were the Indians, with whom the French could make alliances. If English sea power failed, the colonies would be encircled. It took some time for this fact to disturb Pennsylvanians. Their geographical location seemed to promise safety; the powerful Quaker leaders were conscientiously opposed to all things military, including preparation against attack; and the numerous German farmers and artisans cared nothing for British supremacy. Then, in the spring and summer of 1747, Spanish and French privateers appeared in the Delaware River, one of them raiding a settlement less than sixty miles from Philadelphia. The War of the Austrian Succession was suddenly something that had to be reckoned with.

Franklin's *Plain Truth: Or, Serious Considerations on the Present State of the City of Philadelphia, and Province of Pennsylvania*, which appeared in November, is his most effective piece of propaganda. Its purpose was to arouse a divided community to the desperate necessity of unity and action. Like Thomas Paine's *Common Sense* it is an appeal to emotion rather than to reason, directed to almost every special interest which might suffer if the worst should happen and the city and province be attacked. Like Paine, too, Franklin offered a specific course of action, one quickly followed.

Plain Truth has upon its title page a long Latin quotation from Cato, not for ornament but to satisfy the learned that military preparedness had classical precedent. Its first paragraph ends with a proverb, "When the Steed is stolen, you shut the Stable Door," a warning the most illiterate could understand. Every other British colony has taken measures for its defense, Franklin notes. The wealth of Pennsylvania, unprotected, must certainly be a temptation to an enemy which has been exploring the river approaches, is known to have spies everywhere, and very probably has subverted unscrupulous men within the province itself. Remember, Franklin says, the eighth chapter of Judges, which he quotes at length. The French Catholics have converted many Indians, and it may not be long before the scalping parties which have already raided New York will be ravaging the back country of Pennsylvania. City and country are alike in being threatened, and their interests are the same. Trade is in dire danger, and if trade declines bad debts will multiply and land values decrease. The enemy may count upon Quaker pacifism, although Franklin thinks some Quakers will fight in self-defense. Preparedness will cost money, but think of the loss from plundering and burning. Well-to-do Philadelphians may be granted time to flee to the country, but what if there is a sudden attack, "perhaps in the Night! Confined to your Houses, you will have nothing to trust to but the Enemy's Mercy. Your best Fortune will be, to fall under the Power of Commanders of King's Ships, able to controul the Mariners; and not into the Hands of *licentious Privateers*. Who can, without the utmost Horror, conceive the Miseries of the Latter! when your Persons, Fortunes, Wives and Daughters, shall be subject to the wanton and unbridled Rage, Rapine, and Lust, of *Negroes, Molattoes*, and others, the vilest and most abandoned of Mankind." The governing party, not even "Friends" to the people (he is here playing on the formal name for the Quakers), will not permit the appropriation of the funds necessary for defense, nor is anything to be hoped for from the opposition, who will not lay out their wealth to protect the trade of their Quaker adversaries. " 'Till of late I could scarce believe the Story of him who refused to pump in a sinking Ship, because one on board, whom he hated, would be saved by it as well as himself. But such, it seems, is the Unhappiness of human Nature, that our Passions, when violent, often are too hard for the united Force of *Reason, Duty,* and *Religion*." What must be done, therefore, will have to be done by the "middling People" — farmers, shopkeepers, and tradesmen. They are strong enough to muster 60,000 men, exclusive of the Quakers, and all of them are acquainted with the use of firearms. Englishmen have shown before that they can fight, and there are thousands of "*brave* and *steady*" Germans. If the hints of the author, "A Tradesman of Philadelphia," are well received, he will within a few days lay before the people the form of an association, "together with a practicable Scheme for raising the Money necessary for the Defence of our Trade, City, and Country, without laying a Burthen on any Man." The tract then concludes with a prayer.

Here Franklin addressed himself to selfish interests, fear, and prejudice — national, social, racial, and religious. The humble inquirer is forgotten, together with caution other than that which might conciliate the more militant Quakers. *Plain Truth* made him enemies in high places, chief among them Thomas Penn, the proprietor, but it got results. The extralegal association for defense which he proposed was organized almost immediately, despite the objection that it constituted a private army which might be a potential source of danger to government. The money was raised by a lottery which Franklin showed the "middling" people how to run. Arms were procured and the province readied for a battle which fortunately never came, the exhausted great powers of Europe signing the Treaty of Aix-la-Chapelle in 1748. The association thereafter languished, but Franklin was now a man of political influence. He exerted himself again in large affairs in 1754, during the Albany Congress, at which he proposed a plan of colonial union and editorialized in the *Gazette* for that cause, printing the first American newspaper cartoon: a segmented snake, representing the several colonies, above a caption reading "Join, or die." He also took a leading part in the American phase of the Seven Years' War, but never again did he display the sustained passion of the propagandist which *Plain Truth* reveals.

During his two long stays in London Franklin's tasks were essentially diplomatic. His first assignment was to get some settlement of a dispute about taxes which had soured the relations between the Pennsylvania assembly and the Penn family, who retained immense proprietary rights in provincial lands. Later his job was to represent the colonial interests to the British ministry, increasingly hostile as its measures for taxation were opposed by the Americans, and to the British public, which tended to be indifferent to issues so remote. Because of these responsibilities, Franklin's writing between 1757 and 1775 was predominantly political, although he did not neglect science and occasionally found time for such *jeux d'esprits* as the "Craven Street Gazette" of 1770, a fictitious newspaper prepared for the Stevenson family, with whom he lodged for many years.

Over 125 anonymous contributions to English newspapers between 1765 and 1775 have been identified as Franklin's. In addition he had a hand in a number of important pamphlets and sometimes appeared in public to testify, as an expert witness, on American opinion. Facing a hostile or apathetic audience, he was usually ingratiating and conciliatory, appealing to the British concern for national interests and fair play. Only at the end did he despair of settling the quarrel without separation and bloodshed.

Of his pamphlets the most considerable was *The Interest of Great Britain Considered, with Regard to Her Colonies and the Acquisition of Canada and Guadaloupe* (1760). Written toward the end of the Seven Years' War, it strongly urged the annexation of Canada as a condition of peace. Strange as it may now seem, there were some Englishmen who preferred to acquire Guadaloupe, an island group in the West Indies where sugar was already being produced in large quantity. One of their arguments for leaving Canada to the French was that British America was already large enough, since if it grew stronger it might become dangerous to Great Britain. In preparing his answer to this line of reasoning Franklin had the help of an English lawyer-friend, Richard Jackson, and the tone of the piece is largely legalistic. Here and there, however, Franklin's feelings enliven things, as in his suggestion that the growth of the colonies could be checked less cruelly if Parliament should emulate the Egyptian treatment of the Israelites and pass a law requiring midwives to stifle every third or fourth child at birth.

In February 1766, Franklin appeared before the House of Commons in the course of a debate on the repeal of the Stamp Act. He made an impressive showing, not that he was an accomplished orator but because of his talent as a face-to-face persuader. His answers to questions, stenographically reported, reveal a well-planned strategy for dealing with an audience partly friendly and partly hostile. Usually he replied in a sentence or two, but he added more when he saw the chance to appeal to British self-interest or patriotism, and on three or four occasions he spoke at length. Again and again he stood firm on the main point, that the colonies were right in their distinction between external taxes, properly levied for the regulation of commerce, and internal taxes, which they insisted should be imposed only by their own legislatures.

Typical of the many newspaper contributions is "The Causes of American Discontents before 1768," an even-tempered explanation of colonial grievances as they might appear to a disinterested

Englishman. In this and many other letters Franklin's role was to inform rather than to argue; he was what we would now call a public relations man. By 1773, however, he was understandably discouraged, and his two best known newspaper articles are satires: "Rules by Which a Great Empire May Be Reduced to a Small One" and "An Edict by the King of Prussia." He himself said they were "designed to expose the conduct of this country towards the colonies in a short, comprehensive, and striking view, and stated therefore in out-of-the-way forms, as most likely to take the general attention."

The "Rules," one of his most ironic pieces, indirectly but clearly suggests rebellion, and reviews American complaints in highly emotional language. One paragraph will illustrate its method and feeling: "However peaceably your colonies have submitted to your government, shown their affection to your interests, and patiently borne their grievances; you are to suppose them *always inclined to revolt*, and treat them accordingly. Quarter troops among them, who by their insolence may provoke the rising of mobs, and by their bullets and bayonets suppress them. By this means, like the husband who uses his wife ill from suspicion, you may in time convert your suspicions into realities."

The "Edict" is the most effective of what Paul Baender has called Franklin's "duplicative" satires, in which the strategy was to demand that the reader put himself in someone else's place, so that he may feel more keenly feelings which he might otherwise misunderstand. It is also a hoax, whose success greatly pleased its joke-loving author. What Franklin did was to use the very words of the Parliamentary statutes restricting American commerce and manufactures, ranging from the reign of Charles II to that of George III, as if they were enacted by Prussia, a nation with some claim to being Britain's mother country from the time of the Angles and the Saxons. The "Edict" makes clearer than any lengthy argument how shipping and manufacturing interests had "lobbied" for their own advantage over the shipowners, ironmakers, and hatters of the colonies. But by this time, no literary skill could long postpone the appeal to arms.

Having failed to avert the rebellion he dreaded, Franklin returned to Philadelphia long enough to serve on the committee which drafted the Declaration of Independence. By the end of 1776, however, he was back in Europe, this time in Paris, to plead the cause of a new nation and to deal with still another public, this time a most admiring one.

One of his first acts, apparently, was to compose still another hoax. "The Sale of the Hessians" attacks the British employment of German mercenaries in the American war. It is a letter in French, ostensibly written in Rome by the Count de Schaumbergh, to the commander of the German soldiers for whose services the British were paying large subsidies, including lump sums for men killed. Nearly 30,000 Germans were thus hired out by their princes, and in one case the agreement was to count three wounded men as one dead one in reckoning up the account. Franklin's matter-of-fact assumption of the Count's desire to have as many casualties as possible leads to cutting irony.

I am about to send to you some new recruits. Don't economize them. Remember glory before all things. Glory is true wealth. There is nothing degrades the soldier like the love of money. He must care only for honour and reputation, but this reputation must be acquired in the midst of dangers. A battle gained without costing the conqueror any blood is an inglorious success, while the conquered cover themselves with glory by perishing with their arms in their hands. Do you remember that of the 300 Lacedæmonians who defended the defile of Thermopylæ, not one returned? How happy should I be could I say the same of my brave Hessians!
It is true that their king, Leonidas, perished with them: but things have changed, and it is no longer the custom for princes of the empire to go and fight in America for a cause with which they have no concern. And besides, to whom should they pay the thirty guineas per man if I did not stay in Europe to receive them? Then, it is necessary also that I be ready to send recruits to replace the men you lose. For this purpose I must return to Hesse. It is true, grown men are becoming scarce there, but I will send you boys. Besides, the scarcer the commodity the higher the price. I am assured that the women and little girls have begun to till our lands, and they get on not badly. You did right to send back to Europe that Dr. Crumerus who was so successful in curing dysentery. Don't

bother with a man who is subject to looseness of the bowels. That disease makes bad soldiers. One coward will do more mischief in an engagement than ten brave men will do good. Better that they burst in their barracks than fly in a battle, and tarnish the glory of our arms. Besides, you know that they pay me as killed for all who die from disease, and I don't get a farthing for runaways.

Franklin's busy life in France, where he received the adulation usually reserved for matinee idols, was not all grimly political. Living at Passy, then a Paris suburb, he became the center of a group of admirers, many of them women. For their amusement and his own he set up a printing press in his house, upon which were printed, from time to time, short light essays, of a sort sometimes known as *bijoux*. These are usually referred to as the "bagatelles," and there are nineteen of them altogether. The best known are "Dialogue between Franklin and the Gout," "The Whistle," "The Ephemera," and "The Morals of Chess." All exploit an old man's personality or hobbies and, since they were written for a French audience, they have an unusual flavor for English writing — a Gallic delight in the well-turned phrase and the expression of delicate feeling. They are carefully structured, with the tone sustained just long enough for their effect. There is some moralizing, to be sure; that had become a habit of Franklin's.

Every reader has his favorite bagatelle, and few fail to be charmed by one of them or another. My favorite is "The Ephemera," addressed to Madame Brillon, a woman many years Franklin's junior whom he called by the pet name of "Brillante." It is an allegory, "an emblem of human life," which compares men and women to a species of small flies. One white-haired philosopher fly, seven hours old, reflects upon his lot, now that he cannot hope to live more than seven or eight minutes longer. What to him are politics, or scientific investigations, or a name to leave behind him? "For me," he concludes, "after all my eager pursuits, no solid pleasures now remain, but the reflection of a long life spent in meaning well, the sensible conversations of a few good lady ephemeræ, and now and then a kind smile and a tune from the ever amiable *Brillante*."

In that gallant commentary on fame and old age Franklin comes alive more fully then he ever does in the *Autobiography*.

Autobiography is, indeed, an imperfect instrument at best. Memory, whether conscious or unconscious, is tricky and mysterious, and a biographer is sometimes able to get the facts more accurately than he who seeks to explain himself. What the autobiographer does not tell us is sometimes more significant than what he does.

Franklin's autobiography, for example, omits consideration of a vast area of his early life which must have had important psychological effects. He recounts some of his sexual adventures and admits that in his first years in Philadelphia he was resorting to "low Women" to allay "that hard-to-be-govern'd Passion of Youth," but he does not say that a son was born to him in the winter of 1730–31 by a woman who has never been satisfactorily identified. She may have been Deborah Read, whom he took as his common-law wife in September of 1730, regular marriage being impossible because her runaway husband might still have been alive. Deborah was his faithful companion until her death in 1774, but of their life together we know little other than that she brought up William, the illegitimate son, as well as their daughter Sarah, and that she did not have the capacity to share the intellectual growth and social success of her printer husband. It is hard to escape the conviction that the Franklins were always on the wrong side of the tracks, and that some of Benjamin's pleasures in his diplomatic triumphs (he was, some have thought, a bit of a snob in later life) may be explained by his domestic situation.

The *Autobiography* was begun as a letter to William, who had already given Franklin an illegitimate grandson, and for whom some moralizing was no doubt appropriate. (William was later, as the last royal governor of New Jersey, to break with his father over politics.) Franklin wrote eighty-six pages of it in England in 1771; other parts were added later (seventeen pages in 1784 and 117 pages in 1788, all written in France, and a final seven and a half pages in 1790, in Philadelphia). Its piecemeal composition was followed by piecemeal publication, in which Franklin of course had no hand, so that until very recently no reliable text has been available. These circumstances, together with its coverage of only the first part of Franklin's life, make it a remarkably imperfect book.

One much-discussed question about the *Autobiography* has been its style. In the late nineteenth century it was believed that Temple Franklin, editor of the first "official" version in 1818, had systematically substituted Latin words for his grandfather's more vigorous Anglo-Saxon expressions. He was accused of changing "guzzlers of beer" to "drinkers of beer," "Keimer stared like a pig poisoned" to "Keimer stared with astonishment," and making other similar concessions to false gentility. Max Farrand's lengthy examination of the original manuscript, however, has shown that many changes of this kind were probably Franklin's own. In the last months of his life he was apparently much less admiring of a colloquial style than he was in 1771. He seems, indeed, to have grown conservative about language as he grew older, expressing opposition to innovations which he feared might hamper communication between Englishmen and Americans. One wonders what would have been the result had he lived to see the *Autobiography* through the press himself. Or, what is even more frightening, had he edited his own collected works.

For these and various other reasons Franklin is probably best and most fully revealed in those writings with which he had no opportunity to tamper, and particularly in his letters. Of these there are hundreds, to his family (including a lively and favorite sister in Boston, Mrs. Jane Mecom), to his scientific and philosophical friends, and to correspondents who, like Ezra Stiles, invaded his privacy with a slight touch of malice. The majority of his letters date from the latter part of his life. They show his warm feelings for his friends, which were ordinarily warmly reciprocated, the extraordinary range of his interests, and the play of a lively and imaginative mind. That he had a long life of "meaning well" is clear.

It should be evident by this time that I believe Franklin was right in thinking of himself as a writer and that he was seldom as calculating and unemotional a writer as he thought he was. He had a purpose in almost everything he wrote, usually persuasion. He believed written persuasion to be distinct from oral, and he always came back to clarity, brevity, and purpose. An essay of 1733, discovered by Whitfield J. Bell, Jr., contains a passage which sums up his conception of the difference between writing and speech. "*Amplification*, or the Art of saying Little in Much," it reads,

should only be allowed to Speakers. If they preach, a Discourse of considerable Length is expected from them, upon every Subject they undertake, and perhaps they are not stock'd with naked Thought sufficient to furnish it out. If they plead in the Courts, it is of Use to speak abundance, tho' they reason little; for the Ignorant in a Jury, can scarcely believe it possible that a Man can talk so much and so long without being in the Right. Let them have the Liberty then, of repeating the same Sentences in other Words; let them put an Adjective to every Substantive, and double every Substantive with a Synonima; for this is more agreeable than hauking, spitting, taking Snuff, or any other Means of concealing Hesitation. Let them multiply Definitions, Comparisons, Similitudes and Examples. Permit them to make a Detail of Causes and Effects, enumerate all the Consequences, and express one Half by Metaphor and Circumlocution: Nay, allow the Preacher to tell us whatever a Thing is negatively, before he begins to tell us what it is affirmatively; and suffer him to divide and subdivide as far as *Two and fiftieth*. All this is not intolerable while it is not written. But when a Discourse is to be bound down upon Paper, and subjected to the calm leisurely Examination of nice Judgment, every Thing that is needless gives Offence; and therefore all should be retrenched, that does not directly conduce to the End design'd.

The final judgment upon the question of whether or not Franklin was a great writer rests upon the evaluation of his purposes. If the advancement of science and the resolution of political differences are of major importance, he was. If the exploration of the depths of human psychology is the primary purpose of literature, he was not. If the great thing for the writer to do is to present a thought-provoking or satisfying philosophy of life, the question is debatable. Purpose aside, however, and greatness left to individual opinion, Franklin has one telling advantage over most American writers who must be read in the context of their time. People do read him.

LEWIS LEARY

Washington Irving

EW writers have successfully stretched a small talent farther
than Washington Irving. He was an alert, ingenuous man
who liked to be liked, and who tried to write what other people expected of him. His success was at once the measure of his own placid
adaptability and of assurance among most of his contemporaries
that literary excursions should be pleasantly trivial, skipping over
surfaces without disturbing deeper matters of trade or politics, the
opening of the West or decisions on what democracy should be.
People who spoke their minds sharply, like Philip Freneau or Fenimore Cooper, held Irving in great scorn, but almost everyone else
admired him. He was comfortable to have around, for he seldom
raised his voice, and he flattered his countrymen's assumption that
they were, in truth, gentlefolk who could sip appreciatively on Old
World culture at the same time that they built new traditions of
strength and hardihood.

Irving made himself heard at a time when his country needed
someone like him. No longer was quizzical Ben Franklin, sage but
uncouth, to represent the best in native accomplishment. People
had already begun to talk of him as a despoiler of polite language
and cultivated taste. His influence made for penny-pinching vul-
garities, so that even poetry from the New World often spoke of

commerce as a be-all and end-all. Many Englishmen of discrimination seemed to agree with Dr. Samuel Johnson that there was something degenerate about most Americans. Few were surprised at the scorn in Sydney Smith's tone as he asked in 1820, "Who reads an American book?"

When Washington Irving's *The Sketch Book* appeared at just that time, as if to provide by its popularity an answer to the question, literature of the United States gave first promise of eventual maturity. It had lived through a difficult, war-torn childhood, and for years was to struggle through an awkward adolescence. Clothed often in castoff garments, pampered, and praised for the wrong things, nurtured more often in parlor or library than in its spacious backyard, it nonetheless grew, its voice wavering and cracking, until finally, by the time of Irving's death in 1859, it had learned to communicate with authenticity and persuasion. During the years between, when Emerson and Hawthorne spoke most clearly, when Thoreau was thought strange and Poe shocking, when Melville and Whitman wrote of matters beyond the experience of many men, then Irving was more famous and respected than any of these, the dean indeed of American letters, envied by Cooper, admired by Longfellow, whose deft extensions of Irving's moods made him seem his logical successor.

Neither Irving nor Longfellow is esteemed so highly now, but neither is forgotten. The latter's songs still occasionally gladden or gently lull, and Irving, at the very least, has presented his country with the inestimable gift of two characters and a name. Either Rip Van Winkle or Ichabod Crane would be recognized at once if he walked down almost any American street. Their adventures have become as much a part of native lore as Captain Smith's rescue by Pocahontas, Tom Sawyer's slick whitewashing deal, or Paul Bunyan's gargantuan strength and appetite. In much the same sense, the word *knickerbocker* has become, through Irving's use of it, more than a designation for a baggy Dutch garment: it describes a period in the history of native culture, and an attitude toward literature and life; it appears today almost one hundred times in the Manhattan directory, to identify, among others, a fashionable corps of cadets, a brewery, a bookshop, a professional basketball team, and a manufacturer of plastics.

But Irving's reputation during his lifetime rested on greatly more than this, and a candid revaluation of his writing today suggests more also. He had two effective voices. As Diedrich Knickerbocker, he spoke of native themes, with crusty vigor — almost everything of Irving's which is most affectionately remembered is put in the words of that unpretentious and sometimes impolite old gentleman. As Geoffrey Crayon, he was decorous and superbly polished, beloved as an ambassador of good will between the New World and the Old, who lifted the literary embargo on both sides by disproving "the old notion that it is impossible for an *American to write decent English.*" Praised by Scott and Byron and Moore, Irving became a solid, cheerful, adaptable symbol of what a proper man of letters might be. As much as Franklin, he studied the way toward success.

Like Franklin also, he was the last child born in a large family, but without forebears deeply rooted in colonial America, as Franklin's had been. Irving's dour Presbyterian father had come to New York from Scotland only two decades before the birth of his youngest son on April 3, 1783, just as the Revolution drew to a close. In spite of wartime troubles, William Irving had prospered, and was assisted now by his oldest son and namesake, already at seventeen active in the family wine, sugar, hardware, and auctioneering business. The next son, Peter, was two years away from entrance to Columbia College, where he would receive preliminary training toward a medical degree which he was never to use. Seven-year-old Ebenezer was musical, but already promised to be the steadiest of them all, destined for a career in trade. John Treat, five years older than the youngest Irving, would also attend Columbia, to prepare in law. The three sisters married early and moved away, but wrote affectionate letters home which testify to close-knit family ties.

As the youngest, Washington Irving seems to have been a spoiled child, precocious, moody, and sensitive, and subject to alarming bronchial attacks. "When I was very young," he remembered, "I had an impossible flow of spirits that went beyond my strength. Every thing was fairy land to me." From the age of six to fifteen, he was doomed, he said, "to be mewed up the lifelong day in that purgatory of boyhood, a schoolroom." Thereafter, instead of entering college, he read haphazardly in whatever books came to hand, and explored nooks and crannies of little New York: "I knew every spot," he said, "where a murder or robbery had been committed, or a ghost seen." More often, he wandered about the countryside, seeking health, it was explained, in the open air. Sometimes he adventured along the banks of the Hudson River, even above Spuyten Duyvil and Yonkers, through Dutch villages to Tarrytown, where his brother William's wife's family, the Pauldings, lived, "adding greatly to my stock of knowledge," he said, by noting rural habits and customs, and conversing with country people. Passing through Sleepy Hollow to the Pocantico Hills, he could look across the river to the legend-haunted headlands of the lower Catskills.

Between excursions, after 1799, he read law intermittently, finally with Josiah Ogden Hoffman, who had two attractive daughters. During the summer of 1803, he made a long journey with the Hoffmans, by boat and oxcart into Canada, squiring the girls, playing his flute, reciting Shakespeare, and filling notebooks with impressions of moonlight over the Hudson, of trading with Dutch farmers for milk and cheese, of squalid frontier lodgings and overland travel through deep-rutted forest roads, alert for whatever was comic or picturesque or appealed to sentiment.

For he had already, at nineteen, become known to contemporaries as a person of "extraordinary . . . literary accomplishments," deserving of the best "admiration and esteem." When the previous autumn his brother Peter had become editor of the new *Morning Chronicle* in New York, Irving contributed a series of nine sportive letters, from November 15, 1802, to April 23, 1803, over the signature of "Jonathan Oldstyle, Gent." They played with grave pleasantry over the state of manners, dress, and marriage in New York, but with greatest enthusiasm over the state of the theater. The jingoistic drama of the time — brave American sailors in love and at war — was lampooned; actors were caricatured, and musicians who with "solemn and important phizes" produced discordant noise; the managers were chided for not keeping the playhouse clean or the playgoers quiet; and critics were taunted as "pests of society," who attended performances only to "lounge away an idle hour."

Jonathan Oldstyle was so merry and vulgar an old gentleman that a more sedate Irving was later to be ashamed of him, but he spoke zestfully, and colloquially well. He disliked candle-grease dripping on his jacket from the theater chandeliers, and he became tired of dodging apple cores thrown by rowdies in the gallery. Jonathan discreetly ogled the belles who smiled flirtatiously from the boxes, their charms set off to most alluring advantage — here an arched look, there a simper, everywhere bewitching languish. He was sorry that spyglasses were no longer used to observe them more closely. And the critics — "ha! ha!" — how foolish and subversive: "they reduce feelings to a state of miserable refinement, and destroy entirely all the enjoyments in which our coarser sentiments delighted."

Much of what Irving would do best is foreshadowed in these juvenile essays: the physical caricature, which Dickens would admire and imitate — the dapper Frenchman, the persnickety spinster, the talkative old gentleman, the suave but foolish gallant, and the honest countryman "gazing in gaping wonder"; the pose of nostalgia — "Nothing is more intolerable . . . than innovation"; the rich delight in describing food and feasting — "the hissing of frying pans, winding the savory steams of roast or boiled." Most predictive, however, are the style and manner: the tailored sentences, well buttoned with adjectives; the jocular good humor, vulgar sometimes, but seldom ribald; the quip and the laugh and the quick retreat before feelings are deeply hurt; and through all the sense that Irving liked the people at whom he flicked his whimsically bantering wit — "that quiet, shrewd, good-humored sense of the ridiculous" which contemporaries recognized as setting Irving apart "from every other writer in our language," but which never of itself was enough to ensure him place as a major writer.

Perhaps because they did prick republican pretensions and looked shrewdly down their nose on native manners, the Oldstyle essays established young Irving as a kind of social arbiter for young America. Charles Brockden Brown, fresh from minor triumphs as a novelist, invited him to contribute to his *Philadelphia Literary Magazine.* Joseph Dennie, who conducted the *Port Folio* as "Oliver Oldschool," recognized and applauded the literary kinship implied by his choice of pseudonym. During the spring of 1804, Irving almost certainly contributed to Peter's short-lived, astringent *Corrector*, and he continued his precocious career as a wit among men and a favorite with the ladies. His health, however, did not withstand even such pleasantly diversified pastimes, and he was packed off in May for a recuperative voyage to Europe.

The traveling did him good, in health and spirit. He made new friends and learned new manners, and filled notebook after notebook with careful records of what he saw and did, whether reverently viewing castles and cathedrals or in hairbrained escapades with his companions. He endured pirate attacks, excursions through bandit-infested hills, rough rides, bad lodgings, and poor food, picking up smatterings of French, Spanish, and Italian, reading volume after volume of travel adventures written by other men, and flirting with exotic women, now with novices in a convent, at another time with country damsels at a wayside tavern. Even the Italians, he wrote his father, "stared at us in surprise and called us the *wild Americans.*"

In Rome, he met Madame de Staël, and was astonished that any woman could talk so much and so well. In Genoa, he met Washington Allston, the American artist, who almost persuaded him to remain in Italy to study painting. In Paris, he visited the tailors and the theater, and was thrilled to be accosted on the street by handsome, predatory young women. In London, he saw Mrs. Siddons at Covent Garden — in fact, he saw every play he could, and wrote home about them enthusiastically in detail. By the end of twenty-three months, however, Irving admitted that "one gets tired of travelling, even in the gay and polished countries of Europe. Curiosity cannot be kept ever on the stretch; like the sensual appetites, it in time becomes sated." He was happy therefore "once more [to] return to my friends, and sink again into tranquil domestic life."

Back in New York, he entered a scattered round of activities, reserving just enough time for the study of law to allow him to pass his bar examinations late in 1806. He helped Peter translate a travel book from the French; he contributed to the *Literary Picture Gallery*, a periodical dedicated to activities of visitors at Ballston Spa; he wrote occasional verse, including doggerel lines for the opening of the New Park Theater. Perhaps it was of himself that he spoke when later he allowed a character to confess: "I had too much genius for study . . . so I fell into bad company, and took to bad habits. Do not mistake me. I mean that I fell into the company of village literati, and village blues, and took to writing village poetry. It was quite the fashion in the village to be literary."

They were gay blades, those "lads of Kilkenny" — Peter and Gouverneur Kemble, Henry Brevoort, Henry Ogden, James Kirke Paulding, the Irving brothers, Peter and Washington and sometimes William — the "worthies" who met for literary powwows at Dyde's tavern, and for "blackguard suppers" at a porterhouse on Nassau Street: "sad dogs" indeed, fond of conscientious drinking and good fun. Among their favorite haunts was the old Kemble mansion on the Passaic River, about a mile above Newark, which they renamed Cockloft Hall; they transferred to it much of the fictitious adventure set forth in *Salmagundi*, a periodical which, when it appeared in twenty numbers irregularly from January 24, 1807, to January 25, 1808, became the talk and wonder of the town. "If we moralize," they promised, "it shall be but seldom, and on all occasions, we shall be more solicitous to make our readers laugh than cry; for we are laughing philosophers, and truly of the opinion that wisdom, true wisdom, is a plump, jolly dame, who sits in her arm-chair, laughs right merrily at the farce of life — and takes the world as it comes."

Who wrote it was soon suspected — the Irvings, Washington and William and perhaps Peter, and William's brother-in-law, James Kirke Paulding; but who wrote what has never been determined, so mixed and various but unified in temper was the matter set forth as "the whim-whams and opinions of Launcelot Langstaff, Esq., and others." Usually "Anthony Evergreen, Gent.," commented on fashionable society; "William Wizard, Esq.," handled theatrical and literary criticism; "Pindar Cockloft" contributed verse; and Launcelot Langstaff, as proprietor, roamed at will over all subjects. "In hoc est hoax, cum quiz et jokesez. Et smokem, toastem, roastem folksez, Fee, faw fum," they asserted on the title page in a cryptic motto, which was obligingly translated as "With baked and broiled, stew'd and toasted, and fried, boil'd, smok'd and roasted, we treat the town."

"As everybody knows, or ought to know," the first issue began, "what a SALMAGUND is, we shall spare ourselves the trouble of an explanation; besides we despise trouble as we do everything low and mean, and hold the man who would incur it unnecessarily as an object worthy of our highest pity and contempt." Most people, however, have been tempted to look up the word, to discover that it describes an appetizer made of chopped meat (raw), pickled herring, and onions, liberally seasoned with olive oil, vinegar, and cayenne pepper — excellent, some find, with cocktails or beer. No less savory were the elements compounded in *Salmagundi*, expertly mixed to encourage "genuine honest American tastes" rather than fashionable "French slops and fricasseed sentiment." For the convenience of readers, it was printed "on hot-pressed vellum paper, as that is held in highest estimation for buckling up young ladies' hair," in size just right for fitting "old ladies' pockets and young ladies' work bags."

The ladies came in for a great share of attention as the young men from Cockloft Hall labored to "instruct the young, reform the old, correct the town, and castigate the age." The ladies of New York were "the fairest, the finest, the most accomplished, the most ineffable things that walk, creep, crawl, swim, float, or vegetate in any or all of the four elements," but how alarmingly they dressed — in flesh-colored stockings and off-the-shoulder gowns: "*nudity* being all the rage." Actors and critics received sharp flicks, and fashionable upstarts like "Ding Dong," "Ichabod Fungus," and

"Dick Paddle." Open war was declared against local folly and stu-
pidity, especially in the letters of "Mustapha Rub-a-Dub Khan,"
written unashamedly in imitation of Oliver Goldsmith's "Citizen
of the World" essays. Boorish English travelers and foppish French
dancing masters were laughingly derided; even so popular a favorite as Thomas Moore, recently a visitor to America, was reproved
for having "hopp'd and skipp'd our country o'er,"

> . . . sipped our tea and lived on sops,
> Revel'd on syllabubs and slops,
> And when his brain, of cob-web fine,
> Was fuddled with five drops of wine,
> Would all his puny loves rehearse,
> And many a maid debauch — in verse.

All was good humor, laughingly sustained, even when the
satire turned political, like that directed against Thomas Jefferson,
his embargo, his red riding breeches, and his scientific interest in
"impaling butterflies and pickling tadpoles." More bitter invective
was reserved for literary rivals, like Thomas Green Fessenden, an
outlander, recently from New England, who in his *Weekly Spectator* dared criticize *Salmagundi* as a frothy imitation of Addison
and Steele. "From one end of the town to another," he complained,
"all is nonsense and 'Salmagund.' America has never produced
great literature — her products have been scrub oaks, at best. We
should, then, encourage every native sapling; but when, like *Salmagundi*, it turns out to be a *bramble*, and pricks and scratches
everything within its reach, we naturally ask, why it encumbereth
the ground."

Quarreling which turned bitter was not to the taste of the lads
from Cockloft Hall; it was certainly not to Irving's, who for all
his wit, was shy, more fond of conciliation than argument. *Salmagundi* was intended only as "pleasant morning or after-dinner reading, never taking too much of a gentleman's time from his business
or pleasures." It was calculated for the mood of New York, "where
the people — heaven help them — are the most irregular, crazy-
headed, quick-silver, eccentric, whim-whamsical set of mortals that
were ever jumbled together." Though frivolous and derivative,

Salmagundi was expertly done. If it were possible to know what parts of it Washington Irving wrote, they would probably be recognized as almost as good as anything he ever did.

Not only did *Salmagundi* hurt feelings; it was also not profitable — or so the young men claimed when they suspended publication after a year. Footloose again, Irving enjoyed his friends in Washington, Philadelphia, and New York, where he played lightly in chaste drawing-room flirtations with lovely ladies in the highest society and, with gentlemanly disdain, in politics. At Richmond, he helped Josiah Hoffman defend Aaron Burr in his trial for treason. He wrote occasional verse and squibs, and perhaps contributed political commentary to the newspapers, composing what was expected of him — usually at someone else's request. But ever since the decease of *Salmagundi*, he had been casually at work on a book of his own.

He and Peter had started it together, as a parody of a guidebook to New York, but when Peter was called abroad as manager of the family business in Europe, Washington Irving completed it alone — in grief, it has been said, and sadness. For on April 26, 1809 — a date which he never forgot — young Matilda Hoffman died, she on whom Washington Irving's errant attentions had at length settled. His heartbreak was so great, and finally so well known, that it has become a commonplace to suppose that Irving remained all his life a bachelor because of loyalty to Matilda Hoffman's memory: "her image was continually with me, and I dreamt of her incessantly."

But, however sorrowful the months through which Irving brought it to completion, *A History of New York from the Beginning of the World to the End of the Dutch Dynasty*, which appeared in December 1809, remains his first unified and his most joyous book. He wished it thought to have been written by a strange, inquisitive little gentleman named Diedrich Knickerbocker, who had disappeared, leaving behind him the manuscript of this "only authentic history of the times that hath been or ever will be published." Fact was jumbled with fiction, some dates were wrong, some footnotes spurious, but it was a gay, mirth-filled book.

The "unutterable ponderings of Walter the Doubter, the disastrous projects of William the Testy, and the chivalric achievements of Peter the Headstrong" had New York in an uproar; when they reached England, they made Walter Scott's sides, he said, "absolutely sore with laughter." But many people of Dutch descent resented it: horsewhipping was spoken of, and ostracism. Emerson was later to disapprove of Knickerbocker's "deplorable Dutch wit," and Whitman of his "shallow burlesque." More feelings were hurt than Irving had intended.

Yet Knickerbocker's *History* continues lightheartedly to beguile readers of later generations, who enjoy its lovely comic pose — its "Münchausen vein of exaggeration run mad" — without being bothered by attempts to identify every victim of Irving's satire. John Adams may be recognized, and perhaps James Madison; no one will miss Thomas Jefferson, who is ridiculed for his "cocked hat and corduroy small clothes," and his eccentric, democratic manners. What lives, however, are not these things, any more than what lives in *Gulliver's Travels* are the political allusions which scholars discover there. Byron prized Knickerbocker's *History* for its copious style; Dickens is said to have worn out his copy with eager reading; and Coleridge to have stayed up all one night to finish his. Not every modern reader will respond as heartily, but none will find Irving more consistently pleasant to be with than in this boisterous book which he completed at the age of twenty-six.

His laughter is directed at historians, explorers, plump Dutch matrons, and robust Connecticut girls, at Yankee skinflints and parsons, cock-fighting Virginians, the cozy pleasures of bundling and overeating (in luscious detail). As a resident of "the beloved isle of Manna-hata," Knickerbocker looked with suspicion on New Englanders as "pumpkin-eating, molasses-daubing, shingle-splitting, cider-watering, horse-jockeying, notion-peddling" creatures. Colonists to the south "lived on hoe-cakes and bacon, drank mint julips and brandy toddy," and amused themselves with "slave-driving, tavern-haunting, Sabbath-breaking, and mulatto-breeding." Frontiersmen were "a gigantic, gunpowdery race of men . . .

exceedingly expert at boxing, biting, gouging, tar and feathering" — "half man," they were, "half horse, half alligator."

The extravagance, mock gravity, and massive irreverence which was to characterize American humor from Sam Slick through Mark Twain to Faulkner are anticipated as Irving describes a sunbeam falling on the giant red nose of Antony the Trumpeter as he leaned over the side of a ship plying the Hudson, then bouncing off, "hissing hot," into the water "to kill a mighty sturgeon that was sporting beside the vessel." Wouter van Twiller "exactly five feet six inches in height and six feet five inches in circumference," was a man of such extraordinary wisdom that he avoided disturbances of the world by closing his eyes for hours at a time, his active intelligence producing all the while "certain guttural sounds, which his admirers declared were merely the noise of conflict made by his contending doubts and opinions."

Irving's weapon was less often the rapier than what Stanley Williams has described as a "true Dutch blunderbuss, shooting off in all directions." More often than not, the humor is broad, sometimes mirthfully vulgar, as when brave Peter Stuyvesant, harassed in a duel, falls backward "on his seat of honor," to land kerplunk on a meadow "cushion, softer than velvet, which providence or Minerva, or St. Nicholas, or some kindly cow, had benevolently prepared for his reception." No wonder his countrymen were scandalized when Irving compared a Dutch ship to a maiden from New York: "both full in the bows, with a pair of enormous cat-heads, a copper bottom, and a most prodigious poop!"

Legend is created and local legend is utilized as Irving shaped from whatever came to his quick-moving hands a mirage of tradition, through which characters moved in quixotic grandeur, their noble pretensions made absurd, though no less noble, because of the provincial background against which they suffered inevitable, comic defeat. His reading was ransacked for archetypal patterns against which native heroes could be measured: at the Battle of Fort Christina, "immortal deities, who whilom had seen service at the 'affair' of Troy — now mounted their feather-bed clouds and sailed over the plain," until "victory in the likeness of a gigantic

ox-fly, sat perched upon the cocked hat of the gallant Stuyvesant."
How ludicrously small the deeds of warriors in this New World
"when contrasted with the semi-mythic grandeur with which we
have clothed them, as we look backward from the crowned result,
to fancy a cause as majestic as our conception of the effect." With
these words, James Russell Lowell was perhaps the first to recognize that Irving, as much as Cooper, though with lighter touch,
produced a "homespun and plebeian mythos" — in Fielding's terms
a "comic epic" — in which gallant protagonists tested ideals of the
Old World against the frontier requirements of the New.

There was theme and scheme behind the "coarse caricature"
of Knickerbocker's *History*. The *Monthly Anthology* of Boston
greeted it as a book "certainly the wittiest our press has ever produced." In Philadelphia, the *Port Folio* praised its "drollery and
quaintness," its "copious and natural style." Neither recognized it,
as did the *Athenaeum* in London a few years later, as "an honest
and manly attempt to found an American literature. Those who
read it must have exclaimed involuntarily, 'Yes, this is the work
which was wanted. The umbilical cord is severed. America is indeed
independent.'" For not even Irving quite knew what he had done;
when he revised the *History* a few years later, he cleansed it of much
colloquial coarseness, and of caricature which might wound, apparently so intent on being liked that he failed to realize that he
had written the first American book capable of outliving the man
who made it. Only Franklin's *Autobiography* claims precedence,
for reasons quite different.

Irving's book is more irresponsible, more fun, and more literary. Source hunters have searched libraries to discover every influence on it, and none has done the job to another's satisfaction.
Sterne and Fielding were certainly on Irving's mind, imitated or
parodied; Swift, Cervantes, Shakespeare, Rabelais, the King James
Bible, Aesop, Homer, Thomas Malory, and Thomas Paine are all
present, in allusion or idiom; Arthurian legend, Greek myth, and
the ponderous supposings of Cotton Mather's *Magnalia Christi
Americana* jostle one another in exuberant disarray. Historians
have derided or defended his adaptation of fact to fancy, sometimes

locating in some half-forgotten volume in Latin, French, or Dutch the phrase or incident which Irving wove into a fabric not quite like any other.

Knickerbocker's *History* brought some profit (two thousand dollars) and more renown: "I was noticed, caressed, and for a time elated by the popularity I had gained"; but "this career of gayety and notoriety soon palled on me. I seemed to drift without aim or object." A second edition was called for in 1812, another in 1819; it was translated to French and German, and adapted for the stage. But it marked the end of one phase, the most carefree and lavish, of Irving's literary career. Not again would he write with such abandon; seldom would he write so spontaneously well. Grief or circumspection, or the enervating deceleration of spirits called growing up, sobered Irving.

In 1810, he became a partner in the family hardware business, but was apparently expected to devote little time to its routine affairs. Instead, he went to Washington as a lobbyist against restrictions in trade, and there he spent many hours in seeing the town with Paulding, and attending official balls, where he became a favorite of Washington's favorite hostess, Dolly Madison. Back in New York, he prepared a brief biographical introduction for an American edition of the poems of Thomas Campbell, declaring that in "an age when we are overwhelmed by an abundance of eccentric poetry, it is really cheering and consolatory to behold a writer . . . studiously aiming to please."

Irving's consistent demand of literature was that it should please, and more by familiarity than strangeness. As editor for two years beginning in January 1813 of the *Analectic Magazine*, he warned readers against Wordsworth's "new and corrupt fashion of writing," preferring instead the comfortable rhythms of Scott and Byron, the "warm sensibilities and lively fancies" of Thomas Moore. Friends complimented him for having "sacrificed his elegant leisure" thus to contribute to the literary advancement of his country, but Irving was bored and restless. He grumbled about the routine of editorial work and the quality of materials he found to print: "I really stagger under the trash." Paulding contributed an occasional short story, and joined the editor in a series of sketches of naval heroes. Irving himself conducted a column of "literary intelligence," wrote undiscriminating reviews, and published a handful of sketches, among them the "Traits of Indian Character" and "Philip of Pokanoket," which he would later resurrect to fill out the pages of *The Sketch Book*.

Finally, in 1815, "weary of everything and myself," he set out again for Europe, determined "to break off . . . from idle habits and idle associates and fashionable dissipation." There he hoped to "pursue a plan I had some time contemplated, of studying for a while, and then travelling about the country for the purpose of observing the manners and characters of various parts of it, with a view to writing a book which, if I have any acquaintance with my talents, will be far more . . . reputable than anything I have yet written."

In England, he visited with relatives and old friends, explored romantic byways of London, called on Campbell and Moore, breakfasted with Samuel Rogers, went on literary pilgrimages to Kenilworth, Warwick, and Stratford, but most reverently to Abbotsford, where Scott welcomed him cordially. He studied German so that he could read legends which Scott admired. He wrote some tales of his own and assiduously noted impressions, in words or deftly sketched drawings, of each new scene. He helped whenever necessary with the family business, filling in as he could for Peter who was increasingly unwell. When, toward the end of 1817, the commercial enterprises of the Irving brothers faced bankruptcy, William, now in Congress, tried to get government positions for the two brothers stranded in England, and did manage an appointment for Washington, who turned it down, because, he said, "My talents are purely literary. . . . I do not wish to undertake any situation that must involve me in routine duties."

Faced now, in his mid-thirties, for the first time with the necessity of depending on himself for support, Irving took stock of his literary wares: he reworked Knickerbocker's *History* for new publication, thumbed through his journals for usable materials, and reminisced with friends about incidents which might be turned to account. He feared, however, that his mind had lost "much of its cheerfulness and some of its activity." When early in March 1819 he sent home a packet of manuscript, he apologized, "I have attempted no lofty theme, nor sought to look wise and learned. I have preferred addressing myself to the feeling and fancy of the reader rather than to his judgment. My writing, therefore, may seem light and trifling."

But with the appearance in New York two months later of the first number of *The Sketch Book of Geoffrey Crayon, Gent.*, Irving's reputation rose at once to a level from which nothing he had done before or would do again would budge it. A pamphlet of ninety-three pages, in gray-brown paper covers, it contained five sketches, the first four skillfully done but commonplace, and the fifth, "Rip Van Winkle," the slender, indestructible peg on which much of his fame has ever since been hung. Six more numbers were issued in New York, irregularly over the next sixteen months, until September 1820, each greeted with applause and admiration.

When parts of *The Sketch Book* began to appear, without permission or profit, in English periodicals, Irving early in 1820 arranged for a London edition of the whole, first done at his own expense; but soon — thanks to assistance from Scott, to whom in gratitude (or perhaps to set right those readers who supposed Scott had written the pseudonymous work) the edition was dedicated — it was issued by John Murray in two attractive volumes which sold prodigiously well in printing after printing. Of its thirty-two essays and sketches, twenty-six were about England, six of them descriptive of London scenes and five celebrating old-time Christmas festivities at an English country house; two were asides — "The Voyage" and "The Spectre Bridegroom"; and four were on American themes, two of these the Indian sketches from the *Analectic* which had not appeared in the periodical publication of *The Sketch Book* in New York.

Scott thought the book delightful, not so "exclusively American" as Knickerbocker's *History* and *Salmagundi*; William Godwin admitted that he hardly knew an Englishman who could write

so well. Few contemporary readers seemed to agree with Wordsworth that *The Sketch Book*, "though a work of talent, is disfig-
ured by an abundance of affectations"; more thought Irving, as
Southey did, "a remarkably agreeable writer," with touch light
enough "to conciliate any reader." These pleasantly diverting
samples from Geoffrey Crayon's portfolio were shaded with humor
and delicately colored with sentiment, not studied "with the eye
of a philosopher; but rather with the sauntering gaze with which
humble lovers of the picturesque stroll from one shop window of
a print shop to another; caught sometimes by the distortions of
caricature, and sometimes by the loveliness of landscape."

Familiarity added to the charm of the sketches. Scott's influence was plain throughout, his fastidious archaizing and untidy
eloquence, later so distasteful to Mark Twain. Strokes learned
from Addison were clearly discernible, and moods borrowed from
Goldsmith's *The Deserted Village*, Thomson's *The Seasons*, Cowper's *The Task*, and Crabbe's somber rustic vignettes. So soft and
adroitly accommodating was his touch that Irving was constantly
compared to someone else, as if he had not manner or substance of
his own — to Sir Thomas Browne, Fielding, Smollett, Sterne (never
Swift, though sometimes Defoe), but especially to the ruminative
and moralizing essayists of the eighteenth century. As an artist,
he seemed copyist rather than creator: his literary offspring, said
one unkind commentator, "resemble a family of sickly, but pretty
children, — tall, feeble, and delicately slender, with white hair
and white eyes, — dressed in jaconet muslin, trimmed with pink
ribbon."

In England, his "eye dwelt with delight on neat cottages, with
their trim shrubberies and green grass plots," on "the mouldering
abbey overgrown with ivy, with the taper spire of a village church
rising from the brow of a neighboring hill." His landscapes were
stylized in the manner of the Flemish colorists whom he admired.
Broad, traditionally evocative strokes pictured "vast lawns that
extend like sheets of vivid green, and here and there clumps of
gigantic trees, heaping up rich piles of foliage: the solemn pomp
of groves and woodland glades, with deer trooping in silent herds

across them; the hare bounding away to the covert; or the pheasant, suddenly bursting upon the wing; the brook, taught to wind in natural meanderings, or expand into a glassy lake: the sequestered pool, reflecting the quivering trees, with the yellow leaf sleeping on its bosom, the trout roaming fearlessly about its limpid waters; while some rustic temple or sylvan statue grown green and dank with age, gives an air of classic sanctity to the seclusion."

More important than the scene was the mood which it called forth, of serenity — "classic sanctity," wherein each once free-flowing brook is *taught* to wind in what are made to seem, but which are not, "natural meanderings"; or made to "expand into a glassy lake" which calmly reflects the lethargic quiescence which the scene suggests. Geoffrey Crayon's still waters have little depth; the irrepressible bright flow of language with which Diedrich Knickerbocker spoke of old New York had been taught to conform to London manners. Though he admired, Irving said, the elegance and strength, robustness, manliness, and simplicity of the English gentleman, these were not traits which he easily transferred to his laboriously correct, embellished prose. He was not, it can be said, to the manor born.

Even the portraiture which as Geoffrey Crayon he now contrived was less vibrant, and the humor more timidly mannered. A line or two, whimsically suggestive because stylized, was often enough to represent a person — "the little swarthy Frenchman," for example, "with a dry weazen face, and large whiskers." Sometimes the portrait is briefly elaborated, like that of the angler in "broad-skirted fustian coat perplexed with half a hundred pockets; a pair of stout shoes, and leathern gaiters; a basket slung one side for fish; a patent landing net, and a score of other inconveniences." What people looked like was more important than what they were. Even in detailed "character," like that of "John Bull," Irving assiduously balanced every blemish with some appealing trait.

Careful now that feelings should not be hurt, his comic pose was altered. "Wit, after all," he explained, "is a mighty tart, pungent ingredient, and much too acid for some stomachs; but honest good-humor is the oil and wine of a merry meeting." In a world so roiled, who was he to venture a disturbing idea? "If, however, I can by some lucky chance, rub out one wrinkle from the brow of care, or beguile the heavy heart of one moment of sorrow . . . I shall not have written in vain."

Exactly what happened to Irving's comic sense has not been adequately explained. Perhaps it was caution — once burned, twice shy; or perhaps it was maturity, which may be the same thing, or a desire to be liked, which is not. Always dependent on crutches made of other men's literary manner, Irving once had agility enough sometimes to dance a little jig of his own, using the rubber-tipped supports to beat out a muffled accompanying rhythm; or, like some temporarily crippled athlete, had swung from them a breathtaking two steps at a time up some hazardous stairway of ridicule. Now he learned to use them more sedately, careful that his own feet, once bruised by criticism, should touch the ground no more often than necessary, but with his gait so well adjusted to other people's that they hardly noticed his using crutches at all. Some even remarked that he got on very well without them when he adventured in American themes.

But even when he spoke as Diedrich Knickerbocker, Irving was accused of plagiarism. The plot of "Rip Van Winkle" was shamelessly stolen. Passages from the old German tale of "Peter Klaus" have been placed side by side with passages from Irving's narrative, to reveal imitation so blatant that much of Rip's unhappy experience seems little more than direct translation. But such bookish detective work may miss much of Irving's intention. "I wish in every thing I do," he once declared, "to write in such a manner that my productions may have something more than mere interest in narrative to recommend them, which is very evanescent; something, if I may use the phrase, of classic merit, i.e. depending on style . . . which gives a production some chance for duration beyond the whim and fashion of the day."

Something more than style, however, has kept Rip Van Winkle alive, on stage, on screen, and in the hearts of his countrymen. He has become their "muse of memory," Hart Crane once said, their "guardian angel of a trip to the past," and he remains their conscience, accusing and amusing at the same time. As Irving gave local habitation to a myth, perhaps as old as any which has beguiled the mind of man — that of Epimenides, Endymion, Sleeping Beauty, and the seven sleepers of Ephesus — he added such other familiar elements of popular lore as the thunder of the gods, birds of ill-omen, a magic potion, man's canine best companion, and dwarfs who are spectral spirits, transporting Valhalla and the Brocken to the Catskills, where Rip still triumphantly postures as the man-boy American (Huck Finn and Anse Bundren) who never grows up, the New World innocent who yearns to return to prelapsarian freedom from work and responsibility, to retire like Franklin at forty and fly a kite. "A child playing with children," he has been called, "a kid with a dog."

Before Fenimore Cooper or Mark Twain, Henry James, Sinclair Lewis, or William Faulkner, Irving created — it may be thought inadvertently — a symbol of the mythic American, presenting, as Philip Young has pointed out, "a near-perfect image of the way a large part of the world looks at us: likeable enough, up to a point and at times, but essentially immature, self-centered, careless and above all — and perhaps dangerously — innocent. Even more pointedly Rip is a stereotype of the American male as seen from abroad, or in some jaundiced quarters at home: he is perfectly the jolly overgrown child, abysmally ignorant of his own wife and the whole world of adult men — perpetually 'one of the boys' " — a Lazarus come back from the dead, as if to warn his countrymen, and yet a comic figure, in spite of the tragedy of a life slept away. His son is like him, and his grandson is another Rip.

Irving himself was surely not consciously so devious a contriver — it is the critics who have found him out. When in "The Legend of Sleepy Hollow," he adapted parts of Bürger's *Der Wilde Jäger*, and perhaps Robert Burns's "Tam O'Shanter" also, Irving admitted the tale "a random thing, suggested by scenes and stories about Tarrytown"; its borrowed plot was "a mere whimsical band to connect descriptions of scenery, customs, manners." Yet in creating Brom Bones and Ichabod Crane, and the contest between them, he has been recognized as "the first important American author to put to literary use the comic mythology and popular traditions of American character which, by the early nineteenth century, had proliferated widely in oral tradition," demonstrating that "Dutch rowdies of the upper Hudson Valley were frontiersmen of the same stamp as the Ohio riverboatmen and Missouri trappers."

The Dutch of "The Legend of Sleepy Hollow" are indeed different from the chuckle-headed, indolent, pipe-smoking, stoop-sitting Dutch burghers of Irving's earlier writings. Brom is a frontier braggart, burly and roistering, "a Catskill Mike Fink, a ring-tailed roarer from Kinderhook." He is the sturdy backwoodsman who tricks the tenderfoot, acting out for the first time in our literature, says Daniel G. Hoffman, a theme which "has proliferated ever since: in Davy Crockett, in Mark Twain, in thousands of dime novels and popular magazines in which the yokel gets the best of the city slicker." Ichabod, a jack of many trades — schoolmaster, singing teacher, farmer, and eventually a successful lawyer — is rightly designated as Irving's Connecticut Yankee, a comic and less spectacular ancestor of Mark Twain's mechanic, a more optimistic witness to the common man's fate than Melville's Israel Potter. Obtrusively pious, this psalm-singing son of New England, naive and superstitious, but shrewdly ambitious, his head filled with daydreams of quick wealth through union with the "blooming Katrina" and setting out with her toward riches of the frontier, "for Kentucky, Tennessee, or the Lord knows where" — bloodless Ichabod is father to many confident, untrained, blundering, successful native heroes, and is the American cousin certainly of Dickens' Uriah Heep.

Almost all of Irving's better remembered tales thus celebrate victory for the practical man, defeat for the dreamer — as if they were modest or masochistic sardonic parables of his own career. Men like Brom, who understand or defy superstition and know that visions are illusory, come out well. Fancy must be replaced by common sense as one grows older: tales of goblins, or even of high adventure and romance, are for children or childish men. What an ironic twinkle must have accompanied Irving's postscript

notification to readers that even an ungainly visionary like Ichabod
Crane turned out well, when he left daydreaming, as Irving had
not, and turned to law.

As Diedrich Knickerbocker rather than Geoffrey Crayon
speaks, the technique of broadly sketched caricature is managed
with surer touch: readers do not forget Ichabod Crane astride his
boney nag, the short stirrups bringing "his knees nearly up to the
pommel of the saddle; his sharp elbows stuck out like grasshop-
pers'; he carried his whip perpendicularly in his hand, like a
sceptre, and, as his horse jogged on, the motion of his arms was
not unlike the flapping of a pair of wings." Dickens seldom displayed more gustatory fervor than Irving when he described
"the ample charms of a genuine Dutch country tea-table"—the
"doughty doughnut, the tenderer oly koek, and the crisp and
crumbling cruller," the abundance of pies and meats and poultry,
and "delectable dishes of preserved plums, and peaches, and pears,
and quinces . . . all mingled higgledy-piggledy."

Not Hawthorne or Balzac or Frank Norris at his descriptive
best could better have presented Mynheer Van Tassel's spacious
farmhouse, over which "a great elm tree spread its broad branches
. . . at the foot of which bubbled up a spring of the softest and
sweetest water in a little well formed of a barrel; and then stole
sparkling away through the grass to a neighboring brook that bubbled along among alders and dwarf willows." Beneath its low-
projecting eaves were "flails, harness, various utensils of husbandry,
and nets for fishing"; inside the house were "rows of resplendent
pewter, ranged on a long dresser." "In one corner stood a huge
bag of wool ready to be spun; in another a quantity of linsey-wool-
sey just from the loom; ears of Indian corn, and strings of dried
apples and peaches, hung in gay festoons along the walls, mingled
with the gaud of red peppers . . . claw-footed chairs and dark
mahogany tables shone like mirrors; and irons with their accompanying shovel and tongs, glistened from their covert of asparagus
tops; mock-oranges and conch-shells decorated the mantel-piece;
strings of various colored birds' eggs were suspended above it; a
great ostrich egg was hung from the centre of the room, and a cor-

ner cupboard, knowingly left open, displayed immense treasures of old silver and well-mended china."

Without Rip Van Winkle and Ichabod Crane, and Diedrich Knickerbocker to tell their stories, *The Sketch Book* would still be a pleasantly diverting, but an undistinguished, collection. The Christmas sketches, the observations on country customs, the descriptions of Westminster Abbey, Stratford-on-Avon, and Boar's Head Tavern contain painstakingly colored vignettes of people and of venerable scenes. "The Art of Bookmaking" is a good-natured spoof of the manner in which Irving himself culled from writers of the past. His remarks on "The Mutability of Literature" are engaging rephrasings of melancholy certainties about there being no end to the making of books, or to mute, inglorious authors who are fated to write unknown. In his mild rebuke to "English Writers on America," Irving comes perilously close to expressing ideas which might offend.

From this time on, the spirit of Geoffrey Crayon almost completely took charge, and manner became increasingly more important than matter. "I consider the story," Irving repeated a few years later, "merely as a frame on which to spread my materials. It is the play of thought, and sentiment, and language; the weaving in and out of characters lightly, yet expressively delineated; the familiar and faithful presentation of scenes of common life; and the half-concealed vein of humor that is often playing through the whole; — these are what I aim at." But his aim was uncertain: when friends advised him to try longer fiction, he objected that anyone could write a novel — "the mere interest of story . . . carries the reader through pages and pages of careless writing, and the author may be dull for half a volume at a time, if he has some striking scene at the end of it." In composition such as he preferred, the "author must be continuously piquant; woe to him if he makes an awkward sentence or writes a stupid page."

Yet like Poe, who also disputed the effectiveness of longer fiction, Irving did not turn aside from the novel until he had tried to write one and discovered that he did not do it well. Though *Brace-bridge Hall, or, The Humorists* was offered in 1822 as a "medley" of fifty-one sketches centered about an English country house, it is in fact a novel-*manqué*, faintly derisive and winsomely derivative. Squire Bracebridge may have been modeled, as Irving once suggested, on Walter Scott, but General Hardbottle, Lady Lillycraft, the village antiquary, and the faithful family retainers come direct from memories of characters better drawn by Goldsmith and Sterne. Ghost stories, bits of village gossip, essays on falconry, fortunetelling, and love-charms are strung almost haphazardly on a slender thread of romance, which ends with the wedding of Fair Julia, a shy, exemplary English girl, adroitly a caricature of heroines of sentimental fiction.

But most endearing of the sketches in *Bracebridge Hall* are not the village tales which form its substance but the fillers, the stories told as evening pastime at the ancient country house. Suspense is artfully created in "The Stout Gentleman," and exotic charm in "The Student of Salmanaca," but not as successfully as in "Dolph Heyliger" and "The Storm Ship," both re-creations of Hudson River lore drawn "from the MSS. of the late Diedrich Knickerbocker." Once again, however, these native tales were exceptions, for the New World offered little of appeal comparable to that of Europe. In America, Irving explained, all was "new and progressive, and pointed to the future rather than to the past"; there all "works of man gave no ideas but of young existence," without historical associations such as Irving found in England, where he wandered happily, "a grown-up child," he said, "delighted with every object."

"Never need an American look beyond his own country for the sublime and beautiful of natural scenery," he had said in *The Sketch Book*. "But Europe held forth charms of storied and poetical association. There were to be seen the masterpieces of art, the refinements of highly-cultivated society, the quaint peculiarities of ancient and local custom. My native country was full of youthful promise: Europe was rich in the accumulated treasures of age. Her very ruins told the history of times gone by, and every mouldering stone was a chronicle. I longed to wander over the scenes of renowned achievement — to tread, as it were, in the footsteps of antiquity, — to loiter about the ruined castle, — to meditate on the falling tower, — to escape, in short, from the commonplace realities of the present, and lose myself among the shadowy grandeurs of the past." Irving meant what Cooper, Hawthorne, Henry James, and Van Wyck Brooks later were to mean when they spoke of what America lacked which Europe had — the sustaining sense of history, and a decorum bred by tradition; but, perhaps because he said it first, he did not say it as clearly as they.

He searched through Europe now for more tales to retell, in a series of new collections — a German sketch book, an Italian, a Spanish, a French. "There are," he observed, "such quantities of these legendary and romantic tales now littering the press," needing only, as he had said, the polish of style to improve them. So he set out for the Continent in 1823, filling more notebooks with observations on quaint ceremonials, boar hunts, old castles, and bright national costumes — anything calculated to delight the eye or excite the imagination. But he worked by fits and starts, for he was not well, and he was forty: "My sunny days of youth are over." In Dresden, he puttered over translations, entertained himself and his friends with amateur theatricals, and courted young Emily Foster, who thought him too old. In Paris, where French editions of his writings made him seem a man of importance, he collaborated with John Howard Payne on plays, none of which was successful; he considered a book on Napoleon, worked over a series of American tales, planned an edition of English classics and a play based on the life of Shakespeare.

After two dilatory years, hounded by his publisher for new materials but unable to collect enough of any one kind for a new book, in the summer of 1824 Irving threw together what he had into *Tales of a Traveller* — a mélange of German stories, tales of Italian banditti, an abortive novelette, and more American sketches "found among the papers of the late Diedrich Knickerbocker." Though containing some of the liveliest writing which Irving had done since leaving America, and presenting in "The Devil and Tom Walker" his third-best native tale, the collection was not well received. We have heard these stories all before, said *Black-*

wood's: the characters are corpses in clumsy new clothing. Irving was called "indisputably feeble, unoriginal and timorous; a mere adjective of a man, who had neither vigor nor courage to stand alone."

If it were to bring such dubious returns, further travel seemed a wearisome prospect. Irving considered writing a life of Byron, of Cervantes — tempted now to suspect that he was by nature a biographer, which he was; and he worked long hours over a projected American sketch book — and then either destroyed or lost the manuscript. His talent, he thought, was blighted, the romance of life past. When early in 1826, he was invited to join the staff of the American Legation at Madrid, he welcomed the opportunity to settle in one place. He vowed again to work assiduously, and for three years he did.

Irving was wanted in Spain, not as a diplomat, but as a writer, to translate Don Martín de Navarette's recently published collection of documents relating to Columbus. The work was congenial and appealingly sedentary: Irving rummaged with such zeal through old libraries for collateral materials that when Longfellow called on him that spring, he was astounded at the older man's energy — up at six, at his desk through the day. Incidents from Navarette's book were elaborated with bits and pieces from other chronicles, and the whole was polished until it shone attractively as a straightforward narrative of exotic color and maritime adventure. But by the time the four volumes of *The Life and Voyages of Christopher Columbus* were issued in the summer of 1828, Irving was excitedly involved with another book, more surely his own, which he hoped might recapture, though with circumspection, something of the ironic tone of Knickerbocker's *History*.

Assuming the pseudonym of Fray Antonio Agapida, a zealot monk, who distorted history, "marring the chivalry of the camp by the bigotry of the cloister," Irving presented the *Chronicle of the Conquest of Granada* in 1829 as "something of an experiment": a book made "out of old chronicles, embellished, as I am able, by the imagination, and adapted to the romantic taste of the day —

something that was . . . between a history and a romance." William H. Prescott and Francis Parkman were to do this kind of thing better; but Irving did it first, mingling "romance and satire with grave historical details" as he told the story of Boabdil, last Moorish king of Granada, a dashing man in love or battle. But irony filters only dimly through these corpse-strewn fields lighted by flashes of sunlight on the "exterminating scimitar"; as halls resound with shrieks and fountains run red with blood, the spirit of old romance so illuminates each of its one hundred brief and chiseled chapters that Prescott declared Irving's *Granada* was permeated with such "dramatic brilliancy denied to sober history" that it "superseded all further necessity for poetry."

The *Voyages and Discoveries of the Companions of Columbus*, in 1831, was another modified translation, expertly done and well received. Meanwhile, however, Irving had been traveling again — through the "rugged valleys and long, naked, sweeping plains" of southern Spain, where he was captivated by the "proud, hardy, frugal, and abstemious" country people, and by the stories they told and the songs they sang; and he had settled in the old Moorish castle of the Alhambra. Through most of the spring and into the summer of 1829, Irving threw all his energies into a Spanish sketch book which, when published in 1832 as *The Alhambra*, would revive his reputation as "the first English prose-writer of the day," an artist with a true and tender eye for the unusual or picturesque, with feeling for scene at once precise and emotionally expansive.

The luxuriant southern sun, quiet countryside, and remains of oriental splendor in the ancient Moorish stronghold seemed "too beautiful to be real": "As I loiter through these oriental chambers, and hear the murmur of fountains and the song of the nightingale; as I inhale the odor of the rose and feel the influence of the balmy climate, I am almost tempted to fancy myself in the paradise of Mahomet." He admired the refinement of those Moorish "princes of a departed and almost forgotten race, who reigned in elegance and splendor in Andalusia, when Europe was in complete barbarism," their achievements in art and education, their benevolent administration of justice. How splendid was this past, when "lovers of the gay sciences resorted to Cordova and Granada, to imbibe the poetry and music of the east; and the steel-clad warriors of the north hastened thither, to accomplish themselves in the grateful exercises and courteous usages of chivalry."

Irving's love of ancient lore, his feeling for scenery, his sentiment for people as simple, tranquilly suffering, but well-meaning and ultimately good, seldom had been better exercised than in *The Alhambra,* which for generations has vied with *The Sketch Book* as the most popular of his works, anticipating Flaubert, Pierre Loti, Stevenson, and Lafcadio Hearn in luxuriant sensuality. If all seems surface polish and prettiness; if dark areas are lighted with too soft a glow; if "manly defiance of hardships, and contempt of effeminate indulgence" again seem traits inappropriately honored by a person of Irving's haphazard sensibility, *The Alhambra* nonetheless does present him at his burnished best and at his wayward worst. The story of Peregil, the water carrier, in the "Legend of the Moor's Legacy" combines pathos and humor with narrative skill, to produce another minor masterwork; the rest of *The Alhambra* blends to a deliquescent glow which is remembered as pleasant long after details are forgotten.

Fame now completely engulfed Washington Irving, celebrated in the press of two continents as a purveyor of culture from the Old World to the New, and as the good-natured explainer of American idiosyncrasies to Europe: his writings went through half a hundred editions, and were translated into a dozen languages. On leaving the Alhambra in the later summer of 1829, Irving returned to London as secretary to the American Legation there. The next year, he received a medal from the Royal Society of Literature, and he edited Bryant's *Poems* for publication in England, changing some of the words to make them conform to British taste. The year after that, he was awarded an honorary doctorate at Oxford. Then, following a final tour to Stratford and Kenilworth, he set out for home, something he had contemplated doing every year, he said, for the past seventeen years.

His return was triumphant, but his effective literary career was virtually over. He had succeeded for more than two decades in presenting himself to the world, as William L. Hedges has so well explained, as a "somewhat puzzled and alienated observer," beset by whimsey and beguiled by grotesquerie of kinds which during the next twenty years would find more complete expression in the writings of Nathaniel Hawthorne, Herman Melville, and Edgar Allan Poe. The essential characteristic of Irving's early, and better, tales and sketches is, says Mr. Hedges, "that they are told by a man who is not altogether sure of himself"; his fiction "is a fiction of dream, fantastic symbolic projections; it is heavily loaded with imagery functioning as metaphor. . . . It alternately sympathizes with, laughs at, and turns in fear from the stranger, the homeless or orphaned young man, the provincial abroad, the recluse, the eccentric scholar, the teller of tales." Irving had confessed himself "a poor devil of an author," torn by tensions he never completely understood. But he had discovered now a style and a manner. From this time on he would be able to achieve something of composure by capitalizing on his reputation and repeating tested formulas. He would become less harried, more at ease with himself, and less consistently successful.

On May 23, 1832, he once again saw "the bright city" of his birth. New York provided him a hero's welcome, with a ceremonious dinner at the City Hotel, where the halls "rang with bravos, handkerchiefs were waved on every side, three cheers given again and again," as Irving, tears in his eyes, announced that he was home to stay, and that, above all, he loved America: "It was the home of the heart." He visited Saratoga Springs and Niagara Falls, and as the result of a chance meeting with a commissioner to the Indians, made a four-month trip into the Pawnee country of the Southwest, recording excitedly in his journal each new scene of picturesque interest.

Back in New York that winter, among friends now as sedate but not nearly so famous as he had become, plaudits continued to be showered on him. He declined nomination to Congress, as he would later decline nomination by Tammany Hall as candidate for mayor of New York and appointment by President Van Buren as secretary of the navy. Instead he engaged himself to John Jacob Astor — for a tremendous sum, it was rumored — for the purpose of going over that self-made millionaire's papers, to make a book from them about the opening of the West and the fur trade. In 1836, he moved to an old Dutch farmhouse below Tarrytown, which he first named "Wolfert's Roost," and then "Sunnyside," a "little, old-fashioned, stone mansion, all made up of gabled ends, as full of angles and corners as an old cocked hat."

The Crayon Miscellany had appeared in 1835, most of it taken up with the lively *A Tour on the Prairies,* but pieced out with memorials of Abbotsford and Newstead Abbey to make it of book length. Often reprinted as another "minor American classic," a book to be placed beside Parkman's *The Oregon Trail* or even Mark Twain's *Roughing It,* Irving's *Tour* has gone through more than thirty editions in English and twenty in translation. Because, in Irving's words, it is "a simple narrative of everyday occurrence," with "no wonders to describe, nor any moving accidents by flood or field to narrate," it represents to readers with little patience for whimsey or sentimental humor the crown of Irving's work. It offers them a rugged Irving, with trousers tucked inside his boots, gun in hand, fording streams, sprawled (elegantly perhaps) beside a campfire.

Unlike *Astoria,* in 1836 ("Not even WASHINGTON IRVING," said one reviewer, "can beat furs into eloquence"), or *Adventures of Captain Bonneville,* in 1837, both of them, like the Spanish histories, suavely adapted from other men's accounts, *A Tour on the Prairies* recounted Irving's own discovery of the frontier West. He noted the "gypsy fondness" of Creek Indians for brilliant color and gay decorations, the proud independence of the Pawnee ("sons of Ishmael, their hand is against everyone"), and the fine, Roman features of the Osages; their manly independence reminded him, almost twenty years before Thoreau expressed the same thought in *Walden,* that "we in society are slaves, not so much to others as to ourselves; our superfluities are the chains that bind us." Some forecast of the tone of Lambert Strether, who also learned in his middle years that he had never really lived, creeps into Irving's

voice when, over fifty, he admits, "We send our youths abroad to
grow luxurious and effeminate in Europe; it appears to me that
a previous tour of the prairies would be more likely to produce
that manliness, and self-dependence, most in unison with our political institutions."

But, though he spoke of trappers as a "rabble rout of non-
descript beings" who hover like bats "about the frontiers between
civilized and savage life"; though he described his half-breed guide
as "one of the worthless brood engendered and brought up among
the missions," who "fancied himself highly connected, his sister
being concubine to an opulent white trader"; and though he sometimes caught in dialogue the clipped colloquialism of the native
woodsman ("Next to my rifle, I'd as leave lend you my wife"),
Irving's old manner of piquant phrase and romantic extension
crept often into his record of these frontier experiences, especially
when he retold at second hand the stories of hunting and Indian
warfare, tall tales recounted by trappers, and Indian legends which
had "a wild romantic interest heard from the lips of half-savage
narrators." His brief chapter on "The Bee Hunt" may deserve
comparison with William Bartram's account of Florida alligators,
or Thoreau's description of the battle of the ants; but the brief
vignette of forest rangers in bivouac, in a "wild bandit" or "Robin
Hood" atmosphere, is another set piece of the kind at which Geoffrey Crayon had always excelled — an assemblage of particularized
notations, memoranda in an artist's field book: "Some were cooking at large fires made at the feet of trees; some were stretching
and dressing deer skins; some were shooting at a mark, and some
were lying about in the grass. Venison jerked and hung on frames,
was drying over embers in one place; in another lay carcasses recently brought in by the hunters. Stacks of rifles were leaning
against the trunks of trees, and saddles, bridles, and powder-horns
hanging above them, while the horses were grazing here and there
among the thickets."

But pictures like this, carefully drawn from observation, seldom appeared in what Irving now considered his more important
work. He grumbled about imitators who climbed toward fame with

sketch books of their own, none quite done in his painstaking manner, not even Longfellow's *Outre-Mer* in 1834, which spoke of Europe and its legends. John Pendleton Kennedy's *Swallow Barn* in 1832 seemed simply a Virginian adaptation of *Bracebridge Hall*, not to speak of Cooper's *The Pioneers* nine years earlier, which told of an old family mansion on the frontier, and James Hall's *Legends of the West*, which skimmed most of the good stories from that region. Nathaniel Parker Willis had done a *Pencillings by the Way*, and Augustus Longstreet a boisterous *Georgia Scenes*, both in 1835. Irving had no heart for continuing in competition with any of these, or with the younger men like Hawthorne, who admired him, or Poe, who thought him pallid, or Emerson, whose remarks on self-reliance and throwing off shackles of the past may have seemed a rebuke.

Instead, at Sunnyside from 1837 to 1842, Irving rummaged through old notebooks for materials capable of being reworked, "writing away *like fury*," said Longfellow, on "remnants — odds and ends, — about Sleepy Hollow, and Granada. What a pity!" Another Spanish book was on his mind, a history of the conquest of Mexico, but he gave that up when he learned that Prescott was engaged with the subject, turning instead to an even more "American" theme — a life of George Washington which, like the *Columbus*, might examine roots of New World tradition, providing indisputable evidence that strength and resolution and solid sense and gallantry had been from their beginning characteristic of the best of his countrymen.

To the *Knickerbocker Magazine* in New York he contributed sketches and tales — "a hodgepodge of his experiences from the age of eighteen to fifty-eight," which were to be collected in *Wolfert's Roost* in 1855 and in the posthumous volume of *Spanish Papers*. "Mount-Joy: or Some Passages Out of the Life of a Castle-Builder" made good-natured fun of transcendentalists "who render many of our young men verbose and declamatory, and prone to mistake aberrations of their fancy for inspirations of divine philosophy," and both "The Great Mississippi Bubble" and "The Early Adventures of Ralph Ringwood" are sprawling narratives of frontier life which look tentatively toward the lustier ironic realism of Mark Twain.

These better things were few, however, and not greatly different from other contributions by younger Americans who now vaunted their devotion to native scene and theme; but the Irving stamp was on them, certifying their authenticity by a style which shaped whatever subject to his familiar moods. He reworked his biography of Campbell and the sketch of Goldsmith which he had first done in Paris fifteen years before. Few books written during these decorous years were more popularly applauded than his sentimental *Biography and Poetical Remains of the Late Margaret Miller Davidson* of 1841, in which Irving spoke tenderly about the yearnings and aspiring verse of a tremulous, tubercular girl who had died at the age of sixteen, only a year younger than Matilda Hoffman had been when she died.

Early in 1842, Irving accepted appointment as minister plenipotentiary to the court of Spain, a position which came to him as the result of an apparent political about-face which had Fenimore Cooper — just then caged about by legal controversies with Whig opponents — growling in disgust. During the next few years, briefly in England and then in Madrid, Irving played a modestly important role as a diplomat, lending his prestige and suave good humor to negotiations over Cuba, the Oregon boundary dispute, and defense of his country's attitude in the Mexican war, "though I regret to say my endeavors have occasionally been counteracted by the derangement of my health." By the late summer of 1846, he was happy to be back once more at Sunnyside, which he would not leave for long again.

"In the early part of my literary career," he remembered, "I used to think I would take warning by the fate of writers who kept on writing until they 'wrote themselves down,' and that I would retire while still in the freshness of my powers — but . . . circumstances have obliged me to change my plan, and I am likely to write until the pen drops from my hand." Day after day at Sunnyside, he tinkered over old writings and projected new. In 1849 he arranged with George P. Putnam for a revised edition of his works, which would finally grow from fifteen to twenty-one, then to twenty-seven volumes. *Mahomet and His Successors,* over which he had been worrying for almost a quarter of a century, appeared in 1850, to be followed by the miscellaneous *Wolfert's Roost* five years later, a book which it pleased him to find praised in the London *Spectator* as filled with "as much elegance of diction, as graceful a description of natural scenery, as grotesque an earnestness in diablerie, and as quiet but telling a satiric humor, as when Geoffrey Crayon came before the English world, nearly forty years ago."

Meant as praise, these words describe much of Irving's literary fortune, and foretell the inevitable decline of his reputation. For forty years there had been no change. This man of limpid style was without a subject, except as he could find it ready-made, available for transforming to language adroitly adapted to popular taste. Adventures as revealed in old tales or old documents, nostalgic recollection of bygone scenes, and the fallible, lovable, admirable characteristics of people — these were the themes which brought Geoffrey Crayon fame. Diedrich Knickerbocker could do better, and did, slipping into each miscellaneous volume a tale or two giving it body, usually through the creation of characters indelibly drawn.

For it was finally people who interested Washington Irving most — whimsical people, droll manifestations of popular whimwhams; people who drifted as he had drifted, from one project to another, searching for the key to success; or successful people, the heroes of whom Carlyle had written, and the representative men of whom Emerson spoke. Irving's life had been checkered with plans for biographies never completed, of Byron, Napoleon, Cervantes. The lives of English poets which he had supplied as hackwork introductions spurred his ambition to do something larger. The popular success of the little book about Margaret Davidson made him think he could do even better.

He did do greatly better with *Oliver Goldsmith,* one of the most appealing literary biographies of the first half of the nineteenth century. It was "a labor of love," said Irving, "a tribute of gratitude to the memory of an author whose writings were the delight of my childhood, and have been a source of enjoyment to me throughout life." Done in three versions, first in Paris in 1825 as an introduction to the Goldsmith volume in Galignani's series of English Classics, expanded in 1840 as *The Life of Oliver Goldsmith, with Selections from His Writings* in Harper's Family Library, it was published in final form as *Oliver Goldsmith: A Biography* by Putnam in 1849. Though much of its material is drawn from Sir James Prior's and John Forster's more complete studies, Irving's *Oliver Goldsmith* outlives either, partly because, as Hazlitt recognized, its author "binds up his own portrait with Goldsmith's."

Irving admired "the artless benevolence" of Goldsmith, the "whimsical, yet amiable views of human life and nature; the unforced humor, blending so happily with good feeling and good sense, and singularly dashed at times with a pleasing melancholy" — all characteristics which readers for so many years had been accustomed to associate with Irving's own writing. Each, it has been said, looks "at human nature from the same generous point of view, with the same kindly sympathies, and the same tolerant philosophy"; each has "the same quick perception of the ludicrous, and the same tender simplicity in the pathetic"; in each runs "the same quiet vein of humor, and the same cheerful spirit of hopefulness." Irving defended his own literary intentions when he praised Goldsmith's writings because they "sweeten our tempers, and harmonize our thoughts; they put us in a good humor with the world, and in so doing they make us happier and better men."

Veneration and a sense of responsibility got in the way, however, as Irving devoted his final, failing energies to the *Life of George Washington*, the first volume of which appeared in 1855. Planned for three volumes, the work dragged on, filled with fact and anecdote and with massive descriptions of military events; too seldom graced even with vestiges of Irving's former easy prose, it moves by fits and starts, as if pushing desperately toward completion. "The shadows of departed years," he confided to a friend, "are gathering over me." But, he said, "I must get through with the work which I have cut out for myself. I must weave my web, and then die."

Scarcely six months after seeing the fifth and last volume of the *Life of George Washington* through the press, on November 28, 1859, Washington Irving died. At his funeral "thousands from far and near silently looked for the last time on his genial face, and mourned his loss as that of a personal friend and national benefactor." His grave in Sleepy Hollow Cemetery is still carefully attended, and flowers are placed in Christ Episcopal Church in Tarrytown each year on the anniversary of his death. The old house at Sunnyside has been restored, and schoolchildren make pilgrimages there to see the room where Washington Irving wrote.

For his reputation does live on, not perhaps among somber critics, for Irving was not in their sense a dedicated or committed person. But for those who accept in literature what they find there, and who are experienced enough not to expect too much, refreshing discoveries are to be made in reviewing his writings. It will not do to think of Irving as a complicated man. With quick eye, ready tongue, and alert recognition of absurdities, he sits quietly at both ends of the American literary spectrum — an expatriate seeking reverently in Europe for sources of culture, but, like James and Eliot and Pound, most effective in realizing American characters enmeshed in American ideals; and at the same time a native myth-maker who wove indigenous lore into comic tales which become fables. His country's first, but not her best, romantic historian; an early, but unsatisfying, impressionistic biographer; an exotic local colorist before Flaubert popularized the term; a mildly boisterous, thigh-slapping, sidesplitting rural humorist, a comic realist before Thackeray, a caricaturist before Dickens — Irving was tentatively all of these. He writes better than anyone who has written of him, in praise or condemnation; and he shares with each critic the handicap of having little of final importance to write about.

JOSEPHINE MILES

Ralph Waldo Emerson

ROM wise men the world inherits a literature of wisdom, characterized less by its programmatic informativeness than by its strength and brevity of statement. *Proverb, aphorism, maxim* are terms for the succinct wise sayings which we have from every language, from Moses and Jesus, from Confucius, Buddha, and Mohammed, from Heraclitus, Martial, and Marcus Aurelius, from Montaigne and Bacon, down the traditions of time to America's man of wisdom, Ralph Waldo Emerson.

To understand Emerson's writing, we may well try to follow what he has to say in the way that he says it: first, in three maturely characteristic books, his way of setting forth ideas; then in all his writing, from youthful speculation to aging reminiscence, his suiting of thought to event; finally, in specific traits of his style, his individual uses of tradition. The downrightness of Franklin, the elegance of Irving, the sentiment of Longfellow, the outreaching sublimity of Whitman, all have their part in his world, as compacted in his own terms.

One of his most solidly organized and directly speaking books is *The Conduct of Life,* published along with *Representative Men* and *English Traits* in Emerson's mature years and representing the fullness of his achievement. Before these three, he had made many beginnings, in journals, sermons, lectures, poems, and such widely discussed volumes as *Nature* of 1836 and the two *Essays* series. And in the later years, he continued his writing and lecturing, with especial emphasis on the Civil War and the new science. To both beginnings and conclusions, *The Conduct of Life, Representative Men,* and *English Traits* were central. If we look at them first, for Emerson's chief ideas as they concern us, we may then turn to a more historical and a more literary view for further understanding of his purposes and effects.

The *Conduct of Life* begins with one main question: How shall I live? Not, What is the theory of the age, or What is the spirit of the times, or What can we do to reform men? The question is not *What*, but *How*; the questioner not *we*, but *I*; the problem, *to live*. These characteristics of active and personal process establish the tone and the construction of Emerson's whole book, and of his whole work.

Say that you, as reader, have this book in hand, a gracefully compact volume of two hundred pages, how will you most easily follow its thought? By following Emerson's belief that the parts of an idea are given meaning by the whole, as they in their turn give substance to the whole. The parts in *The Conduct of Life* are nine chapters, derived from nine lectures which Emerson had given in sequence to an audience of Boston townspeople gathered together in the 1850's to hear him because of his great reputation for saying well what they needed to hear. What audiences in the 1960's or 1970's might hear on the theme "How Shall I Live?" would depend on the speaker's specialization; they might get a businessman's or a churchman's answer, a scientist's answer, a psychologist's or an artist's answer, an "academic" or "journalistic" answer. For each specialty, there would be a series of informative topics, say, "Automation," or "Renaissance Humanism," or "Zen." In contrast, how surprising in their speculative generality are Emerson's nine: "Fate," "Power," "Wealth," "Culture," "Behavior," "Worship," "Considerations by the Way," "Beauty," and "Illusions." How, the reader may wonder, can he make a whole of these? And where is the information in them? Our modern habit of information-seeking will lead to doubts about such a list of contents. Emerson's own hearers probably felt a different doubt. Bred to churchgoing and sermon-listening, they may have wondered at the nonreligiousness of such titles, their lack of Biblical texts and canons. So this list has a kind of daring to it, for either century, moral yet secular as it is. Few writers except wisdom-writers have the power to span the years by the endurance of their generalities in combination with the immediacy of their references to daily life.

How shall I live? With fate; that is, with the limitations of my inheritance and the natural world. With power, my abilities and energies. With wealth, my gains or losses. With culture, my widest sympathies and affinities. With behavior, my manner of life. With worship, my belief. With considerations, the positive centers for my action. With beauty, the underlying likenesses of the beautiful. And with illusions, the games and masks of my self-deception.

The sequence of answers begins with fate, impersonally and negatively; grows more and more strongly personal through the center in worship; then adds in conclusion a triad of impersonal and negative warnings on the dissonances and consonances of the process of composing a living and a life. The last essay ends as the first ends, with the axiom, the accepted, undemonstrated, intuitive assertion that there is no chance, no anomaly, in the universe; that all is system and gradation; and that the young mortal, the pure in heart, survives with the true, beautiful, and moral gods.

To see more clearly how Emerson established this coherent universe, it is useful to look closely at the form of the first essay, "Fate"; then, to gain a sense of the complementary solidity of individual choice and action, to look at "Wealth" — to relate, that is, life to the living of it. Note the difference from the Christian incarnation, which Emerson had studied to preach and had resigned from preaching. Incarnation draws mind and spirit downward into body, into the crucifixion and redemption of body. For Emerson, the motion is upward, cyclical, opposing and circling into spiral, through the power of every individual soul as it participates in the unifying force of the one soul, the over-soul, which composes all. The positive energy is earthly as well as heavenly.

The essay "Fate" proceeds through a half-dozen steps of four or five pages each. The first step is to make use of the limitations, negations, brute facts, tyrannies of life. The second, in both individual and national inheritance, is to accept the force of such restrictive circumstance. "Nature is, what you may do. There is much you may not. . . . Once we thought, positive power was all. Now we learn, that negative power, or circumstance, is half. Nature is the tyrannous circumstance, the thick skull, the sheathed snake, the ponderous, rock-like jaw; necessitated activity; violent direction; the conditions of a tool, like the locomotive, strong enough on its track, but which can do nothing but mischief off of it; or skates, which are wings on the ice, but fetters on the ground. The book of Nature is the book of Fate." But the third step is to recognize the power of thought in man — "On one side, elemental order, sandstone and granite, rock-ledges, peat-bog, forest, sea and shore; and, on the other part, thought, the spirit which composes and decomposes nature, — here they are, side by side, god and devil, mind and matter, king and conspirator, belt and spasm, riding peacefully together in the eye and brain of every man." The fourth is to see that man's thought not only counters but uses fate, by design, by dream, by will, by moral purpose. "Fate, then, is a name for facts not yet passed under the fire of thought; — for causes which are unpenetrated." The fifth is to see that their interrelations, fate's and thought's, are manifold. The sixth is to think about the spirit of the age as the interworking of event and person, the advance out of fate into freedom, and their rebalancing. The soul "contains the event that shall befall it, for the event is only the actualization of its thoughts; and what we pray to ourselves for is always granted." So finally, the peroration of the pulpit and lecture hall: "Let us build altars to the Beautiful Necessity" which rudely or softly educates man to the perception that there are no contingencies.

The following essay, "Power," stresses again the potential force of man, especially the strength that comes with concentration and habituation of his abilities, and uses the analogy of the energy and husbandry of a machine, which is constructed by man to exclude follies and hindrances, broken threads and rotten hours, from his production.

Coming then to the essay on production, called "Wealth," we may stop to take note of another of Emerson's characteristics as essayist, his sermonlike use of a verse text not scriptural but his own. We note key lines from the poem that stands at the head of this essay:

> And well the primal pioneer
> Knew the strong task to it assigned
> Patient through Heaven's enormous year
> To build in matter home for mind.

The whole poem is a treatise, a history, a four-beat, irregularly rhyming re-creation of past wealth, of wheat, metal ores, coal, and then the binding threads of city and trade, the ties of nature and of law which hold even in the most youthful being.

In the essay itself, the theme is set early: "How does that man get his living? . . . He fails to make his place good in the world, unless he not only pays his debt, but also adds something to the common wealth." "Wealth," says Emerson, "has its source in applications of the mind to nature, from the rudest strokes of spade and axe, up to the last secrets of art." It is "the greatest possible extension to our powers, as if it added feet, and hands, and eyes, and blood, length to the day, and knowledge, and good-will."

By a law of nature, man feeds himself, fills his own needs. "He is the richest man who knows how to draw a benefit from the labors of the greatest number of men, of men in distant countries, and in past times." Economy is moral when it makes for profound, not trivial, independences. No man, in whatever time, is as rich as he ought to be. Property is an intellectual production; commerce, a game of skill; money, the delicate measure of civil, social, and moral changes. "A dollar in a university, is worth more than a dollar in a jail . . . the value of a dollar is social, as it is created by society." Economy has its own inner balances.

In the essay, Emerson makes four main points about economy, that is, about means related to ends: that each man's expense should proceed from his character; that each man should proceed by system; that each should follow the custom of the country; that each will reap what he sows, for "the counting-room maxims liberally expounded are laws of the Universe." Investment is the final significance: from wealth, to money, to value, to expenditure; from bread, to strength, to thought, to courage, invested toward higher goods. Like "Fate," then, "Wealth" is organized by a handful of sections, one moving into the next, with an initial question answered early and then finally raised to a higher power.

The idea of culture tempers the ideas of power and wealth by moderating and expanding them. Books, travels, cities, solitude, with all their difficulties, carry man from focused energy to widening thought, from quadruped to human. Superficially, but no less significantly, the *how* of men's life is the *how* of "Manners." Manners are the best ways of doing things, the gentlest laws and bonds. Their basis lies in self-reliance, in thoughtful choice; their grammar of gesture is clearer than English grammar, a part of both nature and character.

"Worship," in turning back from spirit in body to body in spirit, takes note of criticisms made by hearers of the earlier lectures in this series: that there is too much of body in the lectures; that they grant too much power either to animal man or to negative man. But Emerson says he will persist, against all sanctified airs, in recognizing both, the one for praise, the other for blame. Religious worship is a flowering from bodily stems: it needs the vigor of nature. Vigorless worship, institutionalized, dogmatized, sectarian, as in many of the churches of his day, is weak and wrong; where it exists new forms are needed, new channels for spirit to move in. "In our large cities, the population is godless, materialized, — no bond, no fellow-feeling, no enthusiasm. These are not men, but hungers, thirsts, fevers, and appetites walking. How is it people manage to live on, — so aimless as they are? After their peppercorn aims are gained, it seems as if the lime in their bones alone held them together, and not any worthy purpose." We need not fear, on the other hand, if creeds and sects decline. "The public and the private element, like north and south, like inside and outside, like centrifugal and centripetal, adhere to every soul, and cannot be subdued, except the soul is dissipated. God builds his temple in the heart on the ruins of churches and religions."

Vividly in this climactic chapter, Emerson makes clear the bent of his philosophy. It is not methodology, not logic, not systematic analysis or inquiry that concerns him; it is the creation of a pattern of thought and observation in reasonable harmony with certain accepted axioms of intuited belief. First, "We are born believing. A man bears beliefs, as a tree bears apples." Second, morality and intellect are related in growth. "Every man takes care that his neighbor shall not cheat him. But a day comes when he begins to care that he do not cheat his neighbor. Then all goes well. He has changed his market-cart into a chariot of the sun. What a day dawns, when we have taken to heart the doctrine of faith! to prefer, as a better investment, being to doing . . . the life to the year . . ." The word *investment*, echoing from the essay on wealth, carries the sense of treasure used, of active commitment, in faith, to present and future. After a number of examples, for those faint in heart, comes the peroration of "Worship," which we may take for as strongly and briefly phrased a conclusion as Emerson ever came to. "And so I think that the last lesson of life, the choral song which rises from all elements and all angels, is, a voluntary obedience, a necessitated freedom. Man is made of the same atoms as the world is, he shares the same impressions, predispositions, and destiny. When his mind is illuminated, when his heart is kind, he throws himself joyfully into the sublime order, and does, with knowledge, what the stones do by structure."

To this larger theme of detail in the sublime order, the last three essays in *The Conduct of Life* devote themselves.

"Considerations" deals with true and false bonds, true and false allegiances and centers, for groups and for individuals. "Our chief want in life, is, somebody who shall make us do what we can. This is the service of a friend." This is the service, too, of a good minority in a government, and of any heroic, obligable nucleus — to loose false ties, to give us the courage to serve and to be what we are.

"Beauty" also stresses such relations of harmony. Like science, beauty extends and deepens us, takes us from surfaces to the foundations of things. That which is beautiful is simple, has no superfluous parts, serves its end, stands related to all things, is the mean of many extremes. Each of these qualities Emerson illustrates further; the structure of this essay is a series of exemplifications moving toward the highest power of beauty — to relate.

He concludes with an essay on deceptive relations, "Illusions," to remind us what we are so conscious of today — false fronts, masks. He will not allow us to rest easy; we must ride a beast of ever-changing form. With the young mortal and the gods together in the realm of pure truth, Emerson ends his advices on the conduct of life, catching up in his last sentences what he had set forth in his first: "If we must accept Fate, we are not less compelled to affirm liberty, the significance of the individual, the grandeur of duty, the power of character." He has harped on each string, as he has said, through nine essays, in order to harmonize them. His compositions have been played on these few main themes. Do we grant him his premises, his intuitive beliefs? Whether or no, at least we can grant him his questions and therefore follow where he leads in his ever-varying range of effort to answer.

The Conduct of Life was Emerson's last, most coherent, for many his most admirable, book. We may take it as the mature effort of his thought in his fifties, tried out in journal entries and on lecture platforms, and finally published forth in 1860. Even more than the *Conduct,* the other two books of his maturity, *Representative Men,* 1850, and *English Traits,* 1856, harped on certain strings. The lifelong personal question of *Conduct* — How shall I live? — they asked more historically and descriptively: How do great men and nations live?

We know that one of the much-read books of Emerson's youth was Plutarch's *Lives* — lives of soldiers and statesmen, of men of political action in Greece and Rome. We know that he admired Carlyle's kind of hero, as Divinity, Prophet, Poet, Priest, Man of Letters, King. He might be expected then to give us in *Representative Men* American leaders and prophets, like George Washington, Benjamin Franklin, Thomas Jefferson, or one of the men he most admired in his own day, like Daniel Webster. But we perhaps have learned enough from *The Conduct of Life* to know that Emerson's men will not be such models. He believes in aspiring men, of negative as well as positive quality. To be representative, they may be villains as well as heroes. So we find the six of them: Plato the philosopher, Swedenborg the mystic, Montaigne the skeptic, Shakespeare the poet, Napoleon the man of the world, Goethe the writer — no one a hero or even a heroic type, but each representative of a complex of traits of thought in human kind. Note the introductory essay, "Uses of Great Men." *Uses*, indeed! How shall they live? *For us*.

To begin once more with the assumption of belief: "It is natural to believe in great men. . . . Nature seems to exist for the excellent. The world is upheld by the veracity of good men: they make the earth wholesome. . . . The search after the great man is the dream of youth, and the most serious occupation of manhood." But now when he asks how such men aid us, we see Emerson's surprising yet clearly characteristic point: "Each man seeks those of different quality from his own, and such as are good of their kind; that is, he seeks other men, and the *otherest*." Their service therefore is indirect, not by gift, but by representation, each "connected with some district of nature, whose agent and interpreter he is; as Linnæus, of plants; Huber, of bees . . . Euclid, of lines; Newton, of fluxions." "Every ship that comes to America got its chart from Columbus. Every novel is a debtor to Homer."

One danger is that these men become too much our masters. But change carries them and their kind along. "In some other and quite different field the next man will appear; not Jefferson, not Franklin, but now a great salesman; then a road-contractor; then a student of fishes; then a buffalo-hunting explorer; or a semi-savage western general. . . . With each new mind, a new secret of nature transpires; nor can the Bible be closed until the last great man is born." Nature protects each from every other in his variety; from what varieties can we learn?

From "Plato": "He represents the privilege of the intellect, the power, namely, of carrying up every fact to successive platforms, and so disclosing, in every fact, a germ of expansion." From "Montaigne": "Who shall forbid a wise skepticism, seeing that there is no practical question on which any thing more than an approximate solution can be had?" From "Shakespeare": "The greatest genius is the most indebted man. A poet is . . . a heart in unison with his time and country." From "Napoleon": "He had a directness of action never before combined with so much comprehension."

English Traits, the third in his trio of mature volumes, asks How shall I live? by asking it of a country, and, note, a country to which America was only recently opposed, yet from which it was descended. Oppose Goethe, oppose Montaigne, oppose England: and learn from these oppositions. Why England is England? — this is the way Emerson puts the question now. His steps of inquiry proceed via "Land" to "Race," to "Ability," to "Manners," to "Truth," to "Character," to "Cockayne" (Humor), to "Wealth," to "Aristocracy," to "Universities," to "Religion," to "Literature," to "Result." Each general concern is given its specific English location and form: the land locates the race; aristocracy, the wealth; and humor, the character.

Each section has its theme: "England is a garden." "The English composite character betrays a mixed origin. Everything English is a fusion of distant and antagonistic elements." "The Norman has come popularly to represent in England the aristocratic, and the Saxon the democratic principle." "I find the Englishman to be him of all men who stands firmest in his shoes." "The Teutonic tribes have a national singleness of heart, which contrasts with the Latin races." "The English race are reputed morose." "The English are a nation of humorists." "There is no country in which so absolute a homage is paid to wealth." "The feudal character of the English state, now that it is getting obsolete, glares a little, in contrast with the democratic tendencies." "The logical English train a scholar as they train an engineer. Oxford is a Greek factory, as Wilton mills weave carpet and Sheffield grinds steel." "The religion of England is part of good-breeding." "England is the best of actual nations. . . . Broad-fronted, broad-bottomed Teutons, they stand in solid phalanx foursquare to the points of compass; they constitute the modern world, they have earned their vantage ground and held it through ages of adverse possession. . . . They cannot readily see beyond England."

These brief statements of idea, one for almost each section, let us know how much we can learn, in specific documentation, analysis, anecdote, and the personal experience of the twice-visitor. Together they let us know about the English, that they have gained by opposing, and that we will gain by opposing them.

Emerson has carried his sense of moral unity from person to object, to representative man, to nation and type, and through all of these the active and creating power of inner divinity, of intuition, gives shape to the natural forces of heredity, geography, history. English traits are English fate; within them moves man's powers. His study of England puts Emerson's theories to a strong test; to see what Nietzsche and Spengler have since done with them, would, as Philip Nicoloff suggests, put them to a still stronger test. But it is not a test Emerson would avoid. Form, change, purpose were organic for him in the classic sense, a part of a pattern, as he said, not a romantic caprice. So England could not but add strength to his beliefs; as his beliefs could not but inform that Saxon substance.

These three main volumes in the decade of his maturity were built upon works already established in the heart of New England readers through the two series of *Essays* and the *Poems* of the 1840's. Together these six collections of his thoughts give us Emerson's most formal and formulated wisdom. The startling assertions of such essays as "Self-Reliance" and "The Over-Soul," the contained force of "Woodnotes" and "Threnody," find their stability of focus in the various forms of the question How shall I live? It may now be helpful to consider what in Emerson's earlier world and purpose had helped bring the several forms of this question into being.

The events of Emerson's life in brief summary provide a context for his thought — the *why* of his beliefs. He was born on May 25,

1803, in Boston, in a family of merchants and ministers. His father, the Reverend William Emerson, Unitarian minister and chaplain of the state senate, died in 1811, and his mother turned to boardinghouse keeping to support the children. He attended Boston Latin School from 1812 to 1817 and Harvard College from 1817 to 1821, where he kept journals of his reading and thought, and won prizes for his essays. Encouraged by his Aunt Mary Moody, Emerson early began to write poetry, on the victories of 1812, for example. He taught at his brother William's school for young ladies, studied for the ministry at Harvard, went south to Florida to cure a long-threatening tuberculosis, came back to more preaching, and in 1829 was ordained pastor of the Second Church in Boston, in the same year he was married to the young and fragile Ellen Tucker. She died in 1831, and in 1832 Emerson resigned his pastorate, preached a farewell sermon, and went to England to try to recover strength and purpose.

Though he visited the literary men he most admired, Coleridge, Wordsworth, Carlyle, remarkably it was the botanical world of France's Jardin des Plantes which most gave him what he sought. He returned then to begin in Concord in 1834 his years of leadership in thought and expression. He married Lydia Jackson, and of their four children three survived to later life, the while he lost his eldest, his brothers, and later his mother. He met in the next years new friends, Margaret Fuller, Bronson Alcott, Horace Greeley, the elder Henry James, Hawthorne, Thoreau, Whitman. He began to turn his early practice in sermon-making to lecture-making on the new lecture circuits which were to enlighten the cities, villages, and frontiers of America for the rest of the century. He turned from much-argued-about lectures, like the early "The American Scholar" to much-argued-about publications: *Nature* in 1836, the writings for the *Dial* in 1840–44, the *Essays* of 1841 and 1844, the *Poems* of 1846. He took a number of further trips west and abroad, gave the first of many speeches on problems of slavery, the war, and the nation's leadership, and in the fifties published his three most thematically integrated books — *Representative Men, English Traits,* and *The Conduct of Life* — which took their place alongside the other great volumes of that era, Thoreau's *Walden* and Whitman's *Leaves of Grass*. The sixties brought the Civil War, the death of Lincoln, of Thoreau, of Hawthorne, and a gradual slowing for Emerson: the effort to meet honors at Harvard with new explorations of science and intellect, trips as far as California as guest of his son-in-law, loss of his home by fire, final journeyings abroad, final collecting, despite failing memory, of loved work, like *Parnassus*, and death on April 27, 1882, at Concord.

As a boy, Emerson had looked to his family and town and school for his ideas. What wisdom did he seek in these busy and hard-pressed years? Records of reading in his *Journals* and, more indirectly, in the lists of withdrawals he and his mother made from the Boston Library Society, show his early concern with seeking out belief. His step-grandfather, Ezra Ripley, who lived in the Old Manse in Concord, which was later to be Hawthorne's, and his Aunt Mary Moody, devoted spurrer-on of his thought, both helped lead him in the direction of theology and of moral meditation, so that his readings through his twenties ran as follows: the novels of Sir Walter Scott, Mrs. Inchbald, and Mrs. Edgeworth; Thomas Campbell's long poem *The Pleasures of Hope* and Vicesimus Knox's *Elegant Extracts* in prose and verse; works of Benjamin Franklin, Cicero, Shakespeare, the English essayists like Bacon and Addison, and historians like Robertson; translations of Cervantes, Dante, Euripides, Montaigne, Pascal, Plutarch, Rousseau, *Arabian Nights' Entertainments*, and *Selections from the Popular Poetry of the Hindus*. Scott furnished his world of fictive landscape and romance, Cicero his world of oratorical meditation, Plato his world of speculation about what is true; English prose writers gave a solid professional background, and Eastern lore added a spice to the whole. His first poem, *The History of Fortus*, begun when he was ten, was a romance.

His college studies were standard; among them, first year, Latin, Livy, and Horace, geometry, and Lowth's *Grammar*; second year, Cicero, history, geometry, Blair's *Rhetoric*, Locke's *Human Understanding*; third year, Homer, Juvenal, Hebrew, astronomy, Stewart's *Human Mind*; fourth year, chemistry, political economy,

Butler's *Analogy,* and *The Federalist.* The members of his college
literary club wrote essays and read them aloud.

There are qualities which can be called Emersonian even in
his earliest works, in his two Bowdoin prize essays of 1820 and
1821 when he was not yet twenty, in his first printed essay, his first
sermon, his first lecture. Consider his first Bowdoin essay, on the
assigned topic "The Character of Socrates." It begins, as his essays
were long to do, as his favorite Scott had done, with a poetic epigraph; and note the references: to Plato's academic walk, the Lyceum, which was to be the name for the great American lecture
circuit established a decade later; reference also to *pure* and
stream, terms to be especially characteristic of Emerson's writing;
and reference to the needs of his own country.

> Guide my way
> Through fair Lyceum's walk, the green retreats
> Of Academus, and the thymy vale
> Where, oft enchanted with Socratic sounds,
> Ilissus pure devolved his tuneful stream
> In gentler murmurs. From the blooming store
> Of these auspicious fields, may I unblamed
> Transplant some living blossoms to adorn
> My native clime.

Then this on his main topic: "Socrates taught that every soul was
an eternal, immutable form of beauty in the divine mind, and that
the most beautiful mortals approached nearest to that celestial
mould; that it was the honor and delight of human intellect to
contemplate this *beau ideal,* and that this was better done through
the medium of earthly perfection." How much discussion of Emerson's mysticism would be tempered if it took into account this
approbation of idea's form and substance!

How much too the stress on his individualism would be tempered by a reading of his senior essay of 1821. In it he traces "The
Present State of Ethical Philosophy" from the limits of moral
science set by the Greeks to the church's "obstinacy of ignorance,"
to Cudworth's and Burke's corrections of Hobbes, and the valuable common sense of the modern philosophers Clark, Price, Butler,
Reid, Paley, Smith, and Stewart. Then he makes the important

approving distinction that "The moderns have made their ethical writings of a more practical character than the sages of antiquity. . . . The ancients balanced the comparative excellence of
two virtues or the badness of two vices; they determined the question whether solitude or society were the better condition for virtue. The moderns have substituted inquiries of deep interest for
those of only speculative importance. We would ask, in passing,
what discussion of Aristotle or Socrates can compare, in this respect, with the train of reasoning by which Dr. Price arrives at the
conclusion that every wrong act is a step to all that is tremendous
in the universe." Democratically, too, modern moral philosophy
shows "that a series of humble efforts is more meritorious than solitary miracles of virtue. . . . The plague spot of slavery must be
purged thoroughly out . . . The faith of treaties must be kept
inviolate . . ."

Earlier than most he expressed concern for his country. When
he was nineteen, only a decade past the battles of 1812, in which as
a boy he had served, reinforcing the barricades on Boston's lines to
the sea, he feared the settling down of the national spirit. "In this
merry time," he wrote to a classmate, "and with real substantial
happiness above any known nation, I think we Yankees have
marched on since the Revolution to strength, to honor, and at last
to *ennui*. It is most true that the people (of the city, at least) are
actually tired of hearing Aristides called the Just, and it demonstrates a sad caprice when they hesitate about putting on their
vote such names as Daniel Webster and Sullivan and Prescott, and
only distinguish them by a small majority over bad and doubtful
men. . . . Will it not be dreadful to discover that this experiment,
made by America to ascertain if men can govern themselves, does
not succeed; that too much knowledge and too much liberty make
them mad?"

In his notes for his first sermon, "Pray without Ceasing," he
wrote, "Take care, take care, that your sermon is not a recitation;
that it is a sermon to Mr. A. and Mr. B. and Mr. C." The idea for
this he, a Unitarian, got not only from Thessalonians but from a
Methodist farm laborer, who said to him that men are always

praying. "I meditated much on this saying and wrote my first sermon therefrom, of which the divisions were: (1) Men are always praying; (2) All their prayers are granted; (3) We must beware, then, what we ask." Between this first sermon in Waltham in 1826, and his ordination at Boston's Second Church in 1829, he preached two hundred sermons, learning to dread the demands of Sunday, learning to use one sermon in different places and different ways, yet becoming so habituated that long after he had left the pulpit he still continued to make notes on sermon topics.

In the first Sunday of his Boston ministry, speaking of styles of preaching, he said that preaching should apply itself to the good and evil in men. "Men imagine that the end and use of preaching is to expound a text, and forget that Christianity is an infinite and universal law; that it is the revelation of a Deity whose being the soul cannot reject without denying itself, a rule of action which penetrates into every moment and into the smallest duty. If any one hereafter should object to the want of sanctity of my style and the want of solemnity in my illustrations, I shall remind him that the language and the images of Scripture derive all their dignity from their association with divine truth, and that our Lord condescended to explain himself by allusions to every homely fact, and, if he addressed himself to the men of this age, would appeal to those arts and objects by which we are surrounded; to the printing-press and the loom, to the phenomena of steam and of gas, to free institutions and a petulant and vain nation." In sermon after sermon, "The Christian Minister," "Summer," "The Individual and the State," "Trust Yourself," "Hymn Books," "The Genuine Man," he carries out this active relation. The active verbs of his talks are indicative of his manner.

During the three years of his ministry at Boston's Second Church, the old church of Increase and Cotton Mather in its Puritan tradition, Emerson's reading moved toward the specific wisdoms needed to support him against what his journals had referred to as his own "sluggishness," "silliness," "flippancy," even "frigid fear," along with his lack of unction at "funerals, weddings, and ritual ceremonies," his unwilling absorption in sick calls, in swelling of the poor fund, and in other managements. Here he became more philosophically focused. He borrowed from the library again and again in 1830 de Gérando's *Histoire Comparée des Systèmes de Philosophie* (1804) which provided brief views of the pre-Platonists, pointed to their distinguishing of the ideal from the material, and, especially, emphasized God as unity, first cause, harmony, the law of order by attraction, repulsion, relation. Then Plato abridged by Dacier, a Harvard text, then Thomas Taylor's editions of Plato's *Cratylus*, *Phaedo*, *Parmenides*, and *Timaeus*, which he borrowed many times from 1830 to 1845 and finally bought, for their treasurable emphasis on the soul, its motion, being, and becoming. Then work on Neo-Platonism, possibly Cudworth's *The True Intellectual System of the Universe*, with its concept that nature "doth reconcile the contrarieties and enmities of particular things, and bring them into one general harmony in the whole." Then the philosopher George Berkeley, as against his predecessor Hobbes, on the laws of nature as they discipline us, and on "our delight in every exertion of active moral power." And then at last, along with Boehme and Swedenborg, his own contemporary, Coleridge, in whose *Aids to Reflection, Friend,* and *Biographia*, he found the distinctions between Reason and Understanding, Imagination and Fancy, which Coleridge had adapted from Kant and the Germans and which amounted to the nineteenth century's scientific "reasonable" renaming of the old pair Faith and Reason — that Faith which seems an inward Reason, a powerful and compelling intuition of validity, of the sort which finally enabled Emerson to write in his journal in 1831 the lines of "Gnothi Seauton," "Know Thyself," and to reason himself after his wife's death into a withdrawal from his career, into a year's journey away from America and his own youth.

When in 1832 he resigned his ministry, spoke against church dogma and the communion ceremony, left behind the sorrows of his wife's death and his family's illnesses, Emerson seemed to be seeking in Europe the strong sources of his bookish admirations, in Coleridge, Wordsworth, Carlyle, and others. But what he discovered in the Jardin des Plantes — in the Old World — was its new

world of biological and geological science. Finding his men of letters, except for Carlyle, self-centered, withdrawn, or garrulous, he
found in zoological gardens and institutes of science the invigora-
tion he sought. When he came back to America his ideas, perhaps
under the pressures of a long hard sea voyage, combined youthful
literary and religious studies with newly strengthened views of
science. In a letter of 1834 he wrote, "Is it not a good symptom for
society, this decided and growing taste for natural science which
has appeared though yet in its first gropings? . . . I have been
writing three lectures on Natural History and of course reading
as much geology, chemistry, and physics as I could find." As the editors of his *Early Lectures* say, "The science which Emerson studied
and professed was pre-Darwinian and concerned itself more with
the classification than with the evolution of natural phenomena.
Largely deductive in its theoretical base, it could serve as illustra-
tion of divine law and at the same time offer opportunities for
observation and experimentation."

Emerson's first lecture to laymen in 1833 began, "It seems to
have been designed, if anything was, that men should be students
of Natural History." That Lyceum of which his junior essay had
spoken was off to its great success. "The beauty of the world is a
perpetual invitation to the study of the world." Emerson went on:
"While I stand there [in the Jardin] I am impressed with a singular conviction that not a form so grotesque, so savage, or so beautiful, but is an expression of something in man the observer. . . . I
am moved by strange sympathies. I say I will listen to this invitation. I will be a naturalist." The advantages of the study: health
and useful knowledge, and delight, and improvement of character,
and explanation of man to himself. "Nothing is indifferent to the
wise. If a man should study the economy of a spire of grass — how
it sucks up sap, how it imbibes light, how it resists cold, how it
repels excess of moisture, it would show him a design in the form,
in the color, in the smell, in the very posture of the blade as it
bends before the wind. . . . the whole of Nature is a metaphor
or image of the human Mind. The laws of moral nature answer
to those of matter as face to face in a glass."

Such scientific titles as "On the Relation of Man to the Globe," "Water," and "The Naturalist" alternated throughout his lecturing career, in Boston, New York, Philadelphia, the Midwest, with those of a more historical and biographical order. The lectures of 1835 lauded Michelangelo, Chaucer, Shakespeare, Bacon, Milton, Jeremy Taylor for their earthiness, and Jonson, Herrick, Herbert for their strong and simple sentences and objects. The 1836 series in Boston on "Philosophy of History," and the later series on "Human Culture," "Human Life," "The Present Age," "The Times," stressed the common interests of men, saying of Michelangelo, as of Martin Luther, "so true was he to the laws of the human mind that his character and his works like Isaac Newton's seem rather a part of Nature than arbitrary productions of the human will."

In publication, Emerson's career began from Concord in 1836, when he was just over thirty years old, with a small, not popular, pamphlet called *Nature*, which stated succinctly in its third sentence: "But if a man would be alone, let him look at the stars." This early individual man of Emerson's is a man alone, apart from his friends and even from his own studies and pursuits, an unmediated part of the universe. By "nature," Emerson says, he means "the integrity of impression made by manifold natural objects. It is this which distinguishes the stick of timber of the woodcutter from the tree of the poet." A good local example: "Miller owns this field, Locke that, and Manning the woodland beyond. But none of them owns the landscape."

The main parts of his essay rest upon these distinctions. The causes of the world he calls "Commodity," how things are served and used; "Beauty," how their harmony is perceived, in outline, color, motion, grouping; "Language," how they are signified and symbolized; "Discipline," how they are ordered and distinguished — these are his own versions of Aristotle's classical causes, material, effective, formal, and final. Then in three final sections, Emerson treats man's view of "Idealism," "Spirit," and "Prospects": his perspective through intuitive idea stronger than that through sense or argument; his power, in incarnation, of worship; and his power to speculate, to guess about relations, *whence* and *whereto*. He draws upon *The Tempest*, the Bible's Proverbs, *Comus*, and George Herbert's "Man" to voice his guesses. Both learned and innocent men, he warns, limit their powers and fail to speculate. "The invariable mark of wisdom is to see the miraculous in the common," that is, idea in material, beauty and spirit in commodity and discipline. "What is a day? What is a year? What is summer? What is woman? What is a child? What is sleep? . . . Whilst the abstract question occupies your intellect, nature brings it in the concrete to be solved by your hands. . . . Every spirit builds itself a house, and beyond its house a world, and beyond its world a heaven. . . . Adam called his house, heaven and earth; Cæsar called his house, Rome; you perhaps call yours, a cobbler's trade; a hundred acres of ploughed land; or a scholar's garret. . . . Build therefore your own world. As fast as you conform your life to the pure idea in your mind, that will unfold its great proportions. A correspondent revolution in things will attend the influx of the spirit. So fast will disagreeable appearances, swine, spiders, snakes, pests, mad-houses, prisons, enemies, vanish; they are temporary and shall no more be seen. . . . so shall the advancing spirit . . . draw beautiful faces, warm hearts, wise discourse, and heroic acts, around its way, until evil is no more seen."

Here in its peroration, the essay "Nature" makes the proposals of Emerson's whole lifetime on the simple questions of life, the range and scope of spirit, the fit of historical past and possible future, the nature of evil, the values of fact and of spirit. Emerson's future style too is proposed and exemplified here: the broad speculative generalizations followed by the simplest questions and instances; the speaking to *you*; the quick strides of survey covering miles and centuries; the parallels and dismissals; the earnest recommendations for the life of the universe as for the life of every day.

The poems and the two volumes of essays which follow in the 1840's, as well as some of his most moving lectures, such as "The American Scholar" and the "Divinity School Address," set the fame of Emerson moving into its channels. These accepted works we too may accept, to read them all, rather than to explore them here. The *Essays* followed patterns with which we have already learned to be familiar: from time in "History" to more than time in "Art," from art in "Poet" to religion in "Reformers," ending, as in his more loosely collected essays of the sixties and seventies, with transcendences of age and death. The poems, too, move toward "Terminus," "Farewell," and "In Memoriam."

But two fates, laws of his life, carried Emerson's work to less predictable intensities: one, the force of the slavery question and the Civil War; the other, the force of his concern with the "natural history of intellect" in poetry as in prose. In these we see not seasonal pattern and temporal decline, but the late maturing demanded by event and drawn from the aging seer after his chief works, his solidest books, were done. "Emancipation in the British West Indies," 1844, "The Fugitive Slave Law," 1851 and 1854, "John Brown," 1859, "The Emancipation Proclamation," 1862, "Abraham Lincoln," 1865, all carry the weight of a pressing issue.

Thoreau is said to have rung the bell for the public meeting at the Concord Court House in 1844, at which many citizens opposed Emerson's attitudes on emancipation. Emerson began: "Friends and Fellow Citizens: We are met to exchange congratulations on the anniversary of an event singular in the history of civilization; a day of reason; of the clear light; of that which makes us better than a flock of birds and beasts; a day which gave the immense fortification of a fact, of gross history, to ethical abstractions."

How he delights in the fact of the West Indies' final emancipation, in the fact of "the steady gain of truth and right," in the intelligent self-interest despite the voluptuousness of power. So in America in the fifties, the Whig *must*'s, the Liberal *may*'s, need to combine. So we need, like John Brown, to see the facts behind the forms. So, "this heavy load lifted off the national heart, we shall not fear henceforward to show our faces among mankind." And Providence makes its own instruments, "creates the man for the time." In verse, the Concord "Ode," read July 4, 1857:

> United States! the ages plead, —
> Present and Past in under-song, —

Go put your creed into your deed,
Nor speak with double tongue.

And the "Boston Hymn," read January 1, 1863, in Boston, when
the President's Emancipation Proclamation went into effect:

God said, I am tired of kings,
I suffer them no more;
Up to my ear the morning brings
The outrage of the poor. . . .

To-day unbind the captive,
So only are ye unbound;
Lift up a people from the dust,
Trump of their rescue, sound!

Pay ransom to the owner
And fill the bag to the brim.
Who is the owner? The slave is owner.
And ever was. Pay him.

Emerson has said, "I compared notes with one of my friends who
expects everything of the universe and is disappointed when anything is less than the best, and I found that I begin at the other
extreme, expecting nothing, and am always full of thanks for moderate goods." Yet his intuition that God need not be so modest
could find expression in God's own voice in this hymn and thus
raise the responsive shouts of a Boston audience.

The work of his last active years, of the postwar sixties, was
the work again of the "natural history of intellect." This theme he
still wanted to clarify. "His noun had to wait for its verb or its
adjective until he was ready; then his speech would come down
upon the word he wanted . . ." as his biographer James Cabot
commented. He never spoke impromptu; indeed, in his last years,
he sought so long for the right word that he hesitated to appear
in public. Part of his reticence was that, as he wrote in his journal
of 1859, he wanted no disciples, he spoke to bring men not to him
but to themselves. Harvard Phi Beta Kappa speaker in 1867, as
in 1837, he took up again for Harvard in 1870 the series which
he had projected thirty years before and had given in 1848 and
later, in London, Boston, and New York, again in 1858 as a course

on the "Natural Method of Mental Philosophy," and again in 1866 as "Philosophy for People." Now for a group of thirty students in 1870 and 1871 he would try to bring together what he had to say. He still was not satisfied. Nevertheless: "If one can say so without arrogance, I might suggest that he who contents himself with dotting only a fragmentary curve, recording only what facts he has observed, without attempting to arrange them within one outline, follows a system also, a system as grand as any other, though he does not interfere with its vast curves by prematurely forcing them into a circle or ellipse, but only draws that arc which he clearly sees, and waits for new opportunity, well assured that these observed arcs consist with each other."

This is the way his speaking seemed to a contemporary, W. C. Brownell: "The public was small, attentive, even reverential. The room was as austere as the chapel of a New England Unitarian church would normally be in those days. The Unitarians were the intellectual sect of those days and, as such, suspect. Even the Unitarians, though, who were the aristocratic as well as the intellectual people of the place, found the chapel benches rather hard, I fancy, before the lecture was over, and I recall much stirring. There was, too, a decided sprinkling of scoffers among the audience, whose sentiments were disclosed during the decorous exit. Incomprehensibility, at that epoch generally, was the great offence; it was a sort of universal charge against anything uncomprehended, made in complete innocence of any obligation to comprehend. Nevertheless the small audience was manifestly more or less spellbound. Even the dissenters — as in the circumstances the orthodox of the day may be called — were impressed. It might be all over their heads, as they contemptuously acknowledged, or vague, as they charged, or disintegrating, as they — vaguely — felt. But there was before them, placidly, even benignly, uttering incendiarism, an extraordinarily interesting personality. It was evening and the reflection of two little kerosene lamps, one on either side of his lectern, illuminated softly the serenest of conceivable countenances — nobility in its every lineament and a sort of irradiating detachment about the whole presence . . ."

To think about Emerson not only for himself in his own time and for us in ours, but in the larger context of tradition, we need to think of the qualities which relate him to others, as an author to other authors, as a writer of prose wisdom to other such writers. What place does Emerson hold in the tradition, of his own English literature and of the larger world of wisdom? This question cannot be answered by considering his ideas as if they were separable from his presentation of them. Rather, his presentation of them gives them their special identifiable character. We need to discover the special traits and traditions of this essayist of ours, how he differed from any other we may know — from Cicero and Seneca on old age, from Montaigne on life and friendship, from the Elizabethan essayists whom he read with such pleasure as a boy, from the sermons he heard, from the eighteenth- and nineteenth-century philosophic and journalistic prose which he kept reading in the English reviews, from Carlyle whom he admired so directly, from his own American contemporaries, from the wisdom-literature of China, Persia, India, from his own Bible.

If we read the beginning of his perhaps most famous essay, "Self-Reliance," which followed "History" in introducing his popular series of *Essays* in the 1840's, we may catch his way of expression. In the atmosphere of three quotations to the effect that "man is his own star," Emerson begins: "I read the other day some verses written by an eminent painter which were original and not conventional. The soul always hears an admonition in such lines, let the subject be what it may. The sentiment they instil is of more value than any thought they may contain. To believe your own thought, to believe that what is true for you in your private heart is true for all men — that is genius. Speak your latent conviction, and it shall be the universal sense; for the inmost in due time becomes the outmost, and our first thought is rendered back to us by the trumpets of the Last Judgment. Familiar as the voice of the mind is to each, the highest merit we ascribe to Moses, Plato and Milton is that they set at naught books and traditions, and spoke not what men, but what *they* thought. A man should learn to detect and watch that gleam of light which flashes across his mind from within, more than the lustre of the firmament of bards and sages."

The tone of this whole beginning is at once particular and personal: "I read . . . your own"; general and confident: "the soul always hears"; evocative: "the trumpets of the Last Judgment"; wide-reaching: "Moses, Plato and Milton"; recommendatory: "speak . . . learn"; figurative: "that gleam of light . . . more than the lustre of the firmament."

In this combination of qualities, Emerson's style is more focused and condensed than Cicero's, say, or Seneca's, or Montaigne's, setting its generalities in specific actions and analogies. It is not what we traditionally call a classic style, either in Latin or in English, because it does not carry the tone of a full and logical unfolding of the thought, but rather moves as if by flashes of illumination. This is not to say that it is unlogical, merely that it does not give the effect of explicit stress on logical connections. Nor does it stress the literal qualifications, descriptions, with which classical prose is concerned. Both adjectives and connectives are relatively subordinated to direct active verbs. This is to say that Emerson characteristically in this paragraph and throughout this essay, as still in "Illusions" twenty years later, writes a very active, predicative style, one in which the structure is basically simple statement, for which both modification and connective addition are only minimally necessary, and the sentences are relatively short, the central statements relatively unqualified.

There is scarcely another essayist like this among the famed of English prose. Closest to Emerson are sermon-makers like the pre-Elizabethan Latimer, or Tyndale in his translation of Paul to the Romans, or narrative writers, the Bunyan of *Pilgrim's Progress*, the Joyce of Molly Bloom's soliloquy; and these are styles we do not probably think of as Emersonian. Yet even less so are the styles of classic arguers in the tradition of Hooker, Bacon, and Locke, or of the soaring describers he loved: Sir Thomas Browne, for example, or his own contemporaries like Carlyle, or what he himself called the "mock-turtle nutriment as in Macaulay."

But there is one writer in the tradition with whom he is

closely allied, one whose works in prose and poetry were Emerson's own favorite youthful reading: Ben Jonson. Jonson was as singular in his own time as Emerson in his: their sense of the English language as best used in active concise statements, making connections by implication, was a sense shared in its extreme by few others, and therefore especially lively both in its singularity and in its function as bond between them. Even their use of specific connectives and the proportion of relative clauses to causal clauses and locational phrases are striking. Not Plutarch, not Montaigne, not Bacon, but specifically the aphoristic Jonson of *Timber* is Emerson's direct model.

Emerson's critics, and he himself, have often complained of the sentences which seemed to repel rather than to attract one another. But lack of connectives does not necessarily mean lack of connections. The thought moves from general to particular, and from key word to key word. Such thought is logical, even syllogistic: the general, all men are mortal; the particular, a man; the conclusion, a man is mortal; you and I participate in this truth. But the *and*'s and *therefore*'s have been omitted, or have been used with relative infrequency. In other words, the logical relation of all to one is present, but not the explicit links in the steps of relation. Further, Emerson might begin with what we would call an untenable premise: "All men are immortal." He would feel this intuitively, "the blazing evidence of immortality," the "gleam of light which flashes across his mind from within," and so he would base upon it his logical argument for any one man and for us. And still further, he would treat key words like *man* in a special way, including in them all their degrees of evaluative reference from lowest to highest; so that "man" would mean man in his limitless degree of spirit, as well as in his limiting degree of body, thus supporting by definition, implicit or explicit, the relation between *man* and *immortal* which the syllogism makes. It is as if Emerson were essentially satisfied to say, "All men are men (with all men's limitations and potentialities); a man acts like a man." The connective *therefore*'s and adjectival *immortal*'s are minimal; the subject-predicate *Men are, a man is*, central.

In the early sermons, according to Kenneth Cameron's index-concordance, key terms are *God, Jesus, man, memory, mind, nature, self, soul, truth*. These suggest three centers, religious, psychological, scientific. Then in *Nature*, key terms are *action, beauty, God, man, mind, nature, poet, soul, spirit, thought, truth, world*. The changes make clear Emerson's motion away from religion in the shape of person toward religion in the sense of creation of beauty, whereby *action, thought*, and *world* are taken up into the forms and purposes of *spirit*, and thus made beautiful by their harmony.

Index terms tend to be nouns; but if we look more closely at the recurrent language of specific prose texts, early and late, we will see how strong and traditional are Emerson's verbs, especially those of feeling, knowing, thinking, how evaluative and discriminating his adjectives, as for example in "Self-Reliance," *divine, good, great, new, own, other, same, strong, such, true*, and in the later "Fate" and "Illusions," *fine, find*, and *hold*. The nouns of these essays also parallel the concordance listings for the whole work: the early *action, being, character, fact, friend, truth, virtue*; the later *circumstance, element, form, fate*; and the shared *God, law, life, man, mind, nature, nothing, power, thought, time, world*. The shift in emphasis from early *action* and *character* to later *circumstance* and *fate* is represented in the structure of the prose, as of the poetry also: an unusually high proportion of verbs and low proportion of connectives in the early work and "Self-Reliance" establishing later a proportion of about ten verbs and fewer adjectives to twenty nouns, achieving the precarious and shifting balance between action and circumstance which he argues for.

Poetry and prose for Emerson are not far apart. In syntax, in vocabulary, in idea, their likenesses are greater than their differences. The main differences are the larger proportion of sensory terms in the poetry, and the framing by meter and rhyme. His first poems appeared not in the volume called *Poems* but as epigraphs for essays. He saw poems as epigraphs, like Biblical verses, texts for sermons. Therefore his poetic allegiances were divided — on the one hand to the succinctness of a Jonson, as in prose, yet on the other to the materials and moods of his own day, which were freer, more natural, more exploratory.

His was a sensorily active and receptive vocabulary like that of the English eighteenth and American nineteenth centuries, its especial impact being in its direct joining of man and nature, a nature *wise* and *good*, an *air, sky, sea, star* related to *joy, form, beauty*. This stylistic joining of human and natural realms as both natural, though differently, is like the metaphysical joining, as in Cowper's "church-going bell," which Wordsworth with his more literal connecting processes disapproved; it made condensations of Emerson's widest extensions.

To this outreaching vocabulary he did at least consider suiting a freer form. Like Carlyle, he wearied of the "Specimens" of English verse he had read. Carlyle had written him in the 1830's, ". . . my view is that now at last we have lived to see all manner of Poetics and Rhetorics and Sermonics . . . as good as broken and abolished . . . and so one leaves the pasteboard coulisses, and three unities, and Blair's Lectures quite behind; and feels only that there is *nothing sacred*, then, but the *Speech of Man* to believing Men! [which] will one day doubtless anew environ itself with fit modes, with solemnities that are *not* mummeries." Emerson's own *Journals* of this time (1839) expressed his interest not only in Pope's couplets and Scott's quatrains but in freer measures like those characteristic of Wordsworth's "Immortality Ode" — "not tinkling rhyme, but grand Pindaric strokes, as firm as the tread of a horse," suggesting not a restraint, "but the wildest freedom." Later he wrote to Herman Grimm concerning his *Life of Michelangelo*, "I hate circular sentences, or echoing sentences, where the last half cunningly repeats the first half, — but you step from stone to stone, and advance ever." And he expressed to Grimm his corollary lack of taste for drama: "Certainly it requires great health and wealth of power to ventriloquize (shall I say?) through so many bodies . . ." Rather, "The maker of a sentence . . . launches out into the infinite and builds a road into Chaos and old Night, and is followed by those who hear him with something of wild, creative delight." And: "Who can blame men

for seeking excitement? They are polar, and would you have them
sleep in a dull eternity of equilibrium? Religion, love, ambition,
money, war, brandy, — some fierce antagonism must break the
round of perfect circulation or no spark, no joy, no event can
be."

He is aware too of freedom in natural forms. In 1841: "I told
Henry Thoreau that his freedom is in the form, but he does not
disclose new matter. . . . But now of poetry I would say, that
when I go out into the fields in a still sultry day, in a still sultry
humor, I do perceive that the finest rhythms and cadences of poetry
are yet unfound, and that in that purer state which glimmers before us, rhythms of a faery and dream-like music shall enchant us,
compared with which the finest measures of English poetry are
psalm-tunes. I think now that the very finest and sweetest closes
and falls are not in our metres, but in the measures of eloquence,
which have greater variety and richness than verse. . . ." Such
freedom he aimed for in his prose and poetry of the sea, and such
sense of freedom enabled him in 1855 to hail Whitman's new
scope and form.

Yet there is a stronger controlling force for him, his youthful
note-taking interest in pithy statements. As far back as 1820 we
see his mood: "Have been of late reading patches of Barrow and
Ben Jonson; and what the object — not curiosity? no — nor expec-
tation of edification intellectual or moral — but merely because
they are authors where vigorous phrases and quaint, peculiar words
and expressions may be sought and found, the better 'to rattle
out the battle of my thoughts.'" And in 1840, he stated his philosophical reasons for condensation: "yet does the world reproduce
itself in miniature in every event that transpires, so that all the
laws of nature may be read in the smallest fact."

Then in 1842 he expressed recognition of the power of concentration within scope and range: "This feeling I have respecting
Homer and Greek, that in this great, empty continent of ours,
stretching enormous almost from pole to pole, with thousands of
long rivers and thousands of ranges of mountains, the rare scholar,
who, under a farmhouse roof, reads Homer and the Tragedies,

adorns the land. He begins to fill it with wit, to counterbalance the enormous disproportion of the unquickened earth."

While his chief substance then comes from the protestant naturalism of Sylvester and the eighteenth century, in *air, sea, sky, land, cloud, star,* and its American specifications in *beautiful, river, music, morning, snow, rose,* like Whitman's *grass,* the counter, wry, limiting, and constructing tradition was his aphoristic one, the *good and wise thought, nature, fate, form, time,* of the Elizabethans. When, later in life, Emerson published his collection, *Parnassus,* of the poems he had liked best, the most space went to Shakespeare, the next to Jonson and Herrick, Wordsworth and Tennyson. While the nineteenth-century poets gave him his guide to beauty of reference, the seventeenth century, in poetry as in prose, gave him his form. The Jonson he called master of song he represented by lines which sound like his own:

Come on, come on, and where you go
So interweave the curious knot
As even the Observer scarce may know
Which lines are pleasure, and which not . . .
Admire the wisdom of your feet:
For dancing is an exercise
Not only shows the mover's wit,
But maketh the beholder wise,
As he hath power to rise to it.

So Emerson "studied thy motion, took thy form," giving to cosmos the active limitations of man's rhymes and meters in the shape of aphorism and epigraph, combining, from his favorite readings, the gnomic force of translations from the Anglo-Saxon and Persian with the pith of segments from Jonsonian "Old Plays" used as epigraphs in Scott's novels.

In "Permanent Traits of the English National Genius," for example, Emerson quotes and admires the strength of the Anglo-Saxon verse line:

O in how gloomy
And how bottomless
A well laboreth
The darkened mind

> When it the strong
> Storms beat
> Of the world's business . . .

This is much like Emerson's own "Gnothi Seauton":

> He is in thy world,
> But thy world knows him not.
> He is the mighty Heart
> From which life's varied pulses part.
> Clouded and shrouded there doth sit.
> The Infinite . . .

Such concision he found also when in 1842 he edited the prose and verse of the Persian Saadi's *Gulistan* ("Rose Garden"), a representative collection of wise maxims. As he later explained, "The dense writer has yet ample room and choice of phrase and even a gamesome mood often between his valid words."

Emerson's cryptic and summary comment on more extended thought gave it the close form of meter and rhyme which he was concerned with as a part of the structure of the universe — its recurrent tide in season and in man. For him this form was not "organic" in the sense that we sometimes use the term, as Coleridge used the term, in the individual and spontaneous unfoldment of self as a flower. This Emerson called romantic and capricious. Rather, for him "organic" meant structural, necessary, recurrent in a context of use, in material, formal, and direct cause, that is, as he said, classic.

A close look at the form of his poetry in relation to his prose tells us much of the form of the world for him. Its lines, its regular or varied stresses, its coupled or varied rhymes, are part of the body, the law, of nature. With and against them the poet's free spirit works. Similarly, names are part of the categorizing force of nature. With and against them, through metaphor, the seeing of likeness in difference and difference in likeness, the seeing poet's vision of image and symbol, of individual entity, works. Similarly, sentences, generalizations, are part of the law of nature, and with and against them the vital instance works. In structure, in reference, in sound, his poetry gives us, even more closely than his prose, and with the focus in which he believed, the presence of all in one, the interplay of likeness and difference in every entity of art.

Among Emerson's best liked poems, "Each and All," "Uriel," "Good-Bye," "Woodnotes," "Merlin," "Concord Hymn," "Boston Hymn," "Brahma," "Days," "Terminus," as among his longer descriptions and shorter fragments, condensations and variations appear in all sorts of degrees, from the strictness of "Concord Hymn" to the obliquities of "Merlin." Even some of his choppiest addenda are likable — "Limits," for example, or "The Bohemian Hymn," or "Water" from "Fragments," or "Nature and Life," or

> Roomy Eternity
> Casts her schemes rarely,
> And an æon allows
> For each quality and part
> Of the multitudinous
> And many-chambered heart.

Or, from "The Poet,"

> That book is good
> Which puts me in a working mood.
>   Unless to thought is added Will,
>   Apollo is an imbecile.
> What parts, what gems, what colors shine, —
> Ah, but I miss the grand design.

This was Emerson's steadiest complaint about his style: that he dealt in parts and fragments and could not achieve the whole, which he himself bespoke. Yet his very worry about this achievement, as about his friendship and love, is indicative of their importance to him, their religious center for him. We must not take at face value his fears of coldheartedness, of infinitely repellent particles; these were the recalcitrances of substance in which his spirit worked. "It is very unhappy, but too late to be helped, the discovery we have made that we exist. That discovery is called the Fall of Man." Yet "we are sure, that, though we know not how, necessity does comport with liberty," and "a part of Fate is the freedom of man." These are the principles of his life; they are guides, too, to the form of his art. In the speculative turns of

"Merlin," as in the steady pace of "Brahma" and "Days," is the strength of freedom joined with measure.

The essay "The Poet" makes specific application of these beliefs. Ideally, the poet is the sayer, the teller of news, utterer of the necessary and causal. "For the Universe has three children, born at one time, which reappear under different names in every system of thought, whether they be called cause, operation and effect; or, more poetically, Jove, Pluto, Neptune; or, theologically, the Father, the Spirit and the Son; but which we will call here the Knower, the Doer and the Sayer. These stand respectively for the love of truth, for the love of good, and for the love of beauty. These three are equal. Each is that which he is, essentially, so that he cannot be surmounted or analyzed, and each of these three has the power of the others latent in him and his own, patent."

The poet, by saying, makes new relations, heals dislocations and detachments, shows defects as exuberances, as in Vulcan's lameness, Cupid's blindness. "Every new relation is a new word." The world is thus "put under the mind for verb and noun" without an explicit connective. It is important to realize what this sense of saying means to Emerson's own poetry. It means that as a poet he is not an imagist, not a symbolist, but specifically a figurist. That is, he accepts image and symbol as vital, from the natural world; and then his contribution as poet is to show them in new relation. "He knows why the plain or meadow of space was strown with these flowers we call suns and moons and stars . . ." There is the metaphoric way of speaking. He names now by appearances, now by essences, delighting in the intellect's sense of boundaries, and then in the ascension of things to higher kinds, that is, in both being and becoming, the inebriation of thought moving to fact — even in algebra and definitions, the freedom of trope. Emerson blames mystics, as he would blame modern ritualistic symbolizers, for too many fixities. "The history of hierarchies seems to show that all religious error consisted in making the symbol too stark and solid." "Let us have a little algebra" — a little relation and proportion! "I look in vain for the poet whom I describe. We do not with sufficient plainness or sufficient profoundness address ourselves to life, nor dare we chaunt our own times and social circumstance."

Is Emerson a philosopher? Yes, if we agree with William James (as John Dewey quotes him in a *Southern Review* article of 1937): "Philosophic study means the habit of always seeing an alternative, of not taking the usual for granted, of making conventionalities fluid again, of imagining foreign states of mind." In this way Emerson prepares for James, for Dewey, for Charles Peirce, the great American pragmatists. In this way too he prepares more metaphysically for Nietzsche's Dionysus. But Emerson was not systematic and Germanic. Critics like René Wellek, writing on Emerson's philosophy, Andrew Schiller on his "gnomic structure," Kathryn McEuen on his rhymes, Frank Thompson on his theories of poetry, Walter Blair and Clarence Faust on his method, Nelson Adkins on his bardic tradition, J. D. Yohannan on his Persian translations, Percy Brown on his aesthetics, Vivian Hopkins and Stephen Whicher on his sense of form, and Frederic Carpenter on his use of oriental materials, all suggest variations on the theme of his fragmentary illuminations. So did his elder critics like Carlyle, Arnold, Santayana.

So did he. When in 1870 he began his final series "On the excellence of Intellect, its identity with nature, its formations in Instinct and Inspiration, and relation to the existing religion and civility of the present," he warned his hearers that this series would consist of "anecdotes of the intellect; a sort of Farmer's Almanac of mental moods," and even defended this method, as we have noted before, in his metaphor of the dotted line. He had reasons for not filling in the lines, for not always writing a smoothly qualified prose, poetry, or philosophy. "I think that philosophy is still rude and elementary. It will one day be taught by poets. The poet is in the natural attitude; he is believing; the philosopher, after some struggle, having only reasons for believing." "I confess to a little distrust of that completeness of system which metaphysicians are apt to affect. 'Tis the gnat grasping the world."

But in his sense of metaphysics as useful, for daily use, he had a great deal of work to do in the world. To feed the hunger of the young for ideas; to think what simple pattern of being could include man's sense of joy in being as well as his fear and falsification of it; to draw the world as newly understood by scientific thought into the world of common intuition; to combine his feeling that "the beauty of the world is a perpetual invitation to the study of the world" with such explanation as to his brother Edward in 1834 that visionary reason and toiling understanding work together, "by mutual reaction of thought and life, to make thought solid and life wise."

A man who has been called monist, dualist, pantheist, transcendentalist, puritan, optimist, pragmatist, mystic, may well feel dubious about the validity of labels, of adjectives. Yet his style shows us how all of these terms fit him and how they work together; over and over he tells us that it is degree he believes in; in degree, the one and the many may work together, god, man, nature may work together; all varieties of difference, from dissimilar to contrasting, will share degrees of likeness. His common term *polarity* referred not to modern positive and negative poles merely, and not to modern negative correlations or annihilations, but to "action and interaction," to differences or counterparts which are unified by a common direction, a north star, a magnetic field, a spirit in the laws and limits of body, a drawing of body along in the direction of spirit — a golden mean with a lodestar.

Emerson's plan for the *Essays*, early set down in his *Journals*, well summarizes his steadiest concerns:

There is one soul.
It is related to the world.
Art is its action thereon.
Science finds its methods.
Literature is its record.
Religion is the emotion of reverence that it inspires.
Ethics is the soul illustrated in human life.
Society is the finding of this soul by individuals in each other.
Trades are the learning of the soul in nature by labor.
Politics is the activity of the soul illustrated in power.
Manners are silent and mediate expressions of soul.

His plan, his tables of contents, his major vocabulary, his syntax, are all of a piece, seeking and finding, in what he sees to be the major activities of man, that unifying vitality of good, that one essential likeness, which he calls *soul*. He could say, "Within and Above are synonyms" — a metaphor crucial to belief in our day — so that "transcendental" could easily mean "a little beyond"; and he was able to say in another town or on a weekday what he had not felt able to say at home and on Sunday. For as one of his small-town congregations said, "We are very simple people here, and don't understand anybody but Mr. Emerson." And as their Emerson said, "What but thought deepens life, and makes us better than cow or cat?"

It was fortunate that there was enough of an artist in this wise man of America's nineteenth century, that he tried not only to advise but to preserve, not only to tell but to make and give; that the artistic power of Renaissance poets and prose writers gave him a means to hold and shape the fluent continuities of a liberal eighteenth- and nineteenth-century romanticism; that sermon structure, like rhyme and meter, gave him ways of holding fast the free Aeolian strains of sky and sea in their relevance to thought and fate and form.

There is no permanent wise man, Emerson says. Yet, "How does Memory praise? By holding fast the best." This is the work for a wise art, a laborious but joyful understanding.

EDWARD L. HIRSH

Henry Wadsworth Longfellow

THE span of Henry Wadsworth Longfellow's life, from 1807 to 1882, arched over the transforming years between two American worlds. The New England of his birth was agricultural and mercantile in its economy, anchored to seaports, rivers, and farms, provincial but refined in its culture, engaged in reconciling inherited, semi-aristocratic values with the ideals of a circumscribed but dynamic republicanism; the New England of his death was shaped by post-Civil War industrialism, with its noisy railroads, smoky cities and grim mill towns, emerging class conflicts, and crumbling pieties. Of the nature of this transformation, and its real import, Longfellow was, like most of his contemporaries, only partly and at moments aware. To the issues and occurrences susceptible of judgment by his clear, unexamined moral principles or his somewhat vague but deeply felt religious convictions, he responded vigorously — to the "shabby" Mexican war, the antislavery movement, and the human misery caused by financial panics. The range of his interests, however, is clearer in his diaries, journals, and letters than in his poetry. Although his poetry is more frequently topical than is sometimes realized, its relation to the age's history is usually indirect: with some exceptions, events and causes served as catalysts rather than as subject matter or primary topics of the verse. Before many contemporary developments, Long-fellow could only confess his bewilderment. Always affective and associative rather than analytic and theoretic in his response to life, he could sense the reality of profound change, and its menace, but he could not criticize it. His characteristic answer was the tireless reassertion of the values cherished by the stable society of his early maturity or drawn from his own love of traditional Western culture and the experiences of his childhood and youth.

Born at Portland, Maine, on February 27, 1807, Henry was the second of eight children, descended from Wadsworths and Long-fellows who had already established their families' provincial importance. His mother, Zilpah, shared his literary interests and inspired him with her own religiously motivated idealism, including a lifelong hatred of war and violence. His father, Stephen, a public-spirited lawyer, a trustee of Bowdoin College, and briefly congressman from Maine, was an efficient adviser to his son, and later provided him with financial aid as well as encouragement at the beginning of his career. Hardly second to happiness at home was the joy provided by life in a coastal city. The nearby woods and the northward sweep of primeval forest beyond them; the color and bustle of the harbor; above all, the restless Atlantic with its changing moods — these were to haunt Longfellow's imagination throughout his life and to give much of his poetry its dominant imagery. In his almost obsessive recall of time and happiness past, Arcadia lay in childhood and its geography was that of the New England coastline. His most intense poetic exercise in personal recollection is "My Lost Youth," whose familiar third stanza echoes the tone of the whole:

> I remember the black wharves and the slips,
>   And the sea-tides tossing free;
> And Spanish sailors with bearded lips,
> And the beauty and mystery of the ships,
>   And the magic of the sea.
>   And the voice of that wayward song
>   Is singing and saying still:
> "A boy's will is the wind's will,
> And the thoughts of youth are long, long thoughts."

In 1821, Longfellow was admitted to Bowdoin College, at Brunswick, Maine, although he did not take up residence there until his sophomore year. Inadequate as the young college was in several respects, its curriculum, modeled on Harvard's, prescribed substantial study of the classical languages, mathematics, scripture, and the branches of philosophy, as well as briefer study of natural science. Longfellow, well prepared by Portland Academy and by his own extensive reading, readily mastered the required subjects and also took the then-rare opportunity to receive part-time instruction in French. As important as his work in course was the informal education he received, especially through his membership in the Peucinian, a literary society with a well-stocked library. The reading and critical discussion of papers at its meetings sharpened Longfellow's growing desire for a literary career. This bias may have been further encouraged by a faculty member, Thomas Coggswell Upham, who came to Bowdoin in 1824 with a missionary zeal for the creation of a native American literature. So well did Longfellow profit from the combined influences of his collegiate years that his academic promise came to the attention of the trustees. In 1825 the new graduate was offered a just-established professorship in modern languages, with the stipulation of a period of European study — at his own expense — as preparation for the position. The offer was quickly accepted, and on May 15, 1826, Longfellow sailed from New York.

The three years in France, Spain, Italy, and Germany were touched with enchantment as Longfellow's romantic imagination responded to a past still visible in monuments and customs, to the storied associations which were, the associationist critics maintained, the source of poetic beauty. Longfellow also laid down solid intellectual foundations, especially in Romance languages and literature, but the new task he envisaged from his steadily American perspective was essentially artistic: to help create a great national literature not by radical novelty, as the so-called "Young American" writers urged, but by transmitting to America a rich European heritage for incorporation into its own culture. His pursuit of this goal through essays, lectures, translations, and adaptations from foreign literature exacted a price: if it did not cause, it certainly intensified the bookish tendency of Longfellow's writings. It also resulted, however, in an important contribution to the increasingly important relationship between American and European literature.

Assuming his professional duties in September 1829, Longfellow discovered that he had virtually to establish a new area of studies and to provide its very materials; between 1830 and 1832 he edited or translated six texts in French, Spanish, and Italian. His labors were rewarded: his competence in basic instruction, skill as a lecturer, and courtesy to students quickly made him an influential teacher. Further, he was making a professional reputation. His translations — the book-length *Coplas de Don Jorge Manrique* appeared in 1833 — attested his linguistic proficiency, in Spanish particularly; he was also publishing essays on southern European languages and literature that demonstrated scholarship. Longfellow's attention in these years was focused primarily on academic achievement; the writing of original poetry, begun before he entered Bowdoin and continued during his college days, had almost ceased after 1825, and his literary ambitions now found outlet in prose sketches of his travels interspersed with tales in the manner of Washington Irving. After an abortive beginning in serial form, the completed account was published in 1833–34 as *Outre-Mer: A Pilgrimage beyond the Sea.*

There were also nonprofessional reasons for satisfaction. After a short courtship, Longfellow was married in 1831 to Mary Storer Potter, a delicately attractive girl interested in mathematics and poetry, who made a self-effacing but effective helpmate. Yet, for all his success, Longfellow found Brunswick distressingly provincial after Europe, and energetically sought a larger public stage. This he attained in 1834, when the distinguished George Ticknor, Smith Professor of Modern Languages at Harvard College, designated Longfellow as his successor. Once more preparatory study abroad, this time in Germanic languages, seemed wise, and the Longfellows left for Europe in April 1835.

The pattern of Longfellow's life was decisively changed by the second European journey. The linguistic goals were accomplished: Longfellow added Dutch, Danish, Icelandic, Swedish, and some Finnish to his store of languages, acquired a thorough knowledge of German romantic literature, and began his lifelong reading in Goethe. It was not intellectual achievement, however, that made the period crucial, but the violent emotional experience originating in his wife's death. Mary's health had always been uncertain; now she was pregnant, and the rigors of a Scandinavian trip exhausted her. Back in Holland, she suffered a miscarriage; infection subsequently developed, and on November 29 she died. Soon after sending her body home for burial, Longfellow received news of the death of his closest friend. Suddenly, it seemed to him, life had taken on the unreality, the transiency, of a dream. Courageously, at times hectically, he pushed on with his work, haunted by loneliness and often acutely depressed.

In the spring of 1836, his spirits slightly improved, Longfellow visited the Tyrol. In July, at Interlaken, he encountered the wealthy Bostonian Nathan Appleton and his family, and with the beautiful, talented, and sensitive young Frances Appleton he fell promptly, passionately in love. In August he had to leave for America, his love unreturned; thus began an extended courtship, long unpromising and broken off by Fanny after publication of the too-autobiographical *Hyperion* in 1839. A chance meeting four years later begot a reconciliation, and on April 17, 1843, Longfellow received a note from Fanny that set him walking at top speed from Cambridge to Boston through a transfigured day, and into one of the happiest marriages on record.

The seven-year wait, however, was not spent in palely loitering. Occupying rented quarters in Brattle Street's dignified Craigie House, now maintained as a Longfellow museum, Longfellow performed with distinction his duties as Smith Professor. Although he came to detest departmental business and the drilling in fundamentals, and conducted a continuous, low-keyed quarrel with Harvard's then-conservative administrative policies, he took real delight, as did his listeners, in the delivery of his scrupulously prepared lectures. He not only gave the expected instruction in the history of European languages, but opened to his students the world of modern German literature, of Jean Paul Richter, Schiller, and, above all, Goethe. His teaching of *Faust*, indeed, was the first such offering in an American college.

More important to his own future, he also resumed writing, the European experience having reawakened the long-dormant creative impulse. In 1839, in addition to the prose *Hyperion*, there appeared *Voices of the Night*, his first collection of poems, some of which, including the sensationally popular "A Psalm of Life," had been previously printed in magazines. *Ballads and Other Poems* followed in 1841; *Poems on Slavery*, written during his return from a brief third European trip, in 1842; and a poetic drama, *The Spanish Student*, in book form, in 1843. The renewed conflict between academic and literary ambitions was increasingly resolved in favor of the latter, until it was settled in 1854 by the cessation of teaching.

Longfellow's success was already making him a public figure, a role for which he was well suited. Striking in appearance, elegant, even dandified in dress, urbane and mildly witty, endowed with innate courtesy and a peculiarly masculine sweetness of temper, he made the very model of a New England gentleman-author, and his genuine talent for friendship rapidly wove a web of lasting relationships that embraced the obscure and the famous alike. When he and Fanny were married on July 13, 1843, his father-in-law's gift was Craigie House itself, and the young Longfellows soon gave it a wide reputation as a center of cultivated hospitality.

The years from 1843 to 1860 were Longfellow's most fruitful. Besides editing and contributing to three collections of verse, he wrote many of his best shorter poems, gathered in *The Belfry of Bruges and Other Poems* (1846) and *The Seaside and the Fireside* (1850), as well as "Paul Revere" and "The Saga of King Olaf," to be used later in *Tales of a Wayside Inn*; a novel, *Kavanagh* (1849); and his most successful long poems: *Evangeline* (1847), *The Golden Legend* (1851), *The Song of Hiawatha* (1855), and *The Courtship of Miles Standish* (1858). Many of the volumes sold in numbers and with a speed unprecedented in American publishing history.

Public acclaim mounted yearly in Europe as in America, while distinguished guests and unimportant strangers descended endlessly upon Craigie House and seriously hindered Longfellow's work. Moreover, his domestic happiness was nearly complete, shadowed only by the death of one of the six children born to the Longfellows. The single source of continuous anxiety was the national scene. Longfellow observed the sharpening prewar tensions closely and with growing concern, until the opening of hostilities left him torn between his abhorrence of slavery and his hatred of war, and dejected by public disaster.

To national tragedy was soon added personal. On July 9, 1861, Longfellow was resting on a couch in his study while, in an adjoining room, his still romantically loved wife was sealing locks of their daughters' hair in packets: a scene so Victorian as to seem a period piece. Then a spark or a drop of hot wax ignited Fanny's flimsy summer dress. Ablaze and in agony she ran to Longfellow, whose efforts to beat out the flames left him critically burned. During the night Fanny died and, while she was being buried, Longfellow lay helpless in bed, his life feared for, his sanity at first despaired of by his friends and himself. Physically he made a thorough recovery, although the circumstances of Fanny's death had a grotesque consequence: the scars on Longfellow's face made further shaving impossible, and thus was created the placid bearded image that was destined to gaze from the walls of a thousand future classrooms. Psychic recovery came more slowly, and the inner wounds never completely healed. The journals for the following months he later destroyed, but evidence of his near-despair survives in communications with his friends.

To this shattering experience Longfellow directly refers only once in all his later poetry, although knowledge of it is necessary to a full understanding of several poems, including the six sonnets prefixed to his translation of Dante, and the tone of his lyrics is pervasively affected by it. The sole direct reference is a sonnet written in 1879, when Longfellow came upon a picture of a mountain in whose ravines lay a cross-shaped deposit of snow, and found there the image of his unrelenting pain:

In the long, sleepless watches of the night,
A gentle face — the face of one long dead —
Looks at me from the wall, where round its head
The night-lamp casts a halo of pale light.
Here in this room she died; and soul more white
Never through martyrdom of fire was led
To its repose; nor can in books be read
The legend of a life more benedight.
There is a mountain in the distant West
That, sun-defying, in its deep ravines
Displays a cross of snow upon its side.
Such is the cross I wear upon my breast
These eighteen years, through all the changing scenes
And seasons, changeless since the day she died.

"The Cross of Snow" was published posthumously; like another sonnet, the "Mezzo Cammin" of 1842, it seemed to Longfellow too personal for print.

Initially forcing himself to resume writing as an escape from grief, Longfellow was soon engaged in some of his most ambitious undertakings. The three series of narrative poems constituting *Tales of a Wayside Inn* were published in 1863, 1872, and 1874 respectively; the translation of the whole of the *Divina Commedia* occupied the years from 1865 to 1867; the *New England Tragedies* appeared in 1868 and *The Divine Tragedy* in 1871, two works that were linked with *The Golden Legend* by prologue, interludes, and epilogue to make up the complete *Christus* in 1872. From 1876 to 1879 Longfellow acted as editor, in practice as editor-in-chief, of the thirty-one volumes of *Poems of Places*, which included several of his own contributions. Meantime, a but slightly diminished flow of shorter poems, including the fine sonnets, continued, filling most of six volumes: *Flower-de-Luce* (1867); *Three Books of Song* (1872); *Aftermath* (1873); *The Masque of Pandora and Other Poems* (1875); *Kéramos and Other Poems* (1878); and *Ultima Thule* (1880).

These last years were for Longfellow the years of apotheosis. The distinctions between the poet and the venerable figure of Craigie House were lost in a chorus of affectionate acclaim, in which the dissenting voices of the younger generation were drowned out.

The last European journey in 1868–69 was an almost royal progress, with honorary degrees conferred by the universities of Oxford and Cambridge, to the cheers of the undergraduates, and with a reception by Queen Victoria. From the Continent, Victor Hugo saluted Longfellow as a man who brought honor to America, and at home the schoolchildren of Cambridge presented him with an armchair made from the wood of the original spreading chestnut tree. In American eyes, he was clearly the uncrowned poet laureate, and he played his part to the end. On March 12, 1882, he finished ten six-line stanzas of "The Bells of San Blas," typically celebrating with nostalgia a past of picturesque devotion when "the priest was lord of the land." On March 15, he also typically added a single-stanza counterstatement:

> O Bells of San Blas, in vain
> Ye call back the Past again!
>   The Past is deaf to your prayer;
> Out of the shadows of night
> The world rolls into light;
>   It is daybreak everywhere.

He had reassured himself and his readers for the last time. Nine days later, after a very brief illness, he was dead at the age of seventy-five, and the spontaneous mourning was international. Enough uncollected poems remained to provide *In the Harbor* (1882), and, in 1883, the impressive fragment of his projected poetic drama, *Michael Angelo*, was separately published. With this his art had reached its period, a fact emphasized by the substantially complete and massive edition of his works in 1886. In its eleven volumes the results of sixty-two literarily active years were assembled for the judgment of posterity.

Longfellow's prose works are, with one exception, of minor importance. *Outre-Mer* contains vivid descriptions of Western Europe in the 1820's, and reflects Longfellow's romantic sensibility in a charming manner, but its studied picturesqueness palls, and it remains inferior to the *Sketch Book* that it too obviously imitates. Longfellow's various essays and articles, important in their day, are now chiefly of historical and biographical interest. Their knowledge has been superseded, and their critical methods and point of view seem outmoded, although they still yield some appreciative insights. The one novel, *Kavanagh*, lacks the technical and imaginative unity necessary to success. Its moderately realistic representation of life in a rural New England community deserves the praise Emerson gave it, and there are some amusingly lively scenes satiric of old-line Calvinism and of the patriotic literary theory that assumed the future greatness of American poetry as a consequence of the greatness of American scenery. The love story, however, is flat and sentimentalized, and the characters are insubstantial, save for the sensitive but ineffectual Mr. Churchill, apparently Longfellow's wry portrait of an aspect of himself. In the end, *Kavanagh*'s intention is obscure, its construction feebly episodic. Only in *Hyperion: A Romance* did Longfellow succeed in extended prose fiction.

Hyperion, the most autobiographical of all Longfellow's works, describes under a thin veil of fiction the personal crisis of 1835–36; by Longfellow's own account, its writing was a therapy by which he worked his way from morbidity to health. The spiritual journey, a frequent theme in his works, is imaged here in a romanticized account of the second European trip. Paul Flemming, the hero, despairing over the loss of his "dear friend," retraces Longfellow's expeditions and experiences; at Interlaken he meets and falls in love with Mary Ashburton (Frances Appleton) and is rejected by her. Finally, restored to mental health, he self-reliantly faces the future alone — a stance that his creator and original was unable to adopt. So immediately identifiable were the persons and events of *Hyperion* that "all Boston" was soon happily gossiping and being scolded by Longfellow for its narrow-minded censoriousness. Only as passing years dimmed the topical interest could *Hyperion* be read as an imaginative representation of a not simply personal but generically youthful and romantic odyssey.

Into *Hyperion* Longfellow poured the accumulations of three years. Traveler's notes, long descriptions, general reflections, anecdotes and tales, extended literary and philosophic commentaries, topics from his Harvard lectures, translations from German literature — all are crowded in, often with little explicit connection, and are set in a romantic-plush style certain to try the patience of post-romantic readers. Longfellow was then under the spell of Jean Paul Richter, whose style, in apparent chaos, mingled the serious, comic, sublime, and grotesque; it delighted in abruptly changing moods, materials, and manners, in archaic phrasing, flamboyant figurative expression, and rhapsody. In varying degree, these qualities are also in *Hyperion*, so that the first impression is of confusion and cloying whimsicality. Beneath the patchwork, however, lies a real unity of emotion and experience.

The symbolism of the central journey is developed in simple, traditional imagery. Beginning on a dark, cold, mist-shrouded December morning in the Rhine valley, the action moves, for the climactic scenes of Book IV, up into the Swiss mountains in full summer, with the sun high and strong. The past is figured throughout by darkness and the grave, and is extended to include not only Flemming's personal past but the historical past whose monuments surround him in Europe; similarly, the present is a brightness into which not only he but mankind must enter. As Flemming's enthrallment began at a grave, so deliverance comes in St. Gilgen's churchyard among the tombs. The liberating formula he finds, as Longfellow actually found it, on a tablet affixed to a tomb: "Look not mournfully into the Past. It comes not back again. Wisely improve the Present. It is thine. Go forth to meet the shadowy Future without fear, and with a manly heart."

The immediate result of this directive Flemming calls almost miraculous, but later he asks, "Can such a simple result spring only from the long and intricate process of experience?" The process of a single experience is precisely what unifies, however loosely, the widely disparate materials of *Hyperion* and revivifies its traditional imagery by providing a freshly individual context. Embodying a conflict that runs throughout Longfellow's life and poetry and displaying at length the recurrent terms and images of that conflict, as well as of its outcome, *Hyperion* forms the literary substratum of a large part of Longfellow's later work.

Outre-Mer and *Hyperion* played a significant part in making

Europe's thought and art available to the American public; so, too, did Longfellow's translations of poetry, which occupy a substantial place in his canon and were produced with varying frequency throughout his career. To translation Longfellow was drawn by his personal, sometimes indiscriminate delight in European literature, as well as by the literary and linguistic challenge of the task itself and the pedagogical usefulness of the results. Spanish, Italian, and German literature furnished the most numerous originals, but there are also translations from French, Danish, Swedish, Anglo-Saxon, and Latin poetry, and even three renditions, by way of extant prose translations, of Eastern poems. The originals are qualitatively a hodgepodge of everything from sentimental trivia to Dante's *Divina Commedia*.

Accepting Goethe's belief that the translator should adopt the author's situation, mode of speaking, and peculiarities, Longfellow scrupulously attempted to minimize the unavoidable sacrifices of translation and to move as close to literal correspondence as other considerations permitted. His earlier translations take measured liberties, such as the use of "equivalent stanzas" in rendering the *Coplas de Don Jorge Manrique*; his later translations are austerely restrictive. The great test was the translation of the *Divina Commedia*. After pondering the insurmountable difficulties of Dante's *terza rima*, Longfellow decided to abandon the rhyming so that he could preserve the tercet structure and achieve literal precision. The justification of this decision is the translation itself, which, in spite of unevenness and deficiencies, reflects something of the linguistic economy and rhythmic severity of the original. Although Longfellow's rendition does not attain the semi-independent poetic value of great verse translations, it remains one of the most faithful and effective Englishings of Dante.

On the value of translation to the practicing poet, Longfellow was of divided mind. Judging from his own experience, he insisted that successful translation evidenced real creative power, and that the act of translating served as stimulus to the poet's own thought and feeling; but he also refers to the attendant dangers. Translation is, in his own words, "like running a ploughshare through the soil of one's mind; a thousand germs of thought spring up (excuse this agricultural figure), which otherwise might have lain and rotted in the ground — still it sometimes seems to me like an excuse for being lazy, — like leaning on another man's shoulder." For Longfellow, whose art was highly responsive to external suggestion, translation probably did start ideas, and it undoubtedly contributed to his notable skill in versification. Nevertheless, his preoccupation with translation, during a period of life normally crucial in the development of independence, may indeed have encouraged a habit of leaning on other men's shoulders that partly explains the limited originality of his own subsequent poetry.

Longfellow's first published poem, "The Battle of Lovell's Pond," derivatively celebrating a skirmish whose importance was monumentally local, appeared in the *Portland Gazette* for November 17, 1820, over the signature "Henry." Between this and the final "Bells of San Blas" stand well over five hundred poems whose variety makes generalization pause. Ranging from such brief, pure song as "Stars of the Summer Night" to the composite *Christus*, which occupies one hundred and sixty double-columned pages in the Cambridge Edition, the poetry includes not only "ode and elegy and sonnet" in abundance, but hortatory, meditative, and imagistic lyrics; poetic dramas; and many kinds of narrative from popular ballad to epic-tinged idyll, of widely varying length and manner. The gamut of quality is almost as extended, the good poems being sometimes obscured by the disproportionately large number of bad or indifferent ones. Some lines of development can be chronologically traced, especially for the long poems, but these, with rare exception, mark tonal and emphatic changes, or shifts in predominant verse forms or genres, rather than fundamental alterations in Longfellow's major ideas or attitudes, which, although modified with time, persist in recognizable form from *Voices of the Night* to the end.

The essential characteristics, even the qualitative variance, of Longfellow's poetry are related to his humanistic although unsystematized views on art. Art, he held, is the revelation of man, and of nature only "through man." His abandonment of nature description, Longfellow explained, meant not that he loved nature less, but man more. This basically traditional attitude receives a distinctively nineteenth-century coloring from Longfellow's understanding of artistic usefulness in terms of "elevation." Poetry, he argued in his 1832 "Defence of Poetry," is an instrument for improving the condition of society and advancing the great purpose of human happiness; in America's democratic society, this implied an endorsement of literature's growing concern with the literate common man. So Longfellow's Michael Angelo, in the drama bearing his name, defines art as

> "All that embellishes and sweetens life,
> And lifts it from the level of low cares
> Into the purer atmosphere of beauty;
> The faith in the Ideal . . ."

Thus poetry, even at the risk of losing itself in the "low cares," will serve to charm, to strengthen, and to teach — a formula in which many critics and poets concurred: Walt Whitman, praising Longfellow as an unrecognized master in the treatment of common occurrences, declared his evocation of the poetic quality of everyday things to be truly representative of the spirit of democracy.

That a useful muse might become too housewifely Longfellow was aware. The nature and the problems of the artistic process make a recurrent theme in his poetry, especially from the two poems "Prometheus" and "Epimetheus" of 1854 to the poems of the 1870's, *The Masque of Pandora*, "Kéramos," and *Michael Angelo*, and the problem most reflective of his own experience was that of the frustrating distance between the exaltation of original inspiration and the flatness of final achievement. Longfellow knew that the highest inspiration is Promethean, and he suspected that great art comes only from the continual isolation and the total commitment of struggling with the gods — the art of a Shakespeare or Dante, before whose accomplishment he openly confessed his own inadequacy. Yet, like many of his contemporaries, he half-feared this heroic posture as a humanly perilous one, a cutting-off of the artist from humanity's common lot, from the world of Pandora's opened box and Epimetheus' humanitarian compassion. How the initial lofty vision could without betrayal and without obscurity be made accessible and instructive to a wide audience was the puzzle. Finding no solution, Longfellow accepted without undue repining the Epimethean role of poetic concern with daily sorrows and hopes, but he was haunted by the figure of Prometheus, symbol of the daring act of imagination essential to the birth of all poetry, even that which apparently ended up in slippers at the fireside.

The major ideas underlying Longfellow's poetry are characteristically expressed in a conventional nineteenth-century terminology that invites partial misreading, partly because of subsequent changes in meaning, especially in connotation, and partly because important terms are often so inclusive as to seem indeterminate. Longfellow's constant appeal to the heart is frequently understood as the consequence of a vague, sentimental notion that the gentler emotions could resolve problems and order life, to the near-exclusion of thought. His usage, however, like that of his contemporaries, reflects an older and wider meaning of *heart*. The word refers not only to the emotions, but also to will and intuitive reason. The heart is the source of insight as well as of joy or grief; it embraces the moral sensibility that accepts or rejects truth and that acts as conscience in its unstudied response to generally self-evident laws. When Longfellow writes,

> "It is the heart, and not the brain,
> That to the highest doth attain . . ."

his use of "heart" is close to that of the Pauline formula, in the phraseology of the Authorized Version, "with the heart man believeth to righteousness." The heart, therefore, may stand for all of man's immaterial nature, save his discursive reason, which is often signified by "brain." Moreover, in his simple division of man into body and soul, Longfellow assigned all thoughts, all feelings, all desires to the soul, not the body, which is only the instrument. "It is the soul," he insisted, "that feels, enjoys, suffers . . ." Thus the affections themselves are spiritual, and, directed to good ends, can properly be called "holy."

Longfellow's frame of ultimate reference is formed by his religious convictions. When he established in 1824 the first Unitarian society at Bowdoin, he was not simply revolting against the
"consociation of 'old sanctities,' " as he once called the college's
conservatively Congregationalist clergy, but affirming the strong
personal faith that pervaded his life and writings. Like his father,
Longfellow in general accepted the teaching of William Ellery
Channing: that man is fundamentally good, endowed by God with
reason, conscience, and an intuitive awareness of the divine; and
that Christianity, the purest faith known to man, is progressing
toward a full realization of its ideals in a universal church of the
future. The core of man's religion is a self-sacrificial love issuing
in noble actions and sentiments, and in humanitarian concern for
human welfare. Not by creeds, whether Athanasian or Calvinistic,
but by deeds is man judged, and his faith made effective.

For so optimistic a belief, the chief problem is that of sin and
evil, and the greatest imaginative failure of Longfellow's poetry
is its inability to probe life's dark or sordid aspects. The causes of
failure were partly temperamental. A natural fastidiousness led
Longfellow to recoil from the physical and spiritual ugliness that
caused him actual pain. Although he was personally subject to
periods of neurotic depression with moments of panic, he regarded
these visitations as transient phenomena that raised no intellectual
question about man's nature or destiny. What experience failed
to provide, faith could not supply. Especially in his long poems,
Longfellow represents or alludes to the malicious, fanatic, and
selfish behavior men are capable of, but he suggests no deeper
cause than a defect incidental to man's present condition, reform-
able although not yet reformed. The chief weakness of *The Golden
Legend* is therefore the characterization of Satan, who, although
cast as a fallen angel, is in action only a badly behaved, treacher-
ous superman, neither terrifying nor awe-inspiring, and almost
cursorily dismissed. Somehow — and Longfellow is never deeply
curious about "how's" — everything will come out all right. So,
at least, his reasoning assured him. Yet his attraction to Dante, the
pessimistic feeling that tinges *Christus*, and the powerful vision

of final nullity in *Michael Angelo* all suggest a sensibility whose perceptions are often at variance with the formulating ideas.

The simply held ideas by which Longfellow attempted to order experience are frequently unable to contain the strong current of feeling that is a distinctive quality of his romantic sensibility. Although he was sharply critical of what he considered the excesses and absurdities of romanticism, his own poetry is saturated with a romantic sense of life's fragility. The crumbling ruins, encroaching darkness, and vivid but fleeting visions are not fashionable accessories, but the authentic images of Longfellow's deepest emotion, as his journals testify. That human life is a dream in which the apparent solidities of time and place dissolve into insubstantial forms is a nearly obsessive theme. To Longfellow, the most powerful flow of time and consciousness is backward, from present to past, from actuality to dream, and into the magic night of communion and reminiscence that gives access to the remembered past. However tempered in expression by his almost classical restraint and social poise, the dominant mood of Longfellow's poetry is a melancholy not unlike that of Washington Irving, compounded of nostalgia, the sadness of personal loss, and the painful awareness of transience and mortality. If there is truth in the comment that Longfellow did not face the primary facts of life and nature, one reason may be his feeling that "facts" are neither primary nor solid, but the phenomena of a dream. So pervasive is dream or reverie in Longfellow's imagination that his most effective lyric or meditative poems are likely to be built on dreamlike associations, and the felicitous "legend style," as he called it, of some of his longer works depends upon an atmosphere of dreamy distance.

When physical surfaces lose their bounds and firmness, the natural world is easily invaded by the circumambient world of spirit. From the early "Footsteps of Angels" to the late "Helen of Tyre," Longfellow's poetry is recurrently haunted by phantoms, as the planes of nature and spirit, always thought by Longfellow to be exactly correspondent, seem to converge at a visionary point somewhere between reality and unreality. Longfellow's belief in the interaction of the invisible world and the world of sense led him actually to experiment with spiritualism a few times. In practice, he found spiritualism unconvincing and unedifying, but he never lost the sense of continuity between this world and another, between the living and the dead, that makes the pervasive mysteriousness of many poems so memorable.

To withdraw into the haunted night, to surrender to nostalgia and reverie, was Longfellow's natural inclination, intensified by his domestic catastrophes and, in his later years, by loneliness. His beliefs and character, however, prohibited such a retreat: the voices of night must be answered by the voices of day, or by aspiration the dreaming night must be made holy with stars. To assert present reality and the possibility of meaningful action in it becomes the necessary countermovement against the pull of the past; it is the thrust of health against incipient morbidity. On the side of reality are religious faith, human love, and the achievements and obligations of civilization; these are the foundations of hope and inescapable duty. Thus the longing for imaginative flight is characteristically confronted by a resolute will: this was the fundamental conflict in Longfellow's experience and, mirrored in his art, provides the only continuous tension in a poetry whose structure and language have little of that quality.

The conflict is often described rather than presented, and the resolution stated rather than achieved. Even in such simple poems, however, there is occasionally a conviction successfully communicated that seems unaccountably to be an increment from the underlying experience itself. In the once over-acclaimed, now over-abused "A Psalm of Life," the conflict exists chiefly as a background for the celebration of triumphant resolve, directly expressed. That this hortatory poem should have a witnessed effect denied to countless other exhortations may be due to a residual force not earned, according to the modern prescription, through the strategy of the poem itself, but subtly transmitted to it as a tone from the prior struggle and its resolution that was indeed earned, since "A Psalm of Life" springs from the same experience that produced *Hyperion*. In Longfellow's more complex didactic poems the countering assertion of hope or purpose is not always poetically successful; at times it is imposed, or inadequate to the strength of the preceding melancholy. But in the best poems it is sufficiently implied in the foregoing situation or images to be a valid climax.

The major ideas of Longfellow are clearly reflected in his poetry considered as a whole; he repeatedly makes explicit reference to them, and indulges in overt teaching based upon them. His poetry, nevertheless, is not a poetry of ideas: certainly it is not philosophic or genuinely reflective, if "reflective" implies extended analysis of experience and systematic deliberation upon it. Except occasionally and on some few subjects, notably art, Longfellow's poems are primarily meditative; they express intuitions of experience, whether personal or literary, their thought usually arising immediately from feeling and remaining closely attached to it, or interwoven with it. Habitually, there is little progressive development of idea or attitude: a poem's underlying experience is made concrete in a described object, situation, or story — an image whose significance is presented sometimes as almost a short allegorization, more often as a correspondence or connotation on another plane. Since the image, from whatever source it is drawn and however simple or complex it may be, not only determines the tone of the whole poem but is also the essential figure of the experience, Longfellow's meditative poetry is, on the whole, fundamentally metaphoric, although in many poems the lack of compression, the extended statement, and the failure to renew conventional images all dissipate metaphor's possible intensity.

Some of Longfellow's important images by their complexity, recurrence, and stability become true symbols, at times restricted or extensively modified by particular contexts, but possessing a sufficiently persistent significance throughout the poetry to express Longfellow's imaginative apprehension of life. A few symbols are based on artifacts or on artistic creation — bells, walled forts or castles, music — but most are drawn from nature. Largely traditional, they are sometimes casually used as cultural hand-me-downs; more often, however, their significance has clearly been rediscovered at a deep level of experience. The most pervasive symbols are archetypal: the darkness of haunted night, oblivion, and the past, whose chill is the coldness of the grave; the warm light of reality, of vital energy, and, for Longfellow, of love, concentrated in the sun; water, whose flow is the motion of feeling, spirit, and time, and whose fluidity Longfellow attributes also to sky, air, and light; the stars of divine or spiritual order and, more personally, of aspiration.

Above all others are the symbols drawn from Longfellow's memory of youthful experience; his landscape of the human situation and of individual inner life is that of the Maine coastline: the sea, the nearby forest, and the narrow habitable strip between. This last, the scene of rational and civilized life, additionally provides a symbol of precarious security, the home centered in the hearth, whose warmth is the focus of human relationships and a protection against the storms without: although Longfellow's fireside scene is likely to be sentimentalized, it occasionally reflects in muted fashion the ancient image of man huddled by his saving fire. The forest, boundless and majestic, frequently wailing in the wind, embodies a primitive life somewhat ominous for civilized man. The sea is Longfellow's deepest and most inclusive symbol; no contemporary writer save Melville was more profoundly or constantly responsive to it. In Longfellow's poetry, the sea is the restless mystery of existence, and its unfathomable source; it is the energy of unconfined and subconscious life, and of liberty. In its effects, it is also paradoxical, merciful and merciless, purifying yet dangerous, at once death-giving and life-giving.

In spite of the importance of images and symbols, however, the typical movement of a poem by Longfellow is toward a formulated decision; that is, however complex the underlying feelings or situation, any tension or conflict, or any balance of opposites, is resolved by a choice amongst the possibilities or by a limiting statement of specific significance. Since the poems ordinarily do not fully present whatever struggle or turbulence there may have been in the originating experience, but only selected, usually subdued aspects of it, the resolution often appears easy or oversimplified. In the best poems, however, the concluding statement is

at once a natural consequence of an imaginative prior development and an explication sufficiently complex to embrace all the
possibilities.

The lyric and meditative poems, and several of the shorter narratives, are characteristically, although not exclusively, developed
in distinguishable stages, moving from image to analogy or statement, or from image to analogy to statement; much more rarely,
from statement to image. In a large number of the poems, the image
is fully presented in one or more initial stanzas or verse paragraphs
and its moral or spiritual significance set forth in the following
ones, frequently with an exact correspondence in the lengths of
presentation and of statement, a balance well exemplified in "Sea-
weed" and "The Beleaguered City." Alternatively, the statement
may be a comparatively brief conclusion, or even a counterstatement of denial, revulsion, or change of direction, as in "The Bells of
San Blas," rather than a climax to what has preceded it. In many
poems, the movement between image and comparison or statement is continuously back and forth, the image being presented
in steps, each of which is accompanied by an immediate reflection
upon it. The poems that do not move by clearly defined stages may
conveniently be designated as one-stage. Classification by stages,
however, can be only approximate: an indicated spiritual significance, for example, may cling so closely to an image, as it does in
"Sandalphon," that it seems simply to be an overtone of it.

In the one-stage poems, the presentation may be hortatory,
descriptive, or narrative; it either produces a direct, uncomplicated, often emotional effect or clearly implies a further meaning
without openly indicating or stating it. Into this category fall most
of the short narratives and also many of the poems most appealing
to modern taste, the quasi-imagistic poems that present a concentrated image with expanding overtones: "Chrysaor," "The Bells
of Lynn," "Aftermath," "The Tide Rises, the Tide Falls" are representative of this group, and "The Ropewalk" is similar in its
reliance on suggestion, although it employs a series of images,
central and associated, rather than one image alone. A few two-
stage poems are also primarily imagistic in effect, some of them,

like "The Warning," developing their analogy closely in terms of the original image, others, like "Snowflakes," using their analogy actually to reinforce the image. However stimulating Longfellow's imagistic poems may be, they are nonetheless too small in number to be typical of his poetry.

The three-stage poems usually consist of initial image, analogy, and explicit statement, with attention more or less evenly distributed among them, a method that is obvious in the three stanzas of the feeble "Rainy Day," whose initial lines run "The day is cold, and dark, and dreary . . . My life is cold, and dark, and dreary . . . Be still, sad heart! and cease repining . . ." For some reason, the three-stage poems include many of Longfellow's bad and indifferent pieces; on the other hand, they also include some of the more completely satisfying meditative verses, such as "Palingenesis" and a sensitively wrought ode, "The Building of the Ship," whose oratorically eloquent, hortatory last stanza begins with the familiar "Thou, too, sail on, O Ship of State!" and makes an illogical but emotionally appropriate and powerful new application of the poem's structural analogy between the construction and launching of a ship and the progress of romantic love climaxed in marriage.

The largest number of Longfellow's shorter poems, including the sonnets and such important compositions as the brief "In the Churchyard at Cambridge" and "Jugurtha" and the lengthier "Fire of Driftwood," "My Lost Youth," and "Morituri Salutamus," are two-stage; if his imagination found any method especially congenial, it is this one, so that his notable achievement in sonnet form is not surprising.

The early two- or three-stage poems usually end in explicit declaration; after the mid-1840's there is increasing reliance on a final metaphor or symbol, as in "Autumn Within":

> It is autumn; not without,
> But within me is the cold.
> Youth and spring are all about;
> It is I that have grown old.

Birds are darting through the air,
Singing, building without rest;
Life is stirring everywhere,
Save within my lonely breast.

There is silence: the dead leaves
Fall and rustle and are still;
Beats no flail upon the sheaves,
Comes no murmur from the mill.

The poem is too short to be widely representative, but it bears the Longfellow impress: the quatrains observe a 2-2 rhetorical division; the lines are four-stress, in falling rhythm; the accommodations of stress and pause to meaning are minor but careful; the language is simple and the word order nearly normal, save for the deliberate departure in the concluding lines; there is a touch of showy pathos in the eighth line; the images are traditional, and, especially in the last two lines, rather "poetic" or literary. The fundamental comparison of inner states and outer seasons allows easy further comparison between seasons and thus inner states, and so moves into the suggestive final revelation of age's fruitlessness in a favorite image: the cessation of sound. In so short a poem, the procedure is abbreviated but clear. The initial image is quickly introduced in three words; its spiritual significance is explicitly stated at once; the comparison is somewhat tenuously explored, and the conclusion intensifies the comparison by shifting the images associated with autumn to the signified spiritual state. Like so many of Longfellow's good if obviously minor poems, this has a personal feeling that manages, even if barely, to come through the conventional scenery; it also has something of Longfellow's typical facility, attended, as often, by the bad and good angels of glibness and grace.

Like much nineteenth-century poetry, Longfellow's seems in retrospect leisurely, even too relaxed. The slow development of ideas, the elaboration of details, the multiplication of parallels, the explication of the already-evident are practices that destroy some of his poems and in varying combinations and degrees characterize most of them. The language, too, bears the stamp of its time in its tendency to expansive statement, its often predictable vocabulary and phraseology, and its fondness for literary diction. Like the sporadic addiction to poetically picturesque subject matter, these qualities are alien to sophisticated modern taste, although whether or to what extent they are necessarily faults is a problem of literary theory and the absoluteness of critical standards. Historically considered, the kind of poetry Longfellow wrote lay within a poetic tradition that with various adaptations served the larger part of a century, and was imaginatively satisfying to the romantic-Victorian sensibility. Within the age's literary conventions, Longfellow used language skillfully and sensitively. At its best, his language is simple and economical, natural in movement, emotionally exact in its use of words and phrases, and restrained in statement. Furthermore, Longfellow's handling of language is largely responsible for his achievement of an impressive tonal range from the formality of semi-epic narrative to the humor-seasoned easiness of the discourse of polite society. He makes the traditional poetic language, with often minimal alteration, express distinctively his own insights and feelings.

As a poet more evocative than creative of experience, Longfellow employs language with a notable awareness of the way in which it becomes charged with meaning from the inescapable situations of human life. Frequently he depends not upon connotations or overtones developed within the context of a poem, but upon a resonance provided immediately by general experience itself and renewed in the poem by allusions to the appropriate common events or situations, or by brief descriptions of them. This habit demands from the reader a supply of significance from his private store and a willingness to accept suggestive reference rather than precise control in the poem — a concession not demanded by great poetry, and by some critics austerely refused to any. It is, however, a concession habitually made to occasional poems, whose otherwise vague or flabby language may acquire exactness from setting and event. When, in "Morituri Salutamus," Longfellow recalls his audience from thoughts of friends dead and buried to

. . . these scenes frequented by our feet
When we were young, and life was fresh and sweet,

the last line is not vaguely sentimental, but, like the poem's title, genuinely moving because emotionally appropriate and provided with definable meaning by the situation: an aging poet addressing the dwindled number of college classmates at certainly their last reunion, held fifty years after graduation.

Like other aspects of his poetry, Longfellow's prosody is remarkable for resourcefulness and variety within traditional limits. His uncommon talent in versification and his absorption in its technical problems led to no prosodic revolution; indeed, a dangerous facility, combined with a taste for euphony, brings his verse at moments close to that of the typical Victorian "sweet singer." Within accepted bounds, however, Longfellow's versatility in rhythmical, metrical, and rhyming patterns and his constant experimentation, directed toward the creation of a unique effect for each poem, reveal a technical mastery rarely approached in American poetry. Although his prosodic variety is most obvious in the surprisingly various patterns of his stanzaic verse, it is perhaps more subtly displayed in meeting the resistance of a set form like the sonnet, where, employing the Italian pattern and almost invariably observing a strict octet-sestet division, Longfellow achieves striking rhythmic differences by ingenious handling of metrical substitution, run-on and end-stopped lines, and caesuras. In freer forms, his skill is no less evident: the extremely uneven blank verse of *The Divine Tragedy* has reflective passages in which comparative rhythmic freedom works with approximately normal word order to produce lines that sometimes collapse into prose but that occasionally attain a thoroughly natural movement barely but unmistakably tightened into poetry, as in the course of the soliloquy by Manahem the Essenian in the third part of the "First Passover":

> The things that have been and shall be no more,
> The things that are, and that hereafter shall be,
> The things that might have been, and yet were not,
> The fading twilight of great joys departed,
> The daybreak of great truths as yet unrisen,
> The intuition and the expectation
> Of something, which, when come, is not the same,

> But only like its forecast in men's dreams,
> The longing, the delay, and the delight,
> Sweeter for the delay; youth, hope, love, death,
> And disappointment which is also death,
> All these make up the sum of human life;
> A dream within a dream, a wind at night
> Howling across the desert in despair,
> Seeking for something lost it cannot find.

The technical virtuosity of Longfellow's art is manifested in several accomplishments: the successful maintenance of falling rhythm in spite of English poetry's strong tendency to rising rhythm; the dexterous control of varied rhythm and free rhyming by an organization based on parallelism, balance, and alliteration; and the giving of widely varied movement to such uncomplicated verse forms as the quatrain. Even so straightforward a narrative as "Paul Revere" shows a meticulous attention to technical detail that partly accounts for the rather complex effect of an apparently simple poem. As a rule, the closer the examination of Longfellow's verse technique, the greater is the appreciation of a diversity that can succeed in the subdued four-line stanzas of his meditative poetry, in the stately hexameters of *Evangeline*, and in the jaunty tetrameter couplets of "The Rhyme of Sir Christopher."

The shorter poems of Longfellow enjoyed a contemporary popularity, in England and other countries as well as in America, that has rarely been rivaled, yet it was not these poems but his long ones on which his reputation chiefly rested, especially the long narratives: *Evangeline, Hiawatha, The Courtship of Miles Standish,* and *Tales of a Wayside Inn.* More recently the major narrative poems have been relegated to the classroom, often at a rather elementary level, in acknowledgment of Longfellow's ability to tell a story in them, and with the implication that he does no more. The nineteenth century knew better: when *Evangeline* was published in 1847, one English reviewer hailed it as "the first genuine Castalian fount which has burst from the soil of America!" In spite of his fanciful image, the critic was properly celebrating what was in fact the first important sustained poem by an American and was endorsing the general acclaim that made Evangeline herself a symbol of the Acadian "cause."

Like all of Longfellow's major poems, *Evangeline* was, in modern academic jargon, "well researched," and one result of Longfellow's reading was to make the poem in part a richly descriptive tour of expanses of western and southern America. The story itself, however, is an altogether simple one, whose essentials were first given to Longfellow by Hawthorne: in the dispersal of the French Acadians in 1755, two lovers, Evangeline and Gabriel, are separated, and for weary years Evangeline attempts to trace Gabriel through the settlements and wilds of the American colonies; finally, aging and losing earthly hope, she becomes a Sister of Mercy in a Philadelphia hospital, where, during a plague, the dying Gabriel is brought and the lovers are reunited just before his death. Gabriel early recedes into the background as the sought rather than seeker, and the focus of the whole poem is upon Evangeline, giving the temperamentally chivalric Longfellow full scope for the development of an idealized, simple woman of absolute fidelity, the kind of heroine most congenial to his imagination. In a realistically represented milieu Evangeline would seem too etherealized but the deliberately legendary treatment of the story and the touch of dreamlike remoteness in the setting create an idyllic effect appropriate to the characterization. Moreover, the idealization of the heroine is closely related to the poem's meaning: Evangeline is increasingly spiritualized by the patiently endured sufferings of her nearly endless journey until she finally emerges as a saintly figure.

The journey of Evangeline and the whole story in which she moves are raised to semiheroic proportions by Longfellow's mythologizing of his materials. Acadia is also Arcadia; the simple lives of the peasants, viewed under a summer sun, recall the Golden Age and Eden, and the murmuring pines and hemlocks color the scene with childhood innocence recalled. With expulsion and separation, a mythic pattern specifically Christian develops: the pious Evangeline is the exiled wayfarer making her dedicated journey through the world to her final renunciation of it and her entering upon the more purely spiritual pilgrimage of return to the true Arcadia of Heaven, where alone reunion can be lasting. When the two lovers at one dramatic point miss each other by the narrowest of margins, it is, as one critic has said, like the touch of God's hand reserving Evangeline for another marriage. Despite the slowness and occasional thinness of the narration, the pattern of *Evangeline* gives the poem substance and dignity.

In creating the hexameter lines of *Evangeline* Longfellow sensibly treated the problem of English hexameter as a practical one, and paid little heed to the theoretic objections that have enlivened criticism since the Renaissance. Encouraged by Goethe's example and by the experiments of Southey and Coleridge, he solved the immediate problems by using a basically dactyllic line with a trochaic close and free trochaic substitution; the minimally necessary spondees he obtained by juxtaposing monosyllabic words and by coaxing the second syllable of trochees into an approximation of spondees. The resultant hexameters give *Evangeline* a slow processional movement; the longer line admits lavish introduction of concrete detail through additional modifying words, and has a pleasantly lingering effect appropriate to idyllic tone, as Longfellow apparently realized, since extended use of hexameters occurs chiefly in his idylls — *Evangeline, The Courtship of Miles Standish,* and "Elizabeth" in *Tales of a Wayside Inn.*

The Courtship of Miles Standish, although published eleven years later, resembles *Evangeline* in measure, in use of a legendary-historical foundation, and in pastoral coloring. The *Courtship,* however, has a vein of humor that leaves readers suspended between sentiment and amusement. The story has long since passed into folklore: how John Alden loved Priscilla Mullins but, out of friendship, wooed her in Captain Miles Standish's behalf, and how, with a false report of Standish's death, John and Priscilla married, with the captain returning just in time to assent. It is not the tale but the telling that has distinction. Longfellow moves through variations of tone with impressive assurance, from satirical humor to romance tinged with sentimentality, through sobriety and comedy alternatively.

The success of the *Courtship* lies principally in its humorous juxtaposition of two extravagant attitudes, each described in appropriate language and imagery, with each other and with common sense. One attitude is embodied in Captain Miles Standish, the hot-tempered commander of a twelve-man army, a swaggerer, a valiant man, and a student of the wars of the Hebrews, Caesar's *Commentaries*, and an artillery guide "designed for belligerent Christians"; on the other side is John Alden, sincere, hardworking, over-scrupulous, compelled to disguise pleasure as duty before he can enjoy it, and fearful lest his preference of love over friendship may be "worshipping Astaroth blindly, and impious idols of Baal." At the center is commonsensical Priscilla, quiet, loving, amused at her suitors' posturings, and busy at the spinning wheel emblematic of settled life with its civilizing domesticity.

The marriage of John and Priscilla, however humorous its preliminaries, is nevertheless, in the barely surviving Plymouth colony that is the setting, an affirmation of faith in America's future and a promise of its fruitfulness. Thus the almost lush description of the climactic bridal day is without serious incongruity set forth in images of religious ritual and of fertility, as the sun issues forth like a high priest, with the sea a laver at his feet, and Priscilla rides on a snow-white bull to her wedding while golden sunlight gleams on bunches of purple grapes. Longfellow again introduces the imagery of Eden and expulsion as he describes the land of privation and hardship lying before John and Priscilla, and adds,

> But to their eyes transfigured, it seemed as the Garden
> of Eden,
> Filled with the presence of God, whose voice was the
> sound of the ocean.

The final balance of sometimes broad humor, romantic sentiment, and gravity is a tonal achievement of no small order.

With *Hiawatha* Longfellow made his chief contribution to nineteenth-century American literature's search for a usable national past, whose necessity to the creation of a native culture was assumed from the analogy of European cultural history. America's antiquity, however, was Indian and primitively tribal, and therefore both racially and culturally alien. The pieties of nationalism nonetheless demanded that the gap between the two worlds be bridged; countless authors valiantly responded, and, with a few notable exceptions, artistically perished in the attempt. To Longfellow the whole effort seemed misdirected, since America's cultural past was essentially European, although he had been long interested in Indian lore and history, and was acquainted with such authorities on Indian life as Heckewelder and Schoolcraft. Typically, he found his own formula for relating the Indian past to the American present in a European national poem, the Finnish *Kalevala*, which suggested the use of legends linked together by the central figure of a culture hero, the creations of myth and folklore being, for the cultivated imagination, more viable than the grubby data of actual primitive living. In American terms, the Indians' passage from savagery to a low level of civilization could be treated as preparatory to the climactic arrival of high civilization represented by the white man, and poetry could thus create the continuity that history had failed to provide. One result of this plan is the weakest moment in *Hiawatha*, when the hero unreservedly recommends to his people the religion and culture of the white man, represented by the Jesuit missionaries: the abrupt transition from a legendary world to that of fictionalized history is unconvincing, as it was probably certain to be, in spite of its theoretical justification as a means of relating Indian and white civilization, the chief desideratum of the age.

Like the creators of the Noble Redman, Longfellow adapted his Indians to contemporary tastes and interests. His hero is a bowdlerized version of a mythic Algonkian chief, and Hiawatha's romance with Minnehaha is conducted by the rules of sentimental fiction. The idealization, however, is largely intended by Longfellow, as a part of the deliberately legendary atmosphere of the narration. Criticisms based on realistic assumptions, whether Emerson's mild blame or Schoolcraft's praise, were, in Longfellow's eyes, fundamentally irrelevant: Hiawatha was, he stated, a kind of "American Prometheus," and the poem was "an Indian Edda," a recognizably poetic romance, based on ancient myths and traditions and thus to be read as an attractively colorful reflection not of Indian actuality, but of primitive imagination.

The language and versification of *Hiawatha* were designed as part of its legendary effect. The trochaic tetrameter meter, suggested by the *Kalevala* and by earlier Indian romances, has an accentuation sufficiently strong to invite easy exaggeration into singsong, an invitation readily accepted by most modern readers. In so long a poem, the conspicuous rhythm, the constant use of parallelism and repetition, the profusion of exotic Indian names, and the simple personifications all finally threaten monotony and make parody irresistible. Critical objections to *Hiawatha*'s verse can be countered only by treating the verse, according to Longfellow's intention, as a part of the primitive machinery. Thus regarded, the verse loses its apparent eccentricity and contributes a suitable effect of chant and of quaintness to the legendary atmosphere Longfellow sought to create. Unfortunately, it also heightens the sense of artifice pervasive in *Hiawatha* and perhaps inseparable from a pseudo-primitive genre.

Present-day concern with myth, legend, and folklore gives *Hiawatha* a more serious interest than it possessed in the recent past, even if the modern reader usually prefers to take his myth neat or as revitalized in current forms. The episodes of *Hiawatha* are based upon now familiar mythic patterns. Hiawatha himself, begotten by the West Wind upon the daughter of moon-descended Nokomis, is a demigod aligning himself with humanity. He teaches his people how to plant and cultivate maize, and begins to instruct them in the arts of civilization, the skills of fishing and agriculture, and the art of picture-writing. With the help of his few close companions and of the helpful animals of folklore, he slays the spirit of evil, the serpent-guarded Magician, and Pau-Puk-Keewis, the champion of the old, anarchic savagery, and finally departs for the Islands of the Blessed. From one standpoint, *Hiawatha* is a set of picturesque variations on mythic themes, and its recapitulation of a whole mythic pattern gives it in its entirety an imaginative strength greater than its incidental faults would apparently support. Its major weakness as a whole arises primarily from its literarily calculated primitivism: the sophistication of its simplicity makes it too manifestly a tour de force.

Longfellow's last major narrative work, *Tales of a Wayside Inn*, was published in three installments over an eleven-year period. The design of the work, a collection of stories in a unifying framework, recalls the *Canterbury Tales*, but Longfellow's self-confessed inability to rival Chaucer makes the Chaucerian work properly a point of reference rather than of comparison. In Longfellow's *Tales*, the stories are clearly primary, the framework a support. The setting is the Red-Horse Inn (now the reconstructed Wayside Inn) in Sudbury, Massachusetts, a hostelry well known to Longfellow and his friends. The narrators, designated by profession, avocation, nationality, or race, are all based upon actual acquaintances of Longfellow's: the Poet was Theophilus Parsons, a translator of Dante; the Musician was the Norwegian violinist Ole Bull; the Sicilian was Luigi Monti, an instructor in Harvard's modern languages department. Their individual characteristics are generalized into more or less typical ones, but there can be no satirical representation or socially or dramatically significant quarreling: the narrators form a friendly and homogeneous group. What is possible is realized — an animated running discussion of topics suggested by the tales and of points of view expressed by the tellers. In flexible tetrameter couplets, Longfellow takes the discussion from aesthetics to religion, and achieves an effect of individually colored discourse sufficient to support the tales and often interesting in itself.

Individually considered, the tales vary greatly in nature, interest, and quality. A few, like "Lady Wentworth" and "Azrael," dwindle into anecdote, and others, like "The Ballad of Carmilhan," are principally evocative of mood or of that ghostly atmosphere that Longfellow could always effectively create. Most of the stories, however, are marked by Longfellow's real narrative talent: the ability to make well-selected, continuously progressing events and vividly, if broadly, drawn characters deliver in a climactic scene some comment upon an aspect of life or a typical movement of human feeling. The accomplishment of the *Tales*, however, lies less in particular stories, as good as several of them are, than in the variety of the gathered narratives. Contrasting with each other in scene, tone, and poetic structure, and held together by the framework, the stories in juxtaposition suggest the inclusive range possible to the simple, immemorial activity of storytelling, and the way in which even traditional tales may reflect attitudes and feelings of the narrators. Many kinds of effects are embraced, from the grimness of "Torquemada" to the broad fabliau humor of "The Monk of Casal-Maggiore" or the vividness of "The Saga of King Olaf," one of the most vigorous of all Longfellow's poems, with its balladlike but well-developed dramatization of the mingled zeal and barbarism of the first Viking champions and enemies of Christianity. Moreover, a few of the tales, like "Emma and Eginhard" and "The Falcon of Ser Federigo," reflect a more realistic and tolerant assessment of human behavior than Longfellow's poetry commonly displays. The reputation of the *Tales* is unavoidably linked to the fortunes of narrative poetry, especially of straightforward narrative; within that limited area, the *Tales* occupies a place of considerable honor.

The major irony of Longfellow's literary career was the commitment of his hopes for distinctive major achievement to the form in which he was most consistently unsuccessful, the poetic drama. From 1849 to 1872 he intermittently labored over what he regarded as "his loftier song" in "sublimer strain," as his greatest work, "the equivalent expression for the trouble and wrath of life, for its sorrow and mystery." The completed *Christus: A Mystery* consists of three parts comprising four poetic dramas, all so manifestly closet dramas that they could be properly described as dramatically organized poems. The first part is *The Divine Tragedy*, the last to be published; the second part is *The Golden Legend*, the first published; the third part, *The New England Tragedies*, consists of two dramas, *John Endicott* and *Giles Corey of the Salem Farms*. The three parts are linked by interludes and the whole *Christus* is provided with an "Introitus" and "Finale." No other works of Longfellow's had such intended scope or received such dedicated attention; and none were so disappointing in result. The twenty-odd years spent in composition, the lapse of time between publication of the parts, and the fact that each part is also a substantially self-contained work explain why the *Christus* seems partly to be an assemblage; indeed, it is surprising that the whole does achieve a loose unity which makes it more than the sum of its parts.

Longfellow's general failure in dramatic form is understandable. His talent was narrative and lyrically meditative, and he could not refrain from reliance on narration and exposition, even to the destruction of dramatic effect. The sequence and relationship of episodes and actions is basically determined, especially in the last two parts of the *Christus*, by narrative not dramatic logic and development. It is thus unfortunate that from 1849 on he increasingly looked to drama as the vehicle of his most important ideas. It is his least pretentious dramatic work, the early *Spanish Student*, that is in many respects the most successfully realized; in spite of its lack of intellectual significance, it is a colorful, pleasant comedy of intrigue, technically more proficient than the later poetic dramas. Two minor dramatic works, *Judas Maccabeus* and *The Masque of Pandora*, have interesting themes but are extremely weak in execution. Only the partly completed *Michael Angelo*, closely related to Longfellow's own life and work, and containing in a few passages some of his strongest poetry, shows an apparently emerging mastery of dramatic form in the 1870's.

The fundamental obstacle to the *Christus'* success, however, is not simply a flawed dramatic technique, but an internal conflict in the work between its ostensible intention and its meaning. Originally planned as a dramatizing of the progress of Christianity, the *Christus* loosely employs the theological virtues of faith, hope, and charity as the basis of organization, *The Divine Tragedy* expressing hope through its representation of Christ's life and mission, the *Golden Legend* depicting faith in its full medieval flowering, and the *New England Tragedies* pointing to the religious freedom of the age of charity or love. The optimism of the design is realized in some scenes and is recurrently asserted as a proposition, but it is not borne out in the *Christus'* development and accumulated feeling, which are finally somber and even pessimistic in their tendency. Longfellow's emotional recoil from several aspects of the contemporary religious scene apparently caused him to lose much of his professed hope for the future and left its mark especially on the first and third parts, the latest composed, of the *Christus*. If the last part inculcates love and tolerance at all, it does so only by exhibiting the horrors of bigotry, and the relentless power of intolerance is in fact the dominant force; in *John Endicott* a series of special providences, occurring near the conclusion, indicate divine displeasure with persecution, but the Quakers are saved only by an intervening royal mandate of that unlikely *deus ex machina*, Charles II; in the final, still grimmer *Giles Corey*, where the maliciously accused though innocent Corey is put to death by pressing, this climactic scene is followed by a hasty, excessively short speech by Cotton Mather predicting that never again will such things happen, a judgment perhaps validated by history, but certainly not by the action or tone of the drama. Furthermore, the interlude preparing for the *New England Tragedies* is a soliloquy by Martin Luther that alternates between an announcement of spiritual freedom recovered from religious tyranny and a condemnation of humanism reflecting the sectarianism and hatred most repellent to Longfellow: it is an unpromising introduction to the latest stage of an assertedly progressive historical movement.

That the *New England Tragedies* made a darkened climax Longfellow was probably aware. He originally planned a third, more confident concluding play based on the simple, pious life of Pennsylvania's Moravian sisterhood. This, however, he never wrote, and its abandonment may be explained by the actual state of his sentiments and especially by the developing mood of the *Christus* itself. The opening "Introitus" finds in the sadness of pre-Christian ages the sign of a coming Redeemer, but the "Finale" is not a celebration of redemption achieved; rather, it is a melancholy review of the Christian centuries, concluding that "the evil doth not cease." The survey is not despairing, but its limited hope is proclaimed in spite of rather than out of Christian history, and hope's realization seems indefinitely postponed: meanwhile

> Poor, sad Humanity
> Through all the dust and heat
> Turns back with bleeding feet,
> By the weary road it came . . .

So the tracing of the human condition comes nearly full circle back to the "Introitus," and is saved from cyclical completion only by Longfellow's characteristic emphasis upon the persistence of the ideal and the possibility of individual Christian action.

Perhaps the most successful part of *Christus* is the *Golden Legend,* which, in spite of an elementary plot, an unmedievally melancholy hero, and a sentimentalized heroine, effectively profits from Longfellow's knowledge of the Middle Ages. Although the deepest intellectual and spiritual life of the medieval world is not mirrored here, the varied contrasts and conflicts of the medieval surface, as well as the immediately underlying crosscurrents, are colorfully represented through skillfully shifted scenes presented in a freely handled answerable verse. An acid portrayal of Goliardic friars is set against a simple, reverentially composed nativity play, and the satiric presentations of wrangling scholastics and of a sensational preacher are placed in a sympathetically imagined background of ringing bells and chanting pilgrims. So picturesquely drawn are the diverse actions of a world where "the will is feeble and passion strong," but where everything is seen in a transcendent light, that the effect is of a pageant arranged by religious and historical feeling, almost rich enough to conceal the weaknesses of the dramatic core.

The Divine Tragedy, composed in three "Passovers" or acts, with an "Introitus" and an epilogue, is based, often closely, on the Biblical account of Christ's life. The faults are many and obvious, ranging from insubstantial scenes to timidity in handling the text of the Bible, but in centering the action upon the effects of divine love and human response to it, Longfellow achieves some genuine thematic and dramatic development. Each "Passover" concentrates upon one aspect of Christus' expanding mission: upon the casting out of demons, which is the ejection of irrationality and fear; the curing of blindness, which is the dispelling of ignorance; and sacrifice, the perilous commitment of love. Recurrent themes and images, and frequent cross references, make the action less episodic than it at first appears to be, and an interpretative chorus is provided by Manahem the Essenian. Above all, a basic unity is found in Longfellow's preoccupation with that most persistent and personal of his themes, the problem of dream and reality. The fear expressed throughout *The Divine Tragedy* is that life is a delusive dream within a dream, and Christus the visionary of an unreal kingdom. The act of faith thus becomes primarily an assertion of reality, its validity being finally confirmed by the appearance of the risen Christus. Yet the haunting fear is too powerfully expressed to be completely dissolved even by an apparently victorious conclusion.

The study of Longfellow's poetic reputation is perhaps more relevant to the history of criticism than to the evaluation of his art. His most literate contemporaries delivered varying decisions, some finding the poetry seriously deficient, others praising it without reservation, most setting a very high value on the best poems while pointing out the weakness of others. It was popular acclaim, hailing the man as much as the poet, that elevated Longfellow to a position no sober critical judgment could sanction. With the emergence of modern literature and the literary wars it evoked, the defenders of the new order found it necessary and not unpleasant to counter the hostility of presumably Victorian attitudes by attacking Victorian ideals and achievements. In America, Longfellow, in his popular canonization, offered himself as the surest target for an assault on the nineteenth century; at the nadir, one influential critic advanced the proposition that Longfellow's poetry has no iota of the poetic character. Later, however, as the early twentieth-century revolution itself receded into the past, it became possible for Longfellow to share in the general revaluation of Victorian literature. To this more objective examination, dating especially from Odell Shepard's reserved but often acute essay prefixed to his selective edition of Longfellow's poems, many studies have contributed, including such recent full-length ones as Law-rance Thompson's reassessment of the young Longfellow's experi-ence, Edward Wagenknecht's two important and sympathetic in-terpretations of Longfellow as person and author, Newton Arvin's uniquely valuable analysis of the poetry as a whole, and Cecil Wil-liams' placing of Longfellow in the American literary tradition. From this continuing reconsideration has come a clear view of the many limitations of Longfellow's talent, but also a new respect for his accomplishment within them.

LEON EDEL

Henry D. Thoreau

OF THE creative spirits that flourished in Concord, Massachusetts, during the middle of the nineteenth century, it might be said that Hawthorne loved men but felt estranged from them, Emerson loved ideas even more than men, and Thoreau loved himself. Less of an artist than Hawthorne, less of a thinker than Emerson, Thoreau made of his life a sylvan legend, that of man alone, in communion with nature. He was a strange presence in American letters — we have so few of them — an eccentric. The English tend to tolerate their eccentrics to the enrichment of their national life. In America, where democracy and conformity are often confused, the nonconforming Thoreau was frowned upon, and for good reason. He had a disagreeable and often bellicose nature. He lacked geniality. And then he had once set fire to the Concord woods — a curious episode, too lightly dismissed in the Thoreau biographies. He was, in the fullest sense of the word, a "curmudgeon," and literary history has never sufficiently studied the difficulties his neighbors had in adjusting themselves to certain of his childish ways. But in other ways he was a man of genius — even if it was a "crooked genius" as he himself acknowledged.

A memorable picture has been left by Hawthorne's daughter of the three famous men of Concord skating one winter's afternoon on the river. Hawthorne, wrapped in his cloak, "moved like a self-impelled Greek statue, stately and grave," as one might expect of the future author of *The Marble Faun*. Emerson, stoop-shouldered, "evidently too weary to hold himself erect," pitched forward, "half lying on the air." Thoreau, genuinely skillful on his skates, performed "dithyrambic dances and Bacchic leaps," enchanted with himself. Their manner of skating was in accord with their personalities and temperaments.

Behind a mask of self-exaltation Thoreau performed as before a mirror — and first of all for his own edification. He was a fragile Narcissus embodied in a homely New Englander. His life was brief. He was born in 1817, in Concord; he lived in Concord, and he died in Concord in 1862 shortly after the guns had spoken at Fort Sumter. A child of the romantic era, he tried a number of times to venture forth into the world. He went to Maine, to Staten Island, to Cape Cod, and ultimately to Minnesota, in search of health, but he always circled back to the Thoreau family house in Concord and to the presence of a domineering and loquacious mother. No other man with such wide-ranging thoughts and a soaring mind — it reached to ancient Greece, to the Ganges, to the deepest roots of England and the Continent — bound himself to so small a strip of ground. "He was worse than provincial," the cosmopolitan Henry James remarked, "he was parochial."

All of Thoreau's writings represent a continuous and carefully documented projection of the self. *Walden* announces itself autobiography — "I should not talk so much about myself if there were anybody else whom I knew as well." The book is an idealized and romantic account of Thoreau's sojourn in the woods. Even its beautiful digressions are a series of masks. In both of his works, *Walden* and *A Week on the Concord and Merrimack Rivers*, as in his miscellaneous essays, we find an ideal self rather than the Thoreau Concord knew. The artist in Thoreau improved on nature in the interest of defending himself against some of nature's more painful truths. However, the facts of literary history offer us sufficient clues to the study of the character and personality of the child christened David Henry Thoreau. (Later he chose to be called

Henry David — a slight rearrangement, perhaps in the interest of euphony, yet symptom of the many rearrangements of the Thoreau self.)

It may be a small matter, but Thoreau, who abjured vanities and called on men to simplify their lives, listed among the meager belongings he took to Walden Pond a three-by-three-inch mirror — he who had all of Walden in which to look at himself. He kept, moreover, a mirror for his soul as well, in the most consistently written and religiously preserved journal of American letters. His life was indeed a life of constant self-contemplation and self-observation. Walden was "my own sun and moon and stars, and a little world to myself." If he looked often into his little mirror and the mirror of the Pond, he listened also, as Narcissus did, to the nymph Echo. He found the echoes of his own voice — so he said — almost the only "kindred voices" that he heard.

His inner quest, which he often made eloquent, was to be both Spartan and Athenian. Men can be one or the other at different times. Thoreau tried to be both at once, and he worked hard to reconcile these irreconcilables. He was the sort of man who needs the constant vision of his countenance to assure himself that he is not dissolving altogether into the elements. The mirror he brought to his hut, the hut itself which he purchased from a shanty dweller and rebuilt, the manner in which he extolled Concord even while scolding it, reveal a different Thoreau from the self-portrait, and from the Thoreau image sentimentalized by generations of nature lovers who have never read him. He shrugged his shoulders at the tools of society, but used them constantly. He had enormous practical gifts; he could use his hands, knew much of the lore of nature, had considerable Yankee shrewdness and what we term colloquially "know-how." But in his moments of insight he recognized, as he did in one of his poems, that he was "a parcel of vain strivings tied/ By a chance bond together,/ Dangling this way and that." What attracts our attention in particular is not so much the "vain strivings," which might be attributed to many men, but the poet's imagining himself to be loosely strung together. Poetry, Thoreau once said, "is a piece of very private history, which unostentatiously lets us into the secret of a man's life." Behind the mask of nature lover, philosopher, man of craft and lore, Thoreau struggled to keep the parcel of himself from becoming unwrapped and scattered. He speaks in the same poem of having "no root in the land," and of drinking up his own "juices." His friends observed this in him; his was an inner rage that consumes. Beneath his outward euphoria lay always a deep melancholy.

Perhaps Thoreau's best known remark, made in *Walden*, was that "the mass of men lead lives of quiet desperation." This is often quoted with the assumption that Thoreau himself was never desperate: that he at least achieved a tranquil and philosophic existence. The Concord farmers, however, who saw Thoreau's zeal and compulsions — the tenacities of this self-appointed "inspector of snow storms and rain storms" — would have regarded his assiduous journal-keeping as a life of greater desperation than their own rude lives of daily work. There is in all of Thoreau's writings an enforced calm; strange tensions run below the surface, deep obsessions. He is so preoccupied with self-assertion as to suggest that this was a profound necessity rather than an experience of serenity.

His struggle for identity gave him great powers of concentration and diligence. He was not a born writer, but he taught himself by imitation to carpenter solid verbal structures and give them rhythm and proportion. He went to school to Emerson, to Carlyle, to the Greeks, to the philosophers of India. He was first and foremost a reader of books — and only after them of nature. He read like a bee clinging to a flower, for all that he could extract from the printed page. He wrote poems, many of them banal; yet he poured a great deal of poetry into the more relaxed passages of his prose. This prose is seldom spontaneous; behind its emulation of the measure and moderation of the ancients one feels strain and subterranean violence. The violence often is converted into contempt and condescension for Thoreau's neighbors and the hardworking farmers of Concord.

Two acts established Thoreau's fame and his myth. The first was his building of a comfortable, heated, plastered cabin be-

side Walden Pond; this he did out of a "prefabricated" hut purchased for a few dollars from an impecunious shanty dweller. He
set it well within the range of the railroad and of his fellowmen
and pretended that he lived self-sufficiently in the wilderness. Here
he dwelt for about two years. He himself tallied exactly twenty-six
months, but he did not deduct the month he lived under his
mother's roof while waiting for the plaster to dry; nor the fortnight
of a trip to the Maine woods. During his stay at Walden he worked
hard, hoeing his beans and determining the rude economy possible
to him in simplifying his life. That he had access to his mother's
cookie jar in town and enjoyed sundry dinners elsewhere, as we
shall see, made no difference to his calculations. In his cabin he
wrote *A Week on the Concord and Merrimack Rivers*; he extolled
solitude and nature and spoke of "the unquestionable ability of
man to elevate his life by a conscious endeavor." How he lived as
America's first conscientious public "dropout" he would describe
later in the memorable *Walden,* originally subtitled "Life in the
Woods."

The second source of his fame and myth was his act of "civil
disobedience." He gave us that valuable formulation of the privilege of dissent. He refused to pay his poll tax and went to jail — for
one night. Someone else paid it — "interfered" said Thoreau — and
the jailer ousted him from his cell. In truth, Thoreau did not fancy
martyrdom. He was always willing to allow others — society — to
do for him what he would not do himself. He was willing to use
existing tools so long as these enabled him to pursue his private
course and in his own distinctive way. "I quietly declare war with
the State, after my fashion," he wrote in his celebrated essay and
his own fashion seems to have been partly explained when he
added, "I will still make what use and get what advantage of her
I can, as is usual in such cases." The man of high principle here
shed his principles. And he behaved also as if no other individuals
existed in society. Whitman discerned in him "a morbid dislike of
humanity."

From this it may be seen that the image of Thoreau which has
reached us is larger than the figure Thoreau's contemporaries

knew. His myth of a lonely life in the woods, of man against society, has provided modern men with thoughts about their place in a tree-impoverished world, whose air is polluted — a world alienated from nature. Thoreau gave permanent form to the dream of men in great anonymous urban communities who want to "get away from it all." He also influenced individuals like Tolstoi and Gandhi who had in them a similar rage of reform; these men, however, possessed a larger sense of their fellowmen than did Thoreau.

In a society of diminishing liberties, Thoreau freed himself personally of some of society's tyrannies without offering any ultimate solution for the problems he so fervently discussed. Kamo-No Chōmei, the Japanese sage, in his *Hojoki*, written almost seven centuries before *Walden*, described his life in a ten-foot-square hut; but he lived in it for thirty years and, in the timeless ways of the East, found his answers within himself. Thoreau, who read the books of the East — though he could hardly have known those of a Japan as yet unopened to the West — did not regard his Walden cabin as a permanent home. He left it as abruptly as he built it, saying he had gone there only "to transact some private business." The *Hojoki* describes a way of life, *Walden* represented largely a gesture.

By the standards of his fellow citizens in Concord Thoreau seemed lazy and shiftless. They judged him with severity, but also with indulgence, for they knew his talents. He was a skillful artisan, a fine surveyor, an active amateur naturalist; and he was highly inventive. His resourcefulness extricated his parents from poverty. But he ran away from his accomplishments in a kind of morbid fear they might enslave him. Emerson, in his truth-seeking eulogy at Thoreau's grave, said that he counted it a fault in him that he had no ambition. And he went on to say that "wanting this, instead of engineering for all America, he was the captain of a huckleberry party." Emerson added, in his characteristic fashion, "Pounding beans is good to the end of pounding empires one of these days; but if, at the end of years it is still only beans!" The observation was severe. Emerson expected perhaps too much from his temperamental disciple. Thoreau wanted to be a writer rather than an em-

pire builder. Nevertheless Emerson discerned in Thoreau's daily
life — despite its egocentric form — a drive to power, and one can
understand the philosopher's disappointment.

His allusion to the huckleberry party has some significance.
Thoreau, when very young, had been taken by his mother to Fair
Haven Hill, where the huckleberries were abundant; and she took
him also at a tender age to the shores of Walden Pond. Small wonder that he clung to "the fabulous landscape of my infant dreams."
These were memorable little journeys and Thoreau's personal geography became identified with the powerful, talkative parent who
loomed large in all the years of his life. His father counted for
much less; he is described as a "mousey" man, ineffectual in business, who apparently abdicated early to the houseful of women —
his wife, her sisters, his daughters — a nest of femininity in which
his younger son was cradled. We can understand therefore why
huckleberry picking on Fair Haven Hill, to which he led the children of the town like some latter-day Pied Piper, was one of Thoreau's fondest pastimes. It was a repeated return to a landscape
glamorized for him long before by his mother's love and attention.
Walden and Fair Haven became symbolic transformations in the
innermost world of Thoreau of the one great attachment of his
life. The umbilical cord might be said to have never been cut. Nature, he once remarked, "is my mother at the same time that she is
my sister. I cannot imagine a woman no older than I."

It is recorded that when Thoreau was about to graduate from
Harvard he asked his mother what career he might follow. She
replied: "You can buckle on your knapsack and roam abroad to
seek your fortune." In early America, with the frontier near at
hand, the remark seems natural enough. Yet Thoreau had a sudden fit of weeping. He read his mother's remark as if she were
sending him away from her. His older sister came to his rescue.
"No, Henry, you shall not go, you shall stay at home and live with
us." Sometime later he said, "Methinks I should be content to sit
at the back door in Concord, under the poplar tree henceforth,
forever." And this was, in effect, what he did — for life. In his
writings he would make a virtue of this embeddedness. He read

the great legends and adventures of man into Concord, as James Joyce later read the Odyssey into Dublin. One could, with the aid of books, possess an imaginary world in a cabin by a New England pond. "My cottage becomes the universe," said the Japanese Chōmei.

This quality of dependence, this clinging to his mother, and all that represented her, Concord, Fair Haven, Walden, caused him to seek — in his quest for a place in the world — models he could emulate, and his first and natural choice fell on his elder brother, John. But the brother died young of tetanus. Thoreau, it is recorded, promptly developed the same symptoms, as if he too had to die. Of the two sons, Henry David Thoreau had been designated, by family decision, to go to a university, although there had been some thought at first of making him a carpenter. Money was found and he went to Harvard. Here he acquired the habit of reading; and here he heard Emerson speak. It was a momentous experience to find so much inspiration in a fellow townsman. Their friendship was to be at the very center of Thoreau's life, for his pliant nature imitated Emerson as he had imitated his brother. Lowell, visiting Concord in 1838, a year after Thoreau's graduation, wrote, "I met Thoreau last night and it is exquisitely amusing to see how he imitates Emerson's tone and manner. With my eyes shut, I shouldn't know them apart." And seventeen years later, F. B. Sanborn, one of Thoreau's biographers, still could notice that "in his tones and gestures he seemed to me to imitate Emerson." Thoreau's prose would always be filled with echoes of Emerson and he adopted certain essential qualities of his style while being addicted at the same time — as Emerson was not — to exaggeration and paradox.

For a while, after graduation, he taught school, but early abandoned this. He then sought the lecture platform, also in imitation of Emerson. From 1841 to 1843 he lived in the Emerson household as a general handyman. He attached himself to Mrs. Emerson; she must be seen as still another in the line of female figures — the sisters, aunts, mother — who had surrounded him from his earliest years. Emerson, in his qualified eulogy, described his handyman's aptitudes: "his senses were acute, his frame well-knit and hardy, his hands skillful in the use of tools." He worked neatly and with precision; he took care of the garden, instructed Emerson in husbandry — he brought the lore of the woods to the author of *Nature*. And his mentor, on his side, encouraged him to write, to keep a journal, and to contribute to the *Dial* where Thoreau helped with editorial chores. Thus he came to know the transcendentalists.

No literary or social historian has yet written the full story of the years of Emerson and Thoreau in Concord although a large literature exists on the subject. We have a charming evocation in Van Wyck Brooks's *The Flowering of New England*: but the painting is too much in the tones of the subjects themselves and while the book abounds in color and local substance it does not convey to us the limitations of this community in which so many high-minded people came and went. It is necessary to read ourselves back into a sparse and hardworking society possessed of a parochial yet strong sense of civic responsibility and Christian duty. At one end of the town there lived for some years an imaginative artist in the Old Manse, Nathaniel Hawthorne, and at the other, with rows of elms between, Mr. Emerson daily communicated his thoughts to his journal, wrote his lectures, and walked in his orchard. There was a great scratching of pens in various parts of the town. Thoreau kept his journal; the Alcotts, father and daughter — that is, Bronson Alcott and Louisa May — wrote regularly in their diaries; William Ellery Channing, the poet, and F. B. Sanborn, the teacher, kept records and later wrote the first biographies of Thoreau. Margaret Fuller came and went. There were other salty characters, not least the much-described Mary Moody Emerson, who used her shroud as a garment of daily wear; and the scholarly Mrs. Ripley, Emerson's long-time friend. On another social scale we must mention Mrs. Thoreau, one of the town's socially ambitious women who was described as having a "regal" presence. The place had some two thousand inhabitants counting farmers beyond the town's radius; and in an age of steadfast labor and isolation from the wider world (it took two hours by coach to cover the fourteen miles to Boston) there was sufficient time and energy to expend on the reforms dear to the heart of New England. Concord had its active Temperance Society; and the Middlesex Anti-Slavery Society dedicated itself unremittingly to the abolitionist cause. Thoreau himself was host to runaways and we know of his conducting one slave to a contact point on the underground railway to Canada. There was also the Concord Social Library, and town meetings were regularly held. The town bell summoned citizens and literary history tells us that the bell ringer refused to do his job when Thoreau called a meeting on behalf of John Brown; Thoreau on this occasion rang the bell himself.

We must remind ourselves of these multiple forces at work in this environment: the liberal causes were espoused passionately in a life of solid if rough creature comfort. We can measure the scale of life by visiting the Old Manse, and walking through its low-ceilinged rooms, and seeing the straight-backed chairs, the black horsehair seats, the frugal adornments, and all that is implied when we speak of plain living and high thinking. In such a society, with men of vigorous talent like Hawthorne and Emerson, and idiosyncratic individuals like Thoreau and Channing, thoughts tended to run to transcendental things. The long cold winters, with the deep snows of that era, were conducive to reading and to writing. Henry James, the novelist, who knew the later Concord, would characterize the town and environs as a kind of "American Weimar." Concord had had, long before, its single moment of history: the shot heard round the world had been fired within hearing and sight of the Old Manse and the battle between the farmers and the British had been watched by the Reverend Mr. Ripley from its windows. Touched thus by primary history, the town's very name gave a lofty tone to the place; and the tones of its discourse would echo through later decades and reflect the civilized American mind in close communion with nature and its own sense of secular and divine order.

It might be said that Thoreau was a born transcendentalist and that Emerson's *Nature* might have been written for him. Going beyond affirmation of a romantic idealism, a faith in the self, in one's feelings and senses as distinct from the prescribing faiths, Emerson urged men to put trust in their "involuntary perceptions" — a highly modern view: today we would say that he urged men to try to be more in tune with their unconscious promptings. Octavius B. Frothingham, the historian of transcendentalism, spoke of the movement as "a wave of sentiment"; and Emerson's biographer, J. E. Cabot, phrased this more vividly when he said it was a stirring "of Puritan thought with a hint of smothered fires." Emerson wrote: "Build your own world. As fast as you conform your life to the pure idea in your mind, that will unfold its grand proportions." No deeper chord in Thoreau could have been touched. Ever after he studied the grandeur of the Self; for Emerson's teaching endowed human consciousness with supremacy in life and severed the bonds that tied man's will to religious dictates. V. L. Parrington would characterize this more harshly as "a mystical egocentric universe wherein the children of God might luxuriate in their divinity." Within these ideas one could find echoes of Rousseau, of Coleridge, of Goethe. The full tide of European romanticism had reached the western shores of the Atlantic. Cabot remarks that Emerson, in *Nature*, did not preach reliance on intuition as a self-conceit or "an exaggerated regard for one's own spiritual experiences," but to some extent this was the form of Thoreau's response. He had come upon a philosophy that would suffice for a lifetime. He was "Emerson's moral man made flesh." He could live for the universe as for Concord; he could sing the sense of the infinite in his own being. "I am a poet, a mystic and a transcendentalist," Thoreau announced. "I came into this world not chiefly to make this a good place to live in, but to live in it, be it good or bad." Nevertheless he preached; and what he preached was "self-improvement." Cabot further tells us that "there was much talk in those days of spontaneity — the right and duty of acting oneself out, and following one's genius, whithersoever it might lead." This Thoreau did. There were complaints that transcendentalism unfitted the young men for business and the young women for society — "without making them fit for anything else." The idealism nevertheless was genuine. Emerson's thoughts were wide and humane, but as often happens, not everyone accurately interpreted the inspired message.

No one has ever examined the "interpersonal" relations between Emerson and his disciples and the manner in which this large-minded man attracted eccentricity to himself — as exemplified notably in Alcott, Thoreau, and Channing. One wonders what needs these acolytes fulfilled in Emerson's life and what sense of power he derived from their pronounced discipleship. We may speculate, however, that there came a moment when Emerson asked himself whether he had acquired a handyman for life. Thoreau embedded himself in his household as completely as in his maternal home; indeed Emerson may have represented for Thoreau both his brother and his mother, in his example and his acceptance. The sage of Concord was alert enough not to accept passively so much ambivalence. His eulogy pronounced over Thoreau's grave is filled with significant asperities, some perhaps unintended. It is also frankly critical, as some of Emerson's journal entries also show. He sought to define Thoreau for himself, writing that the younger man's conversation consisted of "a continual twining of the present moment into a sentence and offering it to me." Thoreau's behavior in this household was as quixotic as when he lived at home. "Why is he never frank?" Emerson asked himself once. And he added, "I have no social pleasure with Henry, though more than once the best conversation." At the end of two years, Emerson urged the young man to launch himself in the world of letters. He obtained employment for him in New York, as tutor to the children of a relative on Staten Island. His motive was generous; he believed that Thoreau, as a poet and a sentient being, would contribute to the literature of the new America. But he was also tactfully elbowing the omnipresent handyman out of his household.

Thoreau went to New York. That he found the life in the city less congenial than the familiar woods and fields of Concord is understandable. Given his difficulties in relating to his human — as distinct from animal — environment, he could discover no comfortable friends in an urban community, even though New York in the early 1840's swarmed with writers and publishers, and Thoreau had helpful letters of introduction. The elder Henry James, whom Thoreau went to see with a letter from Emerson, found him to be "the most child-like, unconscious and unblushing egotist it has ever been my fortune to encounter in the ranks of mankind." The father of the future novelist saw in Thoreau "a sheer and mountainous inward self-esteem." He received him, however, with warmth and friendliness. Thoreau found helpful individuals in Manhattan, but he remained homesick, moody, despondent. Within a matter of months he returned from his exile, but not to the Emerson household. He went back to his family, back to his own room, his books, his papers, his botanical specimens. Shortly after this he built his hut beside Walden. He would re-enter the Emerson household two years later, but only for a well-defined term, to take care of the place while Emerson lectured abroad. The history of this friendship was one of gradual estrangement. "His virtues," Emerson said, "sometimes ran into extremes."

Literary history has never asked itself why Henry David Thoreau, aged twenty-eight, in the midsummer of 1845 — on Independence Day — moved into the Walden cabin and embarked on what he called his "experiment" in simplifying the acts of life. It has accepted Thoreau's own explanation for this limited withdrawal from his family home. He wished, he said, to test the things by which society around him lived. He struck for a kind of personal freedom. The men in Concord, the neighboring farmers, led in his view unsimple lives. They were mortgaged to their encumbered properties and their daily labor. Thoreau would practice a rude economy and avoid enslavement: he would free himself for higher things, mainly reading and writing, and his observation of nature. The historical facts suggest, however, that Thoreau was led to his act by a crisis for which a cabin in the woods offered a radical solution. His life with the Emersons had been an extension of his life at home; he had left home, but had gone only as far as the home of a neighbor. He had then attempted to leave Concord and found not only that he was unable to launch himself in the wider world but that life without Concord was impossible to him. Returned from Staten Island, under the family roof, he at first took up his father's trade of pencil making. With his usual resourcefulness, he at this time studied the composition of the graphite in German pencils; he refined the materials used by his father and this led to an improved pencil and ultimately placed the Thoreaus in a position to sell graphite wholesale. Henry remained, however, at loose ends. He had no intention of pursuing the family business; and he seemed to have nowhere to go.

At this time there occurred a small incident which seemed to shake him to his very roots. The woodsman and naturalist accidentally set fire to the fields and woods of Concord while cooking a catch of fish on the shore of Fair Haven Bay where he had gone with a friend. He summoned help after a two-mile dash through the woods; and returning he found a half-mile of flame before him. While help was coming, Thoreau climbed the highest rock of Fair Haven Cliff. "It was a glorious spectacle," he later wrote in his journal, "and I was the only one there to enjoy it." When sufficient help arrived, Thoreau descended from his perch and joined in the fire fighting. "The fire, we understand," said the Concord newspaper, "was communicated to the woods through the thoughtlessness of two of our citizens, who kindled it in a *pine stump,* near the Pond, for the purpose of making a chowder. As every thing around them was as combustible almost as a fireship, the flames spread with rapidity, and hours elapsed before it could be subdued." The newspaper spoke of the "sheer carelessness" of those who had started the fire. The whole town knew who these individuals were.

If this occurrence had in it an acting out of Thoreau's disdain for his fellowmen in the community, the flames that destroyed three hundred acres of woodland also expressed Thoreau's inner rage and his malaise. To treat the fire as a mere accident, as have most of those who have described it, is to overlook the fact that of all men in Concord Thoreau was the one who best knew that fires may not be lit out-of-doors without serious hazard. There was, however, a singular streak of blindness to certain details in Thoreau — he who prided himself on his practical knowledge and could be, when he was interested, all alertness and observation. Lowell spoke of this some years later when he wrote that "till he built his Walden shanty he did not know that the hickory grew in Concord. Till he went to Maine, he had never seen phosphorescent wood, a phenomenon familiar to most country boys. At forty he speaks of the seeding of the pine as a new discovery, though one should have thought that its gold dust of blowing pollen might have earlier drawn his eye. Neither his attention nor his genius was of the spontaneous kind." And in our time Joseph Wood Krutch has remarked that "reading the *Journal*, it is almost disconcerting to discover that at thirty-four he was not sure of the identity of the common thalictrum of the fields and that a year later he had to have help in naming a Luna moth!" The failure in alertness which led to the fire was but one of various such failures, those of a man in whom reverie could pre-empt immediate reality. The fire permanently established Thoreau in the minds of his fellows at Concord as a "woods-burner." The town could shrug its shoulders at his eccentricities. It could not, however, forgive so strange and serious a lapse which threatened life and its homes.

Thus less than a year before the retreat to Walden, Thoreau's reputation in Concord reached its lowest point. No one accused him of "sloth," for it was known how well he could work when he wanted to. The fire, however, caused some to speak of him as a "damned rascal." His journal of the time tells us nothing. Certain later entries show nevertheless that the incident rankled: he was enraged by its consequences: "Who are these men who are said to be the owners of these woods, and how am I related to them? I have set fire to the forest, but I have done no wrong therein, and now it is as if the lightning had done it. These flames are but consuming their natural food." This was written six years after the event. And he also wrote, "it has never troubled me from that day to this more than if the lightning had done it. The trivial fishing was all that disturbed me and disturbs me still." Only a man deeply troubled would write in this way so long afterward and deceive himself that he wasn't troubled. "I at once ceased to regard the owners and my fault — if fault there was in the matter — and attended to the phenomenon before me, determined to make the most of it. To be sure I felt a little ashamed when I reflected on what a trivial occasion this had happened, that at the time I was no better employed than my townsmen."

Thoreau's decision to move to Walden Pond seems to have been, on one level, a way of withdrawing from a town he experienced as hostile to him while at the same time remaining very close to it; a way also of asserting himself as an active "employed" man by embracing the career of writer and philosopher; an act of defiance which would demonstrate that his was a better way of life than that practiced by his fellows. Deeper still may have been the petulance of the child saying, in effect, to the town and to Emerson "see how homeless I am, you have forced me to live in a shanty away from all of you." He would arouse pity; he would also arouse interest. Some such jumble of motives lay behind his complex decision to give an impression of "hermiting" while not being a hermit. The epigraph he chose for *Walden* directly addresses the townspeople. It is a quotation from the book itself: "I do not propose to write an ode to dejection, but to brag as lustily as chanticleer in the morning, standing on his roost, if only to wake my neighbors up." On a subjective level, *Walden* reflects Thoreau's dejection: in the depths of the epigraph one hears the cry of a man who must vent his rage — and be heard by the entire town! That he was full of spleen during the spring of 1845 just before he built his cabin may be discerned in a letter written to him from New York by the younger William Ellery Channing. Channing seems to have provided the impulse for Thoreau's principal act: "I see nothing for you in this earth but that field which I once christened 'Briars'; go out upon that, build yourself a hut, and there begin the grand process of devouring yourself alive. I see no alternative, no other hope for you. Eat yourself up; you will eat nobody else, nor anything else." There is a fund of psychological truth in Channing's

answer to Thoreau's rage. Thoreau had long been devouring himself; he had said as much in the poem already quoted, "here I
bloom for a short hour unseen,/ Drinking my juices up."

Whatever the deeper motivation, Thoreau's conscious feelings
on his taking up his Walden residence are clearly expressed in his
book: "I went to the woods because I wished to live deliberately,
to front only the essential facts of life, and see if I could not learn
what it had to teach, and not, when I came to die, discover that I
had not lived. I did not wish to live what was not life, living is so
dear; nor did I wish to practise resignation, unless it was quite necessary. I wanted to live deep and suck out all the marrow of life, to
live so sturdily and Spartan-like as to put to rout all that was not
life, to cut a broad swath and shave close, to drive life into a corner,
and reduce it to its lowest terms, and, if it proved to be mean, why
then to get the whole and genuine meanness of it, and publish its
meanness to the world; or if it were sublime, to know it by experience, and be able to give a true account of it in my next excursion."

"Briars" consisted of a dozen acres beside Walden. The land
belonged to Emerson. With his friend's permission, Thoreau began in March 1845, after receiving Channing's letter, to clear a spot
and plan his cabin. Thus was inaugurated what would become the
great Thoreauvian myth; yet it was in its own time little more than
a rural comedy. Concord's idlest citizen, the woods-burning "rascal," a year after making himself notorious, builds himself a small
home on the town's outskirts. He will be a hermit. But he walks to
town almost daily; he chats with the townsfolk; he joins the idlers
around the grocery stove; he visits his home. He dines in the homes
of his friends. The diary of Mrs. J. T. Fields tells us much when
it records Thoreau's filial piety. Thoreau was "an excellent son,"
she noted, "and even when living in his retirement at Walden
Pond, would come home every day." At the same time he is thinking of a chapter in his book called "Where I Lived and What I
Lived For."

Literary criticism, if it wished to treat *Walden* (1854) as a work
of the imagination, might say that every poet lives in fancy rather
than in fact. But literary history, unlike literary criticism, is in

bondage to truth, and the truth is that Thoreau lived one kind of life and transformed it in his work into another — and then scolded his fellows for not following his ideals. Like his mother, who often put on grand airs in the town, Chanticleer crowed out of a world of make-believe. His first sentence in *Walden* announces: "When I wrote the following pages, or rather the bulk of them, I lived alone, in the woods, a mile from any neighbor, in a house which I had built myself, on the shore of Walden Pond, in Concord, Massachusetts, and earned my living by the labor of my hands only." History records, let us note in passing, that he did not write the bulk of these pages in the cabin; he took several years to complete the book, and what he wrote in the hut was *A Week on the Concord and Merrimack Rivers* — *Walden* was written largely in the family home; moreover much material was incorporated into it which belonged to other years than those of his Walden residence. He ends his first paragraph by saying "at present I am a sojourner in civilized life again." The words imply that he had been outside civilization when he lived in his cabin. Let us look at Thoreau's sojourn beyond "civilized life" as it is documented by his latest and most careful biographer, Walter Harding.

"It was not a lonely spot. The well-traveled Concord-Lincoln road was within sight across the field. The Fitchburg Railroad steamed regularly past the opposite end of the pond. Concord village was less than two miles away, and the Texas house [the Thoreau family house] was less than that along the railroad right-of-way. . . . Ellery Channing . . . visited the cabin often . . . It is true that his mother and sisters made a special trip out to the pond every Saturday, carrying with them each time some delicacy of cookery which he gladly accepted. And it is equally true that he raided the family cookie jar on his *frequent* [my italics] visits home. . . . The Emersons, too, frequently invited him to dinner as did the Alcotts and the Hosmers. They had all done so before he went to Walden Pond and continued the custom after he left. Rumor had it that every time Mrs. Emerson rang her dinner bell, Thoreau came bounding through the woods and over the fences to be first in line."

Thoreau's biographer points out that it was doubtful whether he could hear the dinner bell at such a distance, but the joke can be taken as symptomatic of something the town knew — that at Walden Thoreau's ear was cocked to the sounds of Concord: that he led neither the solitary nor the Spartan life his book later described. His mention in *Walden* of his dinings out suggests that he did not allow his "experiment" to change his customary social habits. "To meet the objections of some inveterate cavillers," he writes, "I may as well state, that if I dined out occasionally, as I always had done, and I trust shall have opportunities to do again, it was frequently to the detriment of my domestic arrangements. But the dining out, being, as I have stated, a constant element, does not in the least affect a comparative statement like this." The "comparative statement" included the following sentence: "It was fit that I should live on rice, mainly, who loved so well the philosophy of India."

"Hardly a day went by," Harding comments, "that Thoreau did not visit the village or was not visited at the Pond. . . . Emerson was, of course, a frequent visitor at the cabin. . . . On pleasant summer days Thoreau would often join the Emerson family on a picnic or a blueberrying party. . . . The Alcotts often took their friends out to the pond to see Thoreau. . . . The children of Concord were always happy to go out to Walden Pond and Thoreau was equally happy to have them."

Harding goes on: "Occasionally whole groups of Thoreau's friends came out together to the pond and swarmed into his little cabin. It became quite the fashion to hold picnics on his front doorstep. When it rained, his visitors took refuge inside. He had as many as twenty-five or thirty people inside the tiny cabin at one time. On August 1, 1846, the anti-slavery women of Concord held their annual commemoration of the freeing of the West Indian slaves on his doorstep and Emerson, W. H. Channing, and Rev. Caleb Stetson spoke to the assembled group. Afterward a picnic lunch was served to all the guests." There was also a "Walden Pond Society." This "consisted of those who spent their Sunday mornings out walking around Walden Pond enjoying the beauties of nature. Thoreau was unquestionably the high priest of that sect."

"Despite all the visitors," Thoreau's biographer concludes, "despite all his visits to Concord village and to his parents' home, despite his surveying and fence-building and carpentry, and despite the hours devoted to writing, it must not be forgotten that the experiment at Walden was primarily a period of solitude and of communion with nature for Thoreau." We can only ask, What kind of "experiment" was this — and what kind of "solitude"? By no definition of the word — and certainly not in terms of the traditional isolation and contemplation practiced by philosophers and visionaries throughout history — can Thoreau be said to have lived a solitary or even contemplative life at Walden. He "bivouacked there," wrote F. B. Sanborn, adding that he "really lived at home, where he went every day." He was thus a sojourner in civilized life; he was an observant "suburbanite"; he was simply a man who had at last acquired a room of his own, and accomplished this in a way which attracted the town's attention to himself. Young girls found excuses for knocking on his door and asking him for a drink of water; and if he pretended to be indifferent and handed them a dipper to drink from the pond, nothing could have been more satisfying. From being the town's idler, he was now the center of attention.

Thoreau is distinctly ambivalent in the chapter he writes on solitude. "I find it wholesome to be alone the greater part of the time. To be in company, even with the best, is soon wearisome and dissipating. I love to be alone." Yet he begins the very next chapter in *Walden* — which is called "Visitors" — by saying: "I think that I love society as much as most, and am ready enough to fasten myself like a bloodsucker for the time to any full-blooded man that comes in my way." By invoking his solitude at Walden, Thoreau was cultivating an illusion. He spent many hours alone, to be sure, and wandered far afield on lonely rambles: but no more alone than many an individual in his daily life. The real solitude of Thoreau's time was that of the men and women who traveled to America's heartland and who were totally cut off from society and thrown wholly upon their own resources. They faced danger; they learned the meaning of fear. Thoreau's experiment at no time posed for him any question of true aloneness, or of the terrors of the wilderness. Any momentary anxieties could be overcome by a swift walk to the homes of neighbors and kinfolk. Lewis and Clark, or Francis Parkman, might have laid much greater claim to genuine solitude, and the entire generation that ventured forth in the covered wagons. It may be of some significance that the subtitle "Life in the Woods" included in Thoreau's first edition of *Walden* was later dropped, perhaps in recognition that such a life had not been his true subject. Nor is it altogether clear that Thoreau was capable of facing the solitude of the prairies. In his struggle to keep his bundle of "vain strivings" together, in his deeply embedded state, he would have found the primeval forest terrifying and he would have fled the plains, to recover the protecting and embracing arm of the society he verbally repudiated. Sherman Paul has rightly observed that Thoreau's "stance as a philosopher made it clear that his demands on life were not simple or primitive."

To say this is to suggest that *Walden* is a book about a romanticized solitude Thoreau could not permit himself genuinely to experience. Thoreau's Concord life, in the midst of his eking out of his "scanty fare of vegetables" with fish; his curious account books of his frugality and economy; his proclamation of a style of life he approved of intellectually — but did not truly live — make for a paradoxical book. What are we to say of the passage in *Walden* in which Thoreau's fellowmen are scolded for not being as simple in their ways as he believed himself to be?

The pages he devotes to John Field, a shanty dweller and fishing companion, who struggles to provide for the simplest needs of his family, are an extraordinary piece of egotism written by a self-preoccupied and self-indulgent man. In arguing how simple life could be for Field — were he not misguided by social habits — Thoreau forgets that he speaks as a bachelor, living in a reasonably arrangeable world and squatting on Emerson's land. He closes his eyes altogether to Field's poverty. The passage is as cruel as it is sanctimonious: "I tried to help him with my experience, telling him that he was one of my nearest neighbors, and that I too, who came a-fishing here, and looked like a loafer, was getting my living like himself; that I lived in a tight, light, and clean house, which hardly cost more than the annual rent of such a ruin as his commonly amounts to; and how, if he chose, he might in a month or two build himself a palace of his own; that I did not use tea, nor coffee, nor butter, nor milk, nor fresh meat, and so did not have to work to get them; again, as I did not work hard, I did not have to eat hard, and it cost me but a trifle for my food; but as he began with tea, and coffee, and butter, and milk, and beef, he had to work hard to pay for them, and when he had worked hard he had to eat hard again to repair the waste of his system." This seems to have been delivered without a thought for Field's children, who needed the milk, butter, beef — all the nourishment Thoreau had had when he was a growing child and probably was now having in the hospitable homes of Concord. Hawthorne apparently had listened to this kind of homily, for he once noted that in Thoreau's presence "one feels ashamed of having any money, or a house to live in, or so much as two coats to wear."

"None of the brute creation requires more than Food and Shelter," Thoreau wrote in *Walden*, and when he amplified this he could add only clothing and fuel. Doubtless "brute creation" propagates without thought for the survival of the race; but what we see is that Thoreau left no place in his myth for the simple human affections. He discourses nobly on friendship and in a high intellectual way speaks of the nourishment men may derive from the meeting of their minds. Yet of the impulse to love, this lover of nature and worshipper of the simple life writes in *Walden* that "nature is hard to overcome, but she must be suppressed." By this he meant specifically that man must conquer the urge of sex. Thoreau's historians have strained to provide him with a history of love. There is obscure mention in his annals of a proposal of marriage; but the story is as strange as other episodes in his life. His poems show that he loved the young woman's younger brother; and he seems to have proposed only after his own brother was rejected by

the girl. His constituted character had no room for love for anyone save the ubiquitous "I" of his journal.

Walden is not a document, nor even the record of a calculated
experiment. It is a work of art pretending to be a documentary.
Thoreau talked as if he lived in the wilderness but he lived in the
suburbs. He furnished his home with pieces retrieved from Concord attics. We have seen that he plastered and shingled the cabin
when cold weather came. We know that he took his shoes to the
Concord cobbler; that he baked bread using purchased rye and
Indian meal; that he slept not in rough blankets but between
sheets. He gave himself the creature comforts few Americans in
the log cabins of the West could enjoy. James Russell Lowell, in
his celebrated essay, mercilessly denounces Thoreau's pretensions.
The "experiment" presupposes, he wrote, "all that complicated
civilization which it theoretically abjured. He squatted on another
man's land; he borrows an ax; his boards, his nails, his bricks, his
mortar, his books, his lamp, his fishhooks, his plough, his hoe, all
turn state's evidence against him as an accomplice in the sin of that
artificial civilization which rendered it possible that such a person
as Henry D. Thoreau should exist at all." But the author of *Walden* discovered that his whim of living in the woods caught the
fancy of audiences. Men and women were willing to listen to the
fiction of his rude economy as if he were Robinson Crusoe. It is
perhaps to Daniel Defoe that we may turn for a significant literary
predecessor. The writer who had pretended he was keeping a
journal of the plague year in London, long after the plague, who
could invent a story of a man confronting the loneliness of life on
a desert island, may be regarded as the forefather of Thoreau's
book. The narrative of *Walden* is a composite of Thoreau's experiences in and around Concord. The little facts are so assembled
as to constitute a lively fable. Thoreau blended his wide reading
and his purposeful observations to the need of a thesis: and in his
mind he had proved his "experiment" long before he began it. In
the process of ordering, assembling, imagining, and interpreting,
the artist often took possession of his data in a robust, humorous,
whimsical, paradoxical, hammered style.

Walden has moments of exquisite beauty when the disciplined verbal power finds a tone and a mood expressing Thoreau's deepest artistry: "This is a delicious evening, when the whole body is one sense, and imbibes delight through every pore. I go and come with a strange liberty in Nature, a part of herself. As I walk along the stony shore of the pond in my shirt-sleeves, though it is cool as well as cloudy and windy, and I see nothing special to attract me, all the elements are unusually congenial to me. The bullfrogs trump to usher in the night, and the note of the whippoorwill is borne on the rippling wind from over the water. Sympathy with the fluttering alder and poplar leaves almost takes away my breath; yet, like the lake, my serenity is rippled but not ruffled. These small waves raised by the evening wind are as remote from storm as the smooth reflecting surface. Though it is now dark, the wind still blows and roars in the wood, the waves still dash, and some creatures lull the rest with their notes. The repose is never complete. The wildest animals do not repose, but seek their prey now; the fox, and skunk, and rabbit, now roam the fields and woods without fear. They are Nature's watchmen, — links which connect the days of animated life." The lyrical absorption of the scene into the self and the communication of the senses is eloquent. The prose creates a mood of tranquillity.

So too Thoreau can endow his narrative with the cadence of a child's storybook: "Sometimes I rambled to pine groves, standing like temples, or like fleets at sea, full-rigged, with wavy boughs, and rippling with light, so soft and green and shady that the Druids would have forsaken their oaks to worship in them; or to the cedar wood beyond Flint's Pond, where the trees, covered with hoary blue berries, spiring higher and higher, are fit to stand before Valhalla, and the creeping juniper covers the ground with wreaths full of fruit; or to swamps where the usnea lichen hangs in festoons from the white-spruce trees, and toadstools, round tables of the swamp gods, cover the ground, and more beautiful fungi adorn the stumps, like butterflies or shells, vegetable winkles; where the swamp-pink and dogwood grow, the red alder-berry glows like eyes of imps, the waxwork grooves and crushes the hardest woods in its folds, and the wild-holly berries make the beholder forget his home with their beauty, and he is dazzled and tempted by nameless other wild forbidden fruits, too fair for mortal taste."

Walden belongs with the literature of imaginary voyages which yet possess, within the imagined, a great reality of their own. It contains a rustic charm, a tender lyricism in the pages devoted to the seasons and to animal life around the pond and in the neighboring woods. The book is composed of eighteen essays loosely strung together. They acquire their unity in the central themes of the work. Although Thoreau's residence lasted two years he telescoped it into a single year and drew upon materials out of more distant years. He begins in the early summer, and then goes through the autumn and the winter and the coming of spring, the eternal cycle of the seasons. If anything the winter sequence is the best written and the one most deeply felt. The embedded man is never happier than when the landscape is embedded in snow and the pond frozen over to its depths. Each chapter begins with poetic descriptions in which nature and the self merge; each chapter has its hortatory passages; and one suspects that generations of readers — when they have read Thoreau at all and not simply accepted his myth — have skipped the scoldings and the rooster-crowings and listened only to the poet of nature. F. O. Matthiessen long ago showed us the structure within the seeming discursiveness of *Walden*. Thoreau moves into his cabin after building it, and describes his manner of living; since reading is fundamental to it, his essay on this subject is placed early in the book; after that the sounds of nature and then the threnody of his fancied solitude. The life beside Walden is minutely described in the first six chapters. We then leave the cabin for the beanfield (the land was plowed with another's plow) and the nearby village. There is a long and striking passage on the railroad: Thoreau both likes and dislikes that symbol of power which has cut across the land. Then we come to his neighbors, the animal life, the pond in winter. If he records the cycles of nature and of animal life, he does not altogether record the human cycles from which he has removed himself — the fertilities of nature are scanted; the spring in which *Walden* ends is rather a spring of *r*ebirth.

Thoreau likes his paradoxes. He puns; he fondles placenames and the origin of words. And he is always the self-absorbed Narcissus at his pool: "A lake is the landscape's most beautiful and expressive feature. It is earth's eye; looking into which the beholder measures the depth of his own nature. . . . Walden is a perfect forest mirror, set round with stones as precious to my eye as if fewer or rarer. . . . It is a mirror which no stone can crack, whose quicksilver will never wear off, whose gilding Nature continually repairs." In his delight in this great natural mirror he is also the minute observer; and the pages devoted to the pond itself move from personal image to word pictures of light on water surface, underwater currents, dances of the water bugs, the poetry of the ripples, the great depths, the leaping of fish — a kind of nature ballet written in a prose closer to poetry than most of the poems Thoreau wrote. He cast, as Henry James observed, a kind of "spiritual interest" over all that he observed.

He is at his most imaginative — that is, his ear is perhaps truest to poetry — in the playful chapter in which he tells of his "brute neighbors" beginning with a sylvan dialogue between a Hermit and a Poet. One feels in the writing of these pages echoes of the playfulness of Carlyle; but in terms of posthumous influence this passage may have importance in its striking resemblance to the recurrent rhythms of James Joyce's *Finnegans Wake*. It was inevitable that Joyce, early in his "Anna Livia Plurabelle" section, should pun on "Concord and the Merrimake," for that chapter is compounded of river names and water imagery and associations. Thoreau's "Was that a farmer's noon horn which sounded from beyond the woods just now?" and Joyce's "Is that the Poolbeg flasher beyant, pharphar, or a fireboat coasting nyar the Kishna?" seem to have common stylistic origins and the entire Thoreauvian passage finds strong echoes — in an Irish accent — in passages in *Finnegans Wake*. Thoreau writes: "Hark! I hear a rustling of the leaves. Is it some ill-fed village hound yielding to the instinct of the chase? or the lost pig which is said to be in these woods, whose tracks I saw after the rain? It comes on apace; my sumachs and sweetbriers tremble." This has a singular rhythmic charm and one can find its parallel in Joyce. Did Thoreau and Joyce (who had much in common in their alienated temperaments) derive the rhythms and cadences from some common source? or did the Irish writer, in his exploration of rivers and water music, latch onto the peculiar Thoreauvian trouvaille of this chapter. In the strange world of letters in which songs sung in one country become new songs in another, the words of Thoreau by the Concord River have a powerful kinship with those of Joyce by the Liffey.

The "private business" which Thoreau wished to transact at Walden included the writing of a long-planned book, a record of a journey he had made with his brother John when he was twenty-two. John had died three years later and *A Week on the Concord and Merrimack Rivers* (1849) was both a record and a memorial. It is divided into the days of the week, where *Walden* would be shaped according to the changing seasons — as if Thoreau were saying that youth can count but in hours and days while maturity knows the cycles of eternity. *A Week* contains much that is illustrative of Thoreau's philosophy; yet criticism has rightly called it overwritten and self-conscious; it is a mixture of description and homily, of gathered facts and sensitivity, with Thoreau's own poems interlarded between passages. One might call it a mental scrapbook; only in part is it travel narrative, so that anthologists are often prompted to winnow out the contemplative digressions. "We were bid to a river party — not to be preached at," Lowell remarked. But he praised the language as having "an antique purity like wine grown colorless with age." The book contains the lore of the fisherman and nature lover, a personal sense of scene and landscape and a number of little insets culled from history, as for example, the story of an early settler, a pioneer woman who, taken prisoner by the Indians after they had killed her newborn infant, avenged herself by scalping her captors while they slept and collected a bounty for the scalps. Thoreau tells this bloody tale with historical art. But to reach such passages we wade through the tedium of private sermons set down without feeling for the book's essential unity. In *A Week* Thoreau is learning how to write *Walden.*

If *A Week* remembers, in part, the ecstasy of youth, it is a book written with a sense of lost childhood and adolescence. A significant link between it and *Walden* may be found in a quotation (in *A Week*) from the Chinese writer Mencius (Meng-tzu): "If one loses a fowl or a dog, he knows well how to seek them again; if one loses the sentiments of his heart, he does not know how to seek them again. . . . The duties of practical philosophy consist only in seeking after those sentiments of the heart which we have lost; that is all." It seems clear that between the writing of *A Week* and of *Walden* Thoreau came to feel that the sentiments of his heart were irrecoverable, for in *Walden* we read his celebrated parable which harks back to this quotation. It is set down almost irrelevantly with a remark that readers would pardon some "obscurities, for there are more secrets in my trade than in most men's." "I long ago lost a hound, a bay horse, and a turtledove, and am still on their trail. Many are the travellers I have spoken concerning them, describing their tracks and what calls they answered to. I have met one or two who had heard the hound, and the tramp of the horse, and even seen the dove disappear behind a cloud, and they seemed as anxious to recover them as if they had lost them themselves." The obscurity of the parable disappears when it is placed beside the quotation from Mencius. What is more we can read a deeper secret than the loss of youth's first ecstasies. The symbols Thoreau uses represent the most faithful animals in man's life — his dog, guide, companion, devoted beyond the devotion of humans to his master, and his horse, a bay, a handsome animal, which embodies man's thrust, his drive, his animal instincts. A horse carries man and gives him a sense of support and direction. And finally the loss of the turtledove admits to a loss of love and tenderness, symbol of delicacy and affection. A man so bereft had indeed to seek comfort in cold thought. The parable speaks for an eternal quest for the ideal. It also tells us that Thoreau felt he had lost touch with the deepest part of himself — his instincts, his animal nature, with which all

men must make some kind of truce. And so like the Eastern philosophers whom he read, he transcends this part of himself. He sits by
a pond and meditates but only partly in serenity and humility.
His thoughts often express petulance and anger, of a deeply irrational kind. Behind his mask of peace, Thoreau was not at peace
with himself.

No discussion of Thoreau's writings can overlook his debt to
the East, and particularly to India. Through Emerson he came to
the *Bhagavad Gita*; he read the *Veda* and the *Upanishads* and in
these writings, filled with permissive religiosity, and an exaltation
of the quest for the self, showing the way to renunciation and contemplation, he discovered a body of belief highly congenial to his
own anarchist nature. He understood the East, however, as a West-
erner possessing a philosophy of doing as well as of meditation.
Robert Louis Stevenson recognized this when he wrote, "It was his
ambition to be an Oriental philosopher; but he was always a very
Yankee sort of Oriental."

Thoreau's stance was of a Buddha in Concord; that he called
himself an "inspector of snow storms" in itself underlines the essential difference between him and the Eastern writers he read.
They did not think of themselves as "inspectors" of anything, not
even of their own state of being. Thoreau sought in them confir-
mation of his own feelings and solace for his own needs. His inner
restlessness was too great, he was too troubled to arrive at their
kind of peace. He was eclectic, empirical, bent on self-improvement; and it might suggest the difference between him and the
Eastern philosophers if we remind ourselves that Chōmei lived for
thirty years in his hut and made of it a continuous way of life where
Thoreau, after two years, "left the woods for as good a reason as I
went there." He added, "Perhaps it seemed to me that I had several more lives to live, and could not spare any more time for that
one." The idea of having no time to spare for what he had first
asserted as a transcendent way of existence, and of seeking instead
a pluralistic existence — here the American distinctly parted with
the Oriental. But where he was at one with them was often in his
address to the immediate, in his attempt — not always successful —

to see the object unadorned by subjective distortion. That he often failed we must write down to his inner disorganization. In his moments of serenity he arrived, a poetic fancy aiding, at insight; and he sometimes told these insights in the Eastern manner as we have seen, in enigmatic parables which force realization and awaken thought.

The "private business" Thoreau transacted at Walden represented one side of his mind and art; the public business he embraced thereafter has left its mark on mankind. Thoreau was that well-known figure, a man who can accept no authority but himself and who can become, in his moments of eloquence, the voice of the multitude against abuse of authority. Such individuals often waver between utopia and reality; in dismissing authority they offer no viable solution to man's constant need for order. That man has never achieved such order — as witness the barbaric wars of the twentieth century and the ensuing chaos — only certifies the dilemma. And because the dilemma has been constant in all history, man must reiterate in every age a need for fundamental freedom. Such a reiteration leads to action, nearly always violent, and violent even when it calls itself nonviolent. Coercion in any form, even in passive resistance, is violent. These are the ambiguities and the cruel alternatives fate has offered man, making him an eternal seeker of rationality in an ever-irrational world.

Thoreau was sufficiently rational when in 1846 he came into Concord from Walden to take his shoes to the cobbler and was arrested by the town jailer for failure to pay the poll tax. He had refused to pay because he would have no truck with government and in particular a government which waged the Mexican war and condoned slavery. That the government on its side would simply collect the tax from the jailer if he in turn could not collect it from Thoreau did not concern him. This was of course a cycle of coercion, and Thoreau's action did not alter the iniquity, indeed it compounded it. Bronson Alcott earlier had acted similarly and also been freed by a tax-paying friend. Mrs. Alcott wrote that "we were spared the affliction of his absence and he the triumph of suffering for his principles." Thoreau was distinctly deprived of such a triumph. But his indignation persisted. Two years later he expressed it in his lecture on "Civil Disobedience."

It is his most celebrated essay. He tells the story of his night's imprisonment with considerable charm and a certain whimsicality; the story is set into his simple argument calling upon men to offer noncompliance when their conscience dictates it — what came to be called "passive resistance," Gandhi's *Satyagraha*. In practice it has proved to be a passive way of making revolution; that it also can lead to violence does not alter its effectiveness in certain conditions. It cannot be effective in all conditions: one knows that had humans placed themselves on roadways to stop Nazi tanks, the Nazis would have ridden over them. Thoreau's civil disobedience presupposes a high state of conscience; and it presupposes also a form of principle tolerable only in a society which has moved beyond barbarism. "The only obligation which I have a right to assume is to do at any time what I think right," Thoreau said, and implicit in this is the grandeur of great libertarians but also the violence of John Brown.

"Civil Disobedience" is an unusually cogent statement for Thoreau, who was a man of sentiment rather than of profound thought and who tended often to contradict himself. It remains a remarkable statement on behalf of individualism, as well as man's right to oppose and dissent. In the frame of Thoreau's life, however, it reveals the arbitrary nature of his philosophy. His defense of John Brown, with his espousal of violence in that instance, is hardly the voice of the same man. In both lectures, to be sure, Thoreau condemns government; but the preacher of nonviolence suddenly forgets his preachings. Brown had been wantonly destructive; he had staged a brutal massacre in Kansas and killed innocents. He was a man whose fanaticism might have made him in other circumstances a brutal Inquisitor. Thoreau's involvement in his cause has in it strong elements of hysteria. The passive countenance closes it eyes to truth; it sees only Brown's cause and Brown's hatred of authority. It does not see his cruelty or his counterimposition of authority. The world has wisely chosen to remember "Civil Disobedience" rather than the three John Brown lectures.

Whether the personal anarchism Thoreau preached is possible in every age remains to be seen. In his philosophy Thoreau saw only his own dissent; he seems not to have thought of the dangers of tyranny by a minority, as of a majority.

As we survey the volumes of Thoreau's writings, the two completed books, the miscellaneous essays published posthumously, the poems and letters, what looms largest are the fourteen volumes of Thoreau's journals (1906) to which another volume was added in recent times on discovery of a lost notebook (1958). The journal was the mirror of his days; but it is not an autobiographical record in the usual sense. It is one of the more impersonal journals of literary history. Thoreau made it the account book of his days. There are notes on his readings, his observations of nature, his record of walks, scraps of talk, observations of neighbors; on occasion the journal becomes a log, a statistical record. He began to keep it when he was twenty and he kept it until his death a quarter of a century later. It tends to be discursive, sprawling, discontinuous. One finds in it much matter-of-factness and little feeling. "The poet must keep himself unstained and aloof," said Thoreau and his journal is distinctly "aloof." One discerns in it a continuing note of melancholy; there is little humor; the vein is always one of high seriousness. Mankind is regarded in the mass; the generalizations are large; there is not much leaning toward the precisions of science. Nor can one find any record of growth in these pages, some of them turgid and dull, others lucid and fascinating. From 1837 to 1861 we see the same man writing; he has learned little. If one notes a difference it is that he begins by being philosophical and in the end is more committed to observation.

The journal suggests that Thoreau was incapable of a large effort as a writer. He learned to be a master of the short, the familiar essay; he made it lively and humanized it with his whimsicalities. The method of the journal was carried over into his principal works, the journal providing the raw data, filed always for later use. Perry Miller admirably showed how Thoreau labored to convert these data into literary material. The assiduity with which

he applied himself to his writing ultimately bore fruit. If Thoreau
never forged a style and filled his work with the echoes of other
styles, he nevertheless in the end learned his trade. Possessing no
marked ego at the beginning of his adult life, he created a composite ego; and he learned to write by using a series of rhetorical
tricks. Emerson recognized Thoreau's exaggerated mannerisms
when he noted in his journal that "the trick of his rhetoric is soon
learned; it consists in substituting for the obvious word and
thought its diametrical antagonist. He praises wild mountains and
winter forests for their domestic air; snow and ice for their warmth;
villagers and woodchoppers for their urbanity, and the wilderness
for resembling Rome and Paris." There were times, as in the description of the battle of the ants as if it were the Trojan war,
when this trick of exaggeration is markedly successful. But after
a while it tends to become tedious and seems like a tic, as Perry
Miller remarked. Lowell aptly characterized the style when he
said Thoreau turns "commonplaces end for end, and fancies it
makes something new of them." He added that Thoreau "had
none of the artistic mastery which controls great work to the serene
balance of completeness, but exquisite mechanical skill in shaping
of sentences and paragraphs."

Lowell, Emerson, and of all writers, Robert Louis Stevenson
wrote essays on Thoreau which characterized him more carefully
and perceptively than most of his worshippers have since done.
But because these were essays which were measured and critical
of the man as reflected in his work, they have been dismissed as un-
generous and irrelevant. Indeed Lowell's brilliant essay has been
called "infamous," perhaps because its criticism was uncompromising and lacked the urbanity and delicacy of Stevenson's. Lowell
was a gregarious man; he met the world as he found it; he could
therefore recognize the alienated side of Thoreau and see the profound narcissism of his nature — although he called it by another
name. He said of Thoreau that he made "his own whim the law,
his own range the horizon of the universe," and noted that he
"confounded physical with spiritual remoteness from men." Emerson's judgments were contained in his funeral oration and they are

stated with considerable subtlety. We have but to ponder a remark such as that Thoreau "chose wisely, no doubt, for himself, to be the bachelor of thought and nature" to recognize that Emerson is defining what was most absent from Thoreau's life — human love, and the give and take an individual must learn in his human relatedness. Stevenson noted the absence of "geniality" in Thoreau, "the smile was not broad enough," and like Emerson he spoke of Thoreau's failure to allow himself "the rubs and trials of human society." In a sentence of considerable point for our time, Stevenson equated drug taking with this kind of alienation. "A man who must separate himself from his neighbor's habits in order to be happy, is in much the same case with one who requires to take opium for the same purpose." Perhaps the best known part of Stevenson's essay was his characterization of Thoreau's views of friendship. He "does not give way to love any more than to hatred," wrote Stevenson, "but preserves them both with care, like valuable curiosities. A more bald-headed picture of life, if I may so express myself, or a more selfish, has seldom been presented . . . Thoreau is dry, priggish and selfish. It is profit he is after in these intimacies; moral profit, certainly, but still profit to himself. If you will be the sort of friend I want, he remarks naively, 'my education cannot dispense with your society.' His education! as though a friend were a dictionary. And with all this, not a word about pleasure, or laughter, or kisses, or any quality of the flesh and blood. It was not inappropriate, surely, that he had such close relations with the fish." Emerson spoke with great candor of Thoreau's aggressivity: "There was something military in his nature not to be subdued, always manly and able, but rarely tender, as if he did not feel himself except in opposition. He wanted a fallacy to expose, a blunder to pillory, I may say he required a little sense of victory, a roll of the drum, to call his powers into full exercise. It cost him nothing to say No; indeed he found it much easier than to say Yes. It seemed as if his first instinct on hearing a proposition was to controvert it, so impatient was he of the limitations of our daily thought. This habit, of course, is a little chilling to the social affections; and though the companion would in the end acquit him of any malice or untruth, yet it mars conversation. Hence, no equal companion stood in affectionate relations with one so pure and guileless. 'I love Henry,' said one of his friends, 'but I cannot like him; and as for taking his arm, I should as soon think of taking the arm of an elm-tree.' "

Men will continue to discover these strange ambiguities in the author of *Walden*. If we are to dress a literary portrait of him, we must place him among those writers in whom the human will is organized to a fine pitch in the interest of mental and emotional survival. We must rank him with the "disinherited" and the alienated, with the writers who find themselves possessed of unconquerable demons and who then harness them in the service of self-preservation. Out of this quest sometimes mere eccentricity emerges; at other times art. There are distinct pathological traits in Thoreau, a constant sense — a few have discerned it — of inner disintegration which leads Thoreau in his *Walden* imagery to a terrible vision of human decay. One may venture a guess that this little observed Poesque streak in Thoreau testified to a crisis of identity so fundamental that Thoreau rescued himself only by an almost superhuman self-organization to keep himself, as it were, from falling apart. In doing this he clung obsessively to nature. A much deeper history of Thoreau's psyche may have to be written to explain his tenuous hold on existence in spite of the vigor of his outdoor life: his own quiet desperation, his endless need to keep a journal ("as if he had no moment to waste," said his friend Channing), and his early death of tuberculosis at forty-five in Concord during the spring of 1862. His works were the anchor of his days. He overcame dissolution during his abbreviated life by a constant struggle to assert himself in words. Some such strivings shaped his own recognition of his "crooked genius."

His brief journeys and his writings about them enabled others after his death to put together the volumes published as *Excursions* (1863), *The Maine Woods* (1864), *Cape Cod* (1865), and *A Yankee in Canada* (1866). He had, as he said, "travelled a good deal in Concord"; and it is in that setting that his myth is best recognized and best understood.

RICHARD CHASE

Walt Whitman

NEARLY everyone agrees that Walt Whitman is America's greatest poet. But many Americans agree reluctantly or grudgingly and, perhaps because the influential contemporary critics of poetry — "the new critics" — have either scorned or ignored Whitman, they do not trouble to discern the true qualities of Whitman's poetry but content themselves with admitting that in some undefined way it is "powerful." Yet even those readers who hail Whitman's greatness with enthusiasm and read him with ever-renewed pleasure do not always find it easy to say precisely what it is about the poems that they admire. The true qualities of Emily Dickinson's poetry, for example, or of Wordsworth's or T. S. Eliot's or Donne's can be more readily defined than can the true qualities of Whitman's. And we can more readily state the quality of our pleasure in these poets than we can in the case of Whitman. He is elusive, both as man and as poet.

Consider the first two lines of *Leaves of Grass* (here as elsewhere I quote from the later editions of *Leaves of Grass* without attention to the differences of detail which sometimes exist between these and the early editions):

> One's-self I sing, a simple separate person,
> Yet utter the word Democratic, the word En-Masse.

There is a disconcerting abstractness and generality about that
"One's-self." We would expect the poet to say "Myself," but we
discover that even when he does, in "Song of Myself," he still gives
us very little concrete information about a man named Walt Whitman. The poet described *Leaves of Grass* as in effect an autobiography — "an attempt from first to last, to put a *Person*, a human
being (myself, in the latter half of the nineteenth century in
America) freely, fully and truly on record." But there is much less
of direct, concrete autobiography in *Leaves of Grass* than, say, in
Wordsworth's *Prelude*. In fact we discover, after reading *Leaves
of Grass* carefully, that what Whitman has put on record is not
"myself" but, as the quotation above suggests, a "Person" — or
better, a persona or series of personae. In order to understand
Whitman's enormous, sprawling, uneven book, we will have to
understand something about the origin and nature of these self-
projected images which are only equivocally the "real" Whitman.
And of course Whitman projected images of himself in life as well
as in his poetry (they are often the same ones). He was an inveterate poseur and he had more than a little vanity. His well-known,
carefully cultivated poses include the worldly dandy we briefly
glimpse in the early 1840's; the somewhat Christlike carpenter and
radical of the early fifties; the bearded, well-bathed, burly, bluff
"camerado" of later years; then the male nurse and good gray poet
of his Washington years; and finally the venerable sage of Camden.
Whitman was in his way an intellectual as well as a highly unorthodox poet. He had his neurotic side — covert, bisexual, quirky,
elusive, power-seeking, bohemian, libidinous, indolent. Which is
to say that Whitman's poses were not mere play-acting but arose
from a deep maladjustment to the nineteenth-century America he
lived in. One cannot always be sure whether he became the celebrant of this America in spite of or because of his maladjustment;
both possibilities are involved.

Many modern readers are likely to be made uneasy by Whitman's announcement that he is going to "sing" one's-self. But we
should not forget that traditionally poets, particularly if they were
prophetic or epic poets, did "sing," rather than fabricate what a

contemporary critic of poetry would probably call a "symbolic construct." Of course, Whitman often "sang" stridently and, in the bad sense, "rhetorically." Some American readers will connect with Whitman's singing what they consider his immoderate chauvinism, his spread-eagleism, his sometimes philistine celebration of America's material success. But by now our traditional sense of cultural inferiority, vis-à-vis Europe, has certainly gone by the board and we need no longer be embarrassed by Whitman's vaunting Americanism (the Europeans have always loved it). It is becoming increasingly easy to find his philistinism not only excusable but, on occasion, delightfully characteristic. For example, in "Song of the Exposition" we hear Whitman hailing the Muse of poetry as the "illustrious emigré" who has come to America to observe its advanced technology. She is

> Bluff'd not a bit by drain-pipe, gasometers,
>   artificial fertilizers,
> Smiling and pleas'd with palpable intent to
>   stay,
> She's here, install'd amid the kitchen ware!

These pleasingly comical lines are certainly not among Whitman's greatest utterances, but neither are they likely to do any damage to culture.

Whitman promises to sing "a simple, separate person," yet before we have read very far in *Leaves of Grass* or very much about the poet by his biographers, we see that neither Whitman nor the images of himself that he projects can be described as "simple" — far from it. We see too that there is difficulty in that word *separate*. We discover that the so-called "separate" person, or self, is always merging with other persons or with the "En-Masse" or becoming an abstraction. And sometimes the poems make us feel not only that the "person" is separate in the sense of being self-reliant or integral ("Me imperturbe, standing at ease in Nature"), and in the sense that he is a citizen in a democracy with a vote as good as any other man's, but that this person's separateness becomes a radical alienation which seems to carry him almost to the point of loving death. For Whitman is indeed a poet who can think of death (in the memorable words of Wallace Stevens) as "the mother of beauty."

We note the paradox involved in one of Whitman's key words — *identity* — when we read that besides singing the individual, he is going to "utter the word Democratic." Naturally enough the democratic paradox is the central metaphor of *Leaves of Grass*, arising from the double allegiance of democratic man, on the one hand, to the inviolable integrity of the self and, on the other, to the united body of all men. In Whitman's poems the individual "identity" is always identifying itself and then, as it were, unidentifying itself with the "En-Masse." This often becomes disconcerting and is inevitably one of the origins of the diffuseness, vagueness, and lack of inner structure and dramatic tension which characterize much of Whitman's verse. For example, in "Starting from Paumanok" (the piece that serves as a kind of poetic table of contents for *Leaves of Grass*), we read:

> Victory, union, faith, identity, time,
> The indissoluble compacts, riches, mystery,
> Eternal progress, the kosmos, and the modern reports.

Intriguing perhaps, but it is far from perfectly clear what is being talked about, except that in some way in modern America the individual becomes integral in his separateness to the extent that he is absorbed into the indissoluble union of all men. Out of this paradox arises all the strength and weakness of Whitman's poetry, and it is here that we must begin to look for the meaning of this poetry, rather than in his real or fancied relation to Neo-Platonism, Hegelianism, mysticism, and all the other philosophical or religious isms that Whitman scholars have so much overemphasized.

Ever since D. H. Lawrence's *Studies in Classic American Literature*, critics have been elaborating on Lawrence's perception of the "doubleness" or "duplicity" of our best writers — Cooper, Hawthorne, Melville, Mark Twain, for example. We do not perhaps think of Whitman at first as being available to this kind of approach. We are likely to think of him as the uncomplicated, optimistic, basically unquestioning celebrant of democratic man and his untroubled progress in an open, pragmatic world. And of course

Whitman *is* this celebrant. Yet, as I have pointed out, merely by *being* the bard of democracy, Whitman involves himself in "doubleness" and contradiction. Then we recall the poems in which death figures so prominently; we recall the vituperative criticism of democracy in *Democratic Vistas*; we take note of his carefully maintained poses; and we cannot help thinking that there is complexity and contradiction in Walt Whitman, as well as in the other classic authors. "I cannot understand the mystery," Whitman wrote in a notebook perhaps as early as 1847, "but I am always conscious of myself as two." In the notebook he conjectures that the "two" are "my soul and I" and in his poetry he was later to discover many ways of expressing the "two." A central metaphor of the great poem "Crossing Brooklyn Ferry" is Whitman's statement that "I too knitted the old knot of contrariety." And when he gets off the famous (to some people notorious) lines in "Song of Myself,"

> Do I contradict myself?
> Very well then I contradict myself,
> (I am large, I contain multitudes),

he is not merely indulging in bravado or apologizing for contradictions of logic or fact. He is stating a basic truth about himself and his poetry. No doubt Whitman's mind is not so complex or his contradictions so drastic as, say, Melville's. And no doubt his poetry is totally unlike what we often think of as the poetry of paradox — that of Donne and the other metaphysical poets, for example. Nevertheless, the way to understand Whitman and his best poems is to learn what we can about how he knitted his knot of contrariety.

Whitman was in truth the "slow arriver" he called himself, for he was well into maturity when the first edition of *Leaves of Grass* was published in 1855. He had been born in 1819, at West Hills, Long Island, the second of nine children, several of whom turned out to be of unsound mental and physical constitution. His father was a not too successful carpenter, and Walt seems to have derived little from this apparently morose and inarticulate man except a belief in the more radical wing of Jeffersonian-Jacksonian politics.

His mother was the mainstay of the family, as is suggested by the daguerreotype that shows her broad, firm, pensive face. Walt's lifelong attachment to his nearly illiterate mother is one of the remarkable and ennobling facts of his life. His mother was "the most perfect and magnetic character, the rarest combination of practical, moral, and spiritual, and the least selfish, of all and any I have ever known, and by me O so much the most deeply loved." But moving as this utterance is (made on the occasion of his mother's death), we must see in it the origin of Whitman's never successfully established sexuality, with its apparent bisexual quality tending toward the homosexual.

The move of the Whitmans to Brooklyn when Walt was four was only one of several that occurred during his childhood and youth and that contributed to the generally unsettled and anxious life the family lived. As he said in later years "the time of my boyhood was a very restless and unhappy one; I did not know what to do." After a certain amount of desultory schooling, Walt worked in various capacities for newspapers and printers. He even tried his hand at teaching school. But it was newspaper work that he was drawn to, and by 1846 the somewhat indolent young man had worked hard enough at it to become the editor, for two years, of the *Brooklyn Eagle*, a flourishing paper which expressed the opinions of the Democratic party and made Whitman something of a public figure in the rapidly growing town. His life continued to be unsettled, after the *Eagle* editorship, although we do hear of his sometimes assisting his father on carpentering jobs. During the years before 1855 doubtless his real employment was an inner one — the gradual evolution in his mind of the remarkable book he was to publish, setting the type himself, in that year.

There will always seem to be something miraculous about the first edition of *Leaves of Grass*, with its showpiece, the (then untitled) "Song of Myself." How did this editor, saunterer, loafer, schoolteacher, small-time politico, opera-goer, and (as we may guess) mediocre carpenter come to be one of the world's great poets? Of course, there can be no final answer to this question, even if we had many more materials to work with than we have.

There is next to nothing in Whitman's newspaper writing to suggest a gradually emerging set of ideas or a style that in any specific sense forecasts *Leaves of Grass.* Whitman's early notebooks are sparse and hardly suggest, any more than do the few early poems that survive, the qualities of the poetry in the 1855 edition. Lacking these materials, we are tempted to conjecture whether some decisive event in Whitman's life may have at once freed and consolidated his powers of intellect, emotion, and imagination. Whitman worked in New Orleans on a newspaper called the *Crescent* in the spring of 1848, and the so-called "New Orleans episode" has always figured prominently in the speculations of his biographers. Can the not so young man (he was 29) have been awakened emotionally by the Paris of the South? Did he become involved with a woman for the first time — perhaps, as some shadowy evidence suggests, an octoroon? Is there any truth in Whitman's statements in a letter of 1890 to John Addington Symonds that he was the father of six illegitimate children, and that "My life, young manhood, mid-age, times South, etc., have been jolly bodily"? This famous letter, as it goes on, *sounds* like a patent fabrication (which could be beautifully read by W. C. Fields — "Though unmarried I have had six children — two dead — one living Southern grandchild, fine boy, writes to me occasionally"), but it is possible that there is truth in it. Yet Whitman's sexuality seems to have been diffuse, somewhat infantile, and except for periods of anxiety (of which his notebook jottings give evidence) not directed toward women. It is therefore most unlikely that a passionate love affair occurred in New Orleans, or that, even if it did, it could have had much to do with the awakening of emotional power which produced the poems of 1855, a full seven years after his New Orleans sojourn.

The conjecture has also been made that Whitman at some time before 1855, after various unhappy sexual attempts, came to realize that he was homosexual and that his acceptance of this freed him of inhibitions and gave power and form to his imagination. But he seems actually to have been bisexual rather than truly homosexual. The conjecture has also been advanced that Whitman may have had some overwhelming mystical experience which changed the whole course of his life — perhaps like the blinding light that struck down St. Paul on the road to Damascus. The objection to both of these speculations is, first, that there is no evidence for them and, second, that they both assume in Whitman a capacity for sudden and dramatic changes in his nature. Such changes are of course possible in some personalities and have been decisive in the emergence of many poets. But this does not seem possible in the life of Walt Whitman, whose emotional experience, except in his best poems, was diffuse and who, as I have said, accurately described himself as a "slow arriver."

What can be said, then, about the embryon period (Whitman would like the expression) of *Leaves of Grass*? A full discussion, which of course cannot be launched here, might well begin with two quotations from the poet. First there is his statement that "I was simmering, simmering, simmering. Emerson brought me to a boil." Second there is his remark that his journalistic writing (he is talking about his contributions to the *Democratic Review,* but the words apply as well to nearly everything he wrote before *Leaves of Grass*) "came from the surface of the mind, and had no connection with what lay below — a great deal of which indeed was below consciousness. At last came the time when the concealed growth had to come to light."

In Emerson's essays Whitman read much about the self and its all but autonomous power, and the plight and destiny of the self was to become Whitman's real subject. Less serene and isolated from life than Emerson, more instinctively aware of the powers of the unconscious, he was gradually able to free the latent powers of his unconscious mind and through poetry endow the self with these powers, so that the self became for him not merely a moral or mystical entity as it tends to be in Emerson, not merely one term in the political paradox of the self vs. society, but the decisive part of a poetic metaphor — the other part of which is, variously, other selves, nature, or society. The characteristic quality of Whitman's best poetry arises either from the dramatic (often comic) tensions evoked when the self is shown to be in a state of contradiction or

polarity to the not-self or from the lyric harmony, often meditative, retrospective, and "mystical," which is evoked when the self
is felt to be identical with the not-self or some aspect of it. The
poems which do not in some way involve the metaphor of the self
are more likely than not to be inert catalogues, empty rhetoric,
"cosmic," vague, or in other ways unsatisfactory.

We can trace the process by which the idea of the self was endowed with emotional power in Whitman's highly significant
though not entirely successful poem called "The Sleepers," with
its hauntingly dreamlike (though at first apparently miscellaneous)
images of the shipwreck, the "beautiful gigantic swimmer" who
becomes a "brave corpse," George Washington bidding a fatherly
farewell to his soldiers, and above all the mother, who is seen variously as having a shadowy lover, as a "sleepless widow" looking at
the coffin of her husband, and as an Indian squaw who resembles
a goddess. Doubtless it is all too easy to say that Whitman has performed the therapeutic act of becoming able symbolically to represent his unconscious desire to kill his father and possess his
mother; but it is not irrelevant to say so. Whitman at any rate
conceives of the poem as narrating the descent of the conscious
mind into the perilous night and then emerging with new strength.
Before the descent the poet describes himself as "wandering, confused, lost to myself, ill-assorted, contradictory." But his mood
afterwards — aggressive, self-confident, creative — is suggested by
the following:

> I am a dance — play up there! the fit is whirling me fast! . . .
> Onward we move, a gay gang of blackguards! with mirth-
> shouting music and wild-flapping pennants of joy!

This brief discussion will perhaps suggest that there was nothing
mysterious about Whitman's emergence as a poet, except the general mystery of the emergence of genius. We do not, in any case,
require an octoroon or an influx of cosmic light to account for it.

When *Leaves of Grass* appeared in 1855 readers (of whom
there were very few indeed) discovered therein twelve untitled
poems and a preface explaining the poet's view of poetry and its
purpose. The poet, Whitman says, must not content himself with

making beautifully contrived verses. He must be a prophet, a seer, a bard, a teacher, and a moralist. Not that, as a moralist, the poet teaches improving lessons or preaches uprightness. He is a moralist in the sense that he speaks for — "promulges," Whitman likes to say — the future and for democracy. His aim is "to cheer up slaves and horrify despots." But he is a spiritual leader, too; for the age of religion is past and the poet must assume the role of the priest. He must make himself the most perfect of men, the archetype of the spiritually and organically normal. "Of all mankind the great poet is the equable man. Not in him but off from him things are grotesque or eccentric or fail of their sanity. . . . He is the arbiter of the diverse and he is the key." Also the poet is a kind of spokesman for his people. His is not only an individual voice but also the voice of his nation. "He incarnates its geography and natural life and rivers and lakes." But more than that, the poet, seeing "the beauty and sacredness of the demonstrable," abandons the conventional myths of traditional poetry and shapes "solid and beautiful forms of the future," providing his countrymen (as Whitman was to argue more at length in *Democratic Vistas*) with native archetypes of the imagination and modes of instinctive response and feeling which will give coherence to a new and still unformed civilization. He rejects no fact of life from his poems; yet he is not a "realist": his poetry "is to be transcendent and new; it is to be indirect and not direct or descriptive or epic." As for the form of poems, they are to be "organic," evolving free metrical patterns "as unerringly and loosely as lilacs or roses on a bush." And it is significant that Whitman uses the phrase "poems or music or orations or recitation," because his poems often have a musical structure — so much so that sometimes we can follow the patterns of aria and recitative in his poetry as Whitman had learned them from the Italian operas he loved so well. And he thinks too that the poem is in a sense an oration, meant to be "sung" or declaimed; Whitman was in fact a would-be orator and made several attempts to become a public speaker or lecturer.

It is clear that the Bible had a deep influence on Whitman's style. The opening lines of "Song of Myself" are:

> I celebrate myself, and sing myself,
> And what I assume you shall assume,
> For every atom belonging to me as good belongs to you.
>
> I loafe and invite my soul,
> I lean and loafe at my ease observing a spear
>   of summer grass.

If we compare this with any one of innumerable passages from the Bible — say Psalm 8 — we see one of the main origins of Whitman's mode of versification.

> What is man, that thou art mindful of him? And the
>   son of man, that thou visitest him?
>
> For thou hast made him a little lower than the angels,
>   and hast crowned him with glory and honor.
>
> Thou madest him to have dominion over the works of
>   thy hands; thou hast put all things under his feet.

Characteristically, Whitman's "organic" style, like that of Hebrew poetry, is based on the device of "parallelism." His rhythms are those of repetition — of word, image, or idea — and counterbalance of phrases and lines. His poems proceed through cycles of statement and restatement, the restatement providing the poem with momentum because it not only restates but at the same time amplifies, modulates, or qualifies what has been said and prepares us, it may be, for the next rhythmic cycle.

There is no tightly knit over-all structure to "Song of Myself." But in general the "plot" of the poem can be called the gradual universalization of the self. The first four sections present the leading themes and motifs of the piece, make a personal statement about the age and health of the poet (although this was not in the first edition), proclaim the poet's freedom from all "creeds and schools," affirm the elusiveness and yet the autonomy of the self, which is "a mystery" not to be discovered by mere "trippers and askers" and yet is

> Sure as the most certain sure, plumb in the uprights,
>   well entretied, braced in the beams,
> Stout as a horse, affectionate, haughty, electrical.

From the very beginning the poem assumes a dialogue form, as is suitable for a prophet-poet, by addressing "you" — that is, any man or woman in a perfectly equalitarian life (of which the leaves of grass are the general symbol). The tone is both that of the potential lover and that of the teacher.

In section 5, the "plot" of the poem begins. Here the self is imagined to be engaged in a dialogue with itself, as the soul might be imagined to be in dialogue with the body. The emotion evoked is quite frankly autoerotic and this emotion leads Whitman to one of his most beautiful statements of his feeling of being in harmony with all of nature:

> . . . a kelson of the creation is love,
> And limitless are leaves stiff or drooping in the fields,
> And brown ants in the little wells beneath them,
> And mossy scabs of the worm fence, heap'd stones, elder,
>   mullein, and poke-weed.

From this point, though by no means in a straight or continuous line, all "goes onward and outward" (see the end of section 6) in the poem, until toward the end, the identification of the self not only with the nation and with all mankind but with the immortal and the divine — "the great Camerado" — is affirmed. The poem develops into a rhapsody celebrating the democratic life, the fecund creativity of the self, and a benign universe in which death is overcome by a kind of maternal process of reincarnation. This accords well with the Preface and its announced program for the poet as prophet and seer.

But if this were all the poem did, it would be merely one of the better of Whitman's many affirmative and optimistic poem-prophecies, instead of the truly great poem it is. For one thing it is in American literature the first truly *modern* poem. It repudiated the conventional genteel and romantic poetry of Whitman's day and in doing so (it is not too much to say) made modern poetry possible. For although the poem is not "realistic," its assumption is the modern one, that all of experience, and not just that which is innately "poetic" or "proper," is available to poetry. Whitman's other main contribution to modernism — that of bringing a persistent prose element into the lyric style — helped him to give to "Song of Myself" a sense of the immediacy of experience. For example, in lines like

The blab of the pave, tires of carts, sluff of boot-soles,
talk of the promenaders,
The heavy omnibus, the driver with his interrogating
thumb, the clank of the shod horses on the granite floor,

poetry discovered a hitherto little treated subject, the city. In lines like the following we find what later came to be called imagist poetry:

The little one sleeps in its cradle,
I lift the gauze and look a long time, and silently brush
away flies with my hand.

The youngster and the red-faced girl turn aside up
the bushy hill,
I peeringly view them from the top.

The suicide sprawls on the bloody floor of the bedroom,
I witness the corpse with its dabbled hair, I note where
the pistol has fallen.

But it is not only its modernity that makes "Song of Myself" important. There is also the comic quality of the poem. For the happy fact is that Whitman was unable to maintain the high moralistic or "Emersonian" tone he sought to maintain. A purely lawless gaiety and upwelling wit find their way into "Song of Myself." Retrospectively reading Whitman's definition of prophecy which occurs in a tribute to Carlyle in *Specimen Days*, we are not surprised at this. "The word prophecy," he writes, "is much misused; it seems narrow'd to prediction merely. That is not the main sense of the Hebrew word translated 'prophet'; it means one whose mind bubbles and pours forth like a fountain, from inner divine spontaneities revealing God. . . . The great matter is to reveal and outpour the God-like suggestions pressing for birth in the soul." We are not surprised to find that in "Song of Myself" many such inner divine spontaneities have revealed themselves; nor are we surprised that such lawless impulses do not always accord with, and in fact often gaily or whimsically subvert, the moralizing poet who is supposed to be "the most equable of men." The comic tone of the poem, which in the end all but takes command, begins perhaps at section 20, where, after talking rather too long about "the clean-hair'd Yankee girl" who "works with her sewing machine" and what seems like half the rest of the population of the United States, Whitman suddenly asks, "Who goes there? hankering, gross, mystical, nude . . . ?" As I have said elsewhere in writing about Whitman, "Whoever he is, he is not in a position to utter morality." At this point the poem takes on a new vitality and richness. The poet seems liberated from a moral requirement and begins to reveal and outpour what is really pressing for expression. "Speech," which is the "twin of my vision," provokes him by saying *"Walt, you contain enough, why don't you let it out then?"* Doubtless it will depend on one's own sense of what humor is how far one is prepared to respond to "Song of Myself" as a comic poem (although Constance Rourke long ago described it as such in her *American Humor*). But many readers are bound to be drawn to a poet who suddenly exclaims, "Hurrah for positive science! long live exact demonstration," who says with racy insouciance,

> Unscrew the locks from the doors!
> Unscrew the doors themselves from their jambs!

or who can with grave and whimsical astonishment observe, perhaps after reading an article on evolution,

> I find I incorporate gneiss, coal, long-threaded moss,
>   fruits, grains, esculent roots,
> And am stucco'd with quadrupeds and birds all over.

Sometimes, to be sure, it is difficult to know whether one is laughing *at* Whitman or *with* him. What, for example, of a line like "Partaker of influx and efflux I?" At any rate, I think we are laughing (if we laugh at all) *with* Whitman most of the time and certainly when he suddenly announces in section 44 (the seventh inning of the poem, as it were): "It is time to explain myself — let us stand up."

As in all comedy there is in "Song of Myself" an ever-renewed sense of incongruity. For it is not true as D. H. Lawrence, Santayana, and many others have charged that Whitman has no sense

of incongruity or paradox, that he is capable only of a mystic or
pantheistic tendency to "merge" with all things. He does not in his
best poems allow his identity to be absorbed into the mere chaotic
flux of experience. He is a poet, as he tells us near the beginning
of "Song of Myself," who is "both in and out of the game and
watching and wondering at it." He is a poet whose words are
"reminders" of "life untold, and of freedom and extrication." And
indeed the recurring motif of "Song of Myself" is the identification
of the self with other selves, often highly incongruous ones, followed by the extrication of the self from its momentarily assumed
identity. This repeated dialectic act, or assumption and rejection
of masks, accounts for much of the inner brilliance and wit —
which as anyone can see is *not* simply boisterous humor — of "Song
of Myself." In his inferior poetry Whitman loses his capacity to
think of the self as being in a dialectic tension with the not-self, and
he loses his comic muse. I do not of course mean that Whitman's
greatness rests solely in his capacity for comic effects. But I think
there is more truth and self-understanding than at first meets the
eye in his remark to his Camden friends in 1889: "I pride myself
in being a real humorist underneath everything else."

Before leaving the discussion of Whitman's comedy, one
should at least note that according to Constance Rourke the native American humor has two sides to it. It is not only aggressively
and uninhibitedly assertive; often it modulates into meditative or
even elegiac soliloquy. This tone is well woven into the great last
lines of "Song of Myself" with their exquisite and more than a little
artificial wit:

The spotted hawk swoops by and accuses me, he complains
  of my gab and my loitering.

I too am not a bit tamed, I too am untranslatable,
I sound my barbaric yawp over the roofs of the world.

The last scud of day holds back for me,
It flings my likeness after the rest and true as any on
  the shadow'd wilds,
It coaxes me to the vapor and the dusk.

I depart as air, I shake my white locks at the runaway sun,
I effuse my flesh in eddies, and drift it in lacy jags.

I bequeath myself to the dirt to grow from the grass I love,
If you want me again look for me under your boot-soles.

You will hardly know who I am or what I mean,
But I shall be good health to you nevertheless,
And filter and fibre your blood.

Failing to fetch me at first keep encouraged,
Missing me one place search another,
I stop somewhere waiting for you.

The democratic en-masse whom Whitman addressed and celebrated failed spectacularly to purchase the first edition of *Leaves of
Grass*. It went virtually unread except by a few literary people to
whom Whitman sent copies; it received few favorable reviews,
among them one or two Whitman wrote himself. And it would be,
in fact, several years and several editions later before Whitman
began to acquire a reputation, here and abroad — it was in Europe
that Whitman found some of his earliest sympathetic readers and
it is an open question whether to this day he has not always been
better appreciated abroad than at home. And even in his Washington and Camden years, when he did begin to be widely known in
his own country, he was known more as the public figure and the
prophet than as the poet he actually was. Time was required to
dispel the early notoriety of Whitman's poetry, which was damned
as incomprehensible and obscene, and bring real understanding.
One important exception among the readers of the 1855 edition
was Emerson, and his enthusiastic letter, in which he wrote "I greet
you at the beginning of a great career" and expressed a desire to
meet the poet, must have given the disappointed Whitman much
solace. At any rate, Whitman published, in what some of the new
poems show to be a rather defiant mood, a second edition in 1856.
The book was sponsored by Fowler and Wells, publishers of books
on phrenology, a "science" in which Whitman was much interested. There were thirty-two poems and an appendix containing
favorable reviews of the first edition, Emerson's letter, and an open
reply to Emerson.

Of some significance is the fact that in the two outstanding
poems of the new edition — "Song of the Open Road" and "Cross-

ing Brooklyn Ferry" — the self is conceived, as in so much of Whitman's later poetry, as being in motion. In "Song of Myself" the self stood confident and "aplomb in the midst of irrational things." Whitman has begun to lose his sense of the perfect and arrogant autonomy of the self, and now sends it on pilgrimages and voyages whose destination, it must be admitted, is not always clear. "Song of the Open Road" is a kind of American version of the medieval allegories of the itinerary of the soul to God and a forerunner of all those later American writers, from Dos Passos and Robert Penn Warren to Saul Bellow, who have written of the American "on the road." The poem's main virtue is its exuberance and its bracing apostrophe to the free spirit and the free will. One does not even mind the dubious French:

> Allons! with power, liberty, the earth, the elements,
> Health, defiance, gayety, self-esteem, curiosity;
> Allons! from all formules!
> From your formules, O bat-eyed and materialistic priests.

The weakness of the poem is that it does not find an imagery adequate to the emotions that are invoked. Whitman hails "You objects that call from diffusion my meanings and give them shape" but he does not capture enough of these objects in a recognizable structure.

"Crossing Brooklyn Ferry" is one of Whitman's most successful poems, more of a unity, surely, though less ambitious than the most notable poem that derives from it, Hart Crane's "The Bridge." There is nothing of the comic spirit of "Song of Myself" in "Crossing Brooklyn Ferry," or of the excessive assertions of "Song of the Open Road." The mood is meditative and purely lyric. But Whitman's theme is his familiar one: the mystery of identity. Whitman muses on the paradox of individuality, which is at once different from and a part of the flux of nature ("I too have been struck from the float forever held in solution") and which is at once different from and a part of society, represented here by the small world of people momentarily gathered on the ferry. Whitman's assertions about the simple, separate person and the en-masse are here modulated into a quietly beautiful statement of faith in an ordered, harmonious, and benign universe. Union, harmony, and order are well symbolized by the repeated journeys of the ferry, by the ebb and flow of the tides, and by other "similitudes of the past and the future," such as "the fine centrifugal spokes of light round the shape of my head in the sunlit water" and also "the slow-wheeling circles" that are made in the sky by the sea gulls.

Any poem, and particularly one by a poet like Whitman, is likely to be given depth and authenticity if the poet is able to question or doubt himself, whether ironically or by candid admission. The self-doubting, self-proving quality is entirely missing from a poem like "Song of the Open Road," but in section 6 of "Crossing Brooklyn Ferry" Whitman admits that both he and his poems are a mixture of the good and the bad:

> The best I had done seem'd to me blank and suspicious . . .
> I am he who knew what it was to be evil,
> I too knitted the old knot of contrariety.

But it is Whitman's success in finding related symbols for his subject that ensures the success of "Crossing Brooklyn Ferry." The "dumb, beautiful ministers," as he calls the images he sees, "furnish" their "parts" not only "toward eternity" and "toward the soul" but toward the completed form of the poem. One may readily agree with Thoreau that "Song of Myself" and "Crossing Brooklyn Ferry" are the best of Whitman's early poems.

The 1856 edition of *Leaves of Grass* had hardly more public success than the 1855, and Whitman returned to newspaper work, becoming the editor of the *Brooklyn Times*. But he was again able to respond to disappointment by making new plans for his poetry. In 1857 we find him jotting notes on "the great construction of the new Bible. Not to be diverted from the principle object — the main life. . . . It ought to be ready in 1859." This suggests not only that Whitman was determined to go on as a poet but that he had worked out in his mind at least a general plan for the poetical "Bible" *Leaves of Grass* eventually became. Outwardly Whitman would seem to have continued to be self-confident during the years immediately before the third edition of *Leaves of Grass*, which appeared in 1860. He had a respectable job, and he had taken up an apparently convivial social life with the more or less bohemian patrons of Pfaff's beer cellar. William Dean Howells remembered having seen him there on one occasion playing the lion to a group of young men. In shaking hands, Whitman had reached out his hand "to me," says Howells, "as if he were going to give it to me for good and all."

But was all as well with Whitman as it seemed to be? The 1860 edition of the poems contains "Out of the Cradle Endlessly Rocking" and "As I Ebb'd with the Ocean of Life" — two of his finest poems, to be sure, but reflecting a profound melancholy and self-doubt. The fact that the 1860 edition contained the "Calamus" poems and that parts, at least, of "Out of the Cradle" may be read as a dirge for a lost love leads to the supposition that Whitman had found and lost a male lover and that this loss had been a tragedy to him but had released the creative emotions, so different from those in "Song of Myself," which characterize his elegiac mood. This must remain a supposition, however, since the evidence to corroborate or refute it is lacking.

There can be no doubt, at least, that the homosexual overtones of the "Calamus" poems sound far more authentic emotionally than do the heterosexual expostulations of the "Children of Adam" poems which also appeared in this edition. Although the "Children of Adam" group apparently struck Emerson as being too sexual (for he spent an afternoon on Boston Common trying to argue Whitman out of publishing them), they are actually "sexual" only in intention. Whitman is utterly unable to speak of heterosexual love except as a remote abstraction — an inability which led D. H. Lawrence to exclaim "Oh, beautiful generalization! Oh, biological function! 'Athletic mothers of these States —' Muscles and wombs. They needn't have had faces at all."

But the "Calamus" poems, if not among Whitman's best, are at least emotionally convincing and, in the calamus leaves, the phallic calamus root, the dark waters of the pond, the "paths untrodden," Whitman finds images appropriate to the emotion. These are, we are told, the poet's most intimate utterances:

Here the frailest leaves of me and yet my strongest lasting,
Here I shade and hide my thoughts, I myself do
    not expose them,
And yet they expose me more than all my other poems.

The love spoken of in a poem like "Whoever You Are Holding
Me Now in Hand" is not merely abstract. It is tender, yet arduous
and dangerous.

I give you fair warning before you attempt me further,
I am not what you supposed but far different. . . .
The way is suspicious, the result uncertain,
    perhaps destructive.

It is furtive and timorous:

Or else by stealth in some wood for trial,
Or back of a rock in the open air . . .
Here to put your lips upon mine I permit you,
With the comrade's long-dwelling kiss or the
    new husband's kiss,
For I am the new husband and I am the comrade.

Death, one of Whitman's essential themes, is strongly felt in a poem
like "Scented Herbage of My Breast":

Yet you are beautiful to me you faint tinged roots, you
    make me think of death,
Death is beautiful from you (what indeed is finally
    beautiful except death and love?)
O I think it is not for life I am chanting here my
    chant of lovers, I think it must be for death.

The tenderness and yet the danger of comradely love, or "adhe-
siveness," as Whitman calls it, using a phrenological word, are better expressed and more convincing in the personal and confessional
"Calamus" poems than is the "political" assertion of some of the
others that comradely love is the basis (apparently the *only* basis
as we would gather from "I Hear It Was Charged against Me")
of a new democratic society. A more than slightly false ring ema-
nates from lines like "I believe the main purport of these States is
to found a superb friendship, exalté, previously unknown."

    "Out of the Cradle" is one of Whitman's most complex and
beautiful poems. In form it somewhat resembles an opera, begin-

ning with a rich overture in which the themes are stated and the mood evoked:

Out of the cradle endlessly rocking,
Out of the mocking-bird's throat, the musical shuttle,
Out of the Ninth-month midnight,
Over the sterile sands and the fields beyond, where the child
    leaving his bed wander'd alone, bareheaded, barefoot,
Down from the shower'd halo,
Up from the mystic play of shadows twining and twisting
    as if they were alive
Out from the patches of briers and blackberries,
From the memories of the bird that chanted to me,
From your memories sad brother, from the fitful risings and
    fallings I heard,
From under that yellow half-moon late-risen and swollen
    as if with tears,
From those beginning notes of yearning and love there
    in the mist,
From the thousand responses of my heart never to cease,
From the myriad thence-arous'd words,
From the word stronger and more delicious than any,
From such as now they start the scene revisiting,
As a flock, twittering, rising, or overhead passing,
Borne hither, ere all eludes me, hurriedly,
A man, yet by these tears a little boy again,
Throwing myself on the sand, confronting the waves,
I, chanter of pains and joys, uniter of here and hereafter,
Taking all hints to use them, but swiftly leaping
    beyond them,
A reminiscence sing.

This is followed by passages of recitative and aria. One may note, however, that the finale by no means matches the overture in symphonic complexity, being comparatively muted and, despite the suggestive images of the bird, the sea, and the old crone rocking the cradle, relatively downright and matter-of-fact in tone. The conclusion is a short recessional rather than a finale.

The main theme of "Out of the Cradle," although it does not exhaust the meanings of the poem, is the origin of the poet's genius. Whitman asks for and receives from the sea a "clew" or "word," and we are led to understand that his poetic genius origi-

nated in childhood and its first intuition of the alienation and loss
which are the lot of all beings and which culminate in death. "Out
of the Cradle," then, is a poem about the origin of poetry and to
this extent resembles certain books of Wordsworth's *Prelude*. If
this is not clear from the poem itself, we have as guideposts the
two earlier titles Whitman gave to it: "A Child's Reminiscence"
and "A Word Out of the Sea." Is Whitman right in tracing the
origin of his poetry as he does? Surely he is only half right, for the
world of experience posited in "Out of the Cradle," whether in its
origin or its expressed form, is not that of "Song of Myself."

But if the main theme of the poem is clear, it is not so clear
what else, if anything, the poem means. Is it, as is often said, an
"organic" poem, affirming a whole view of reality in which life
and death or love and death are understood as compensatory parts
of a living universal rhythm? One's objection to this opinion might
be based on any number of perceptions about the poem. For example, is the "old crone" who rocks the cradle at the end of the
poem a benign mother, ushering new life, spiritual or otherwise,
into being? One might think so at first, but what of the rather obvious ambivalence the poet feels toward this "old crone" with her
"sweet garments"? Shrouds can be sweet, and we are probably
not engaging in a too ingenious mode of interpretation if we conjecture that at a different level of meaning that cradle is distinctly
coffinlike. Many of Whitman's poems do assert an organic universe
and an immortal and universal rhythm of life, but "Out of the
Cradle" is not one of them. And in fact the quality of experience
conveyed by this poem — the experience, we are told, out of which
poetry is born — involves love without an object, it involves anxiety, alienation, insoluble contradiction, and ultimate despair, a
despair not assuaged by the sentimental resignation with which
it is embraced.

The illusion of a universe in which opposites and contradictions are reconciled is sustained only at the very beginning of the
poem. There the "musical shuttle" out of "the mocking-bird's
throat" draws into a unity that which is "down" and that which
is "up":

>Down from the shower'd halo,
>Up from the mystic play of shadows twining
>   and twisting as if they were alive . . .

And at the beginning of the poem the poet can confidently speak of himself as the "chanter of pains and joys, uniter of here and hereafter." The feeling of reconciliation and harmony rises to an early pitch in the aria of the two birds:

>*Shine! shine! shine!*
>*Pour down your warmth, great sun!*
>*While we bask, we two together.*

But the illusion of unity and continuity is not sustained, or is sustained only fitfully, after this aria. For now the she-bird has suddenly disappeared, and the he-bird sings his melancholy dirge, pouring out meanings, as Whitman says, "which I of all men know."

A reader mindful of Whitman's love of melodrama, of which he encountered plenty in his favorite Italian operas, will find the first ominous note in this ominous poem in the "surging of the sea," for this surging is described as "hoarse," and although we may see nothing necessarily frightening in this at first, the context of the poem forces us to remember that ghosts and other demonic creatures are often said to speak with a hoarse and sepulchral voice. Even the "white arms out in the breakers tirelessly tossing" which Whitman recalls seeing during the childhood experience he is recapturing or re-creating do not seem on reflection to be so attractive and winsome as they do at first. There is something threatening, something beyond human control, something suggestive of a universe indifferent to human destiny, in that tireless tossing. Or perhaps there is something merely suggestive of death, for the arms of a corpse in the sea might toss tirelessly.

The object of love is now unattainable, though there is still the compulsion to pursue it in panic and madness, a pursuit now seen as an activity of nature itself:

>*O madly the sea pushes upon the land,*
>*With love, with love.*

And whereas white and black were once held together in a unison,

> *Two together!*
> *Winds blow south, or winds blow north,*
> *Day come white, or night come black,*

they are now seen in opposition:

> *What is that little black thing I see there in the white?*

The song of the he-bird rises to a pitch of desperate assertion:

> *Shake out carols!*
> *Solitary here, the night's carols!*
> *Carols of lonesome love! death's carols!*
> *Carols under that lagging, yellow, waning moon!*
> *O under that moon where she droops almost*
>   *down into the sea!*
> *O reckless despairing carols.*

And finally the song recedes into a resigned reminiscence of what used to be: "*We two together no more.*"

Although we hear "the aria sinking," "all else" continues; the stars shine, the winds blow, the notes of the bird echo. But "all else" does not continue in a compensatory or organic harmony. Instead the world has fallen apart. There is no object for "the love in the heart long pent" even though it is "now loose, now at last tumultuously bursting." This is a world characterized by loss and alienation — not presided over by a benign Great Mother, as Whitman of all poets might have wished, but haunted and agitated by the "angry moans" of "the fierce old mother incessantly moaning." Through the fissures of a disjoined world there enter the demonic powers always drawn upon by the imagination of melodrama. Does the boy, the poet-to-be, receive comforting and joyous answers to his questions about his destiny? Far from it:

> The undertone, the savage old mother incessantly crying,
> To the boy's soul's questions sullenly timing, some
>   drown'd secret hissing,
> To the outsetting bard.

At this point the bird is addressed as "demon or bird," and it seems impossible not to take "demon" in both of its usual meanings: the poetic genius and a sinister emanation from some unknown realm. The latter meaning is confirmed by the imagery that occurs a little later in the poem, where the bird is called a messenger, as if from some infernal place:

The messenger there arous'd, the fire, the sweet hell within,
The unknown want, the destiny of me.

Perhaps it is also confirmed by the still later phrase "my dusky demon and brother."

The language and imagery in which "Out of the Cradle" culminates, whether we are thinking of the fivefold invocation to death, the dusky demon, or the old crone, do not, it must be clear, reflect a world of pain assuaged, contradictions reconciled, and disruptive powers placated. Nor does the poem assert that poetry originates in such a world — quite the contrary. "Out of the Cradle" is more unflinching, more uncompromising, more extreme in its perception of disorder and anxiety than its critics have seen, although these critics would readily perceive the same qualities in the works of other American writers of dark imagination, such as Poe, Hawthorne, and Melville.

"As I Ebb'd with the Ocean of Life" is a powerful dirge on the inability of man to understand the universe or to convince himself that finally the self has any more substance, stability, and form than the "chaff, straw, splinters of wood, weeds, and the sea-gluten" which the sea casts up and which the poet contemplates as he dejectedly walks along the beach. Here he is not even sure, as he was in "Out of the Cradle," that man can be a struggling creative being; in this poem he seems to be a mere "castaway," a "little wash'd up drift/ A few sands and dead leaves." But like "Out of the Cradle," this poem derives its power both from the sheer lyric beauty of the lines and from an inner contradiction, this time furnished by an ironic self-regard:

O baffled, balk'd, bent to the very earth,
Oppress'd with myself that I have dared to open my mouth,
Aware now that amid all that blab whose echoes recoil upon
    me I have not once had the least idea who or what I am,
But that before all my arrogant poems the real Me stands
    yet untouch'd, untold, altogether unreach'd,
Withdrawn far, mocking me with mock-congratulatory signs
    and bows,

> With peals of distant ironical laughter at every word I
>   have written,
> Pointing in silence to these songs, and then to the sand beneath.

The nadir of despondency reflected in these lines seems not to
have lasted very long, and by 1861 with the coming of the war and
its accompanying excitement, Whitman gradually entered on his
later years of at least partial public acceptance and even fame. He
was destined to write only a few more first-rate poems, though he
wrote many that were good and a great many that were bad. But
he was able to find increasing satisfaction in his mode of life, his
private and public activities, and in his notoriety. The war came
as a kind of tonic to Whitman, as we can see from the vigor and
excitement of the *Drum-Taps* group of poems, which he began to
write in 1861. He thought of the war as promising a spiritual re-
generation to the country, for he had become increasingly disillu-
sioned with the national political and moral condition in the
years that followed his time of active politicking in Brooklyn. And
he saw in the war a new challenge and opportunity for the poet
who was also a patriot-prophet.

In 1862 Whitman embarked upon his Washington years. He
went to Virginia in December of that year to be with his brother
George, who had been wounded at Fredericksburg. He had already
begun to make a sort of career out of his propensity for being a
"wound dresser" and hospital visitor by paying calls to injured
stage and horsecar drivers whom he knew in New York. Now he
decided to settle in Washington in order to bring some cheer to
the wounded soldiers in the improvised and ill-staffed hospitals
there. During these years "Walt Whitman, a kosmos, of Manhattan the son" became more fatherly, and he was a familiar and
welcome sight in the wards, where he brought gifts and comfort
to the soldiers, after his day's work in one of several government
offices where he found employment.

It was in Washington, too, that a Walt Whitman movement
of sorts began to take shape at the instigation of a small group of
admirers like John Burroughs, William O'Connor, and Eldridge,
Whitman's onetime Boston publisher. Although this admiration,

often amounting to the adoration of disciple for master, must have been comforting to a neglected poet and undoubtedly resulted finally in a wider acceptance of his poetry, the effects were not all good. It seems clear that many of Whitman's avid supporters and disciples in these and later years were interested in him as a kind of messiah, or at least as a prophet with a program for democracy, spirituality, "cosmic consciousness," and one thing and another. This perhaps tended to alienate Whitman from his own best genius and to confirm in him the self-publicist that from the beginning had never been bashful about proclaiming the greatness of Walt Whitman.

Whitman published *Drum-Taps* in 1865, and later a sequel that included "When Lilacs Last in the Dooryard Bloom'd." Yet with the exception of the lilacs poem it is hard to agree with the poet when he says that these poems are better than anything he had previously written. There is some truth in the review by the youthful Henry James (a most unfair review on the whole, as James later admitted), with its complaint that the *Drum-Taps* poems are the product of a "prolonged muscular strain." There is indeed more heat than light, more willfulness than beauty in the poet's martial and hortatory utterances. But a poem such as the well-known "Cavalry Crossing the Ford" is a highly successful piece of imagist picture-drawing. And elegiac pieces, like "Reconciliation" and "As I Lay with My Head in Your Lap, Camerado," have a fine lyric quality.

There is more than a little theatricality and a kind of muffled melodrama about "When Lilacs Last in the Dooryard Bloom'd," with its two mysterious "companions" whom the poet calls "the knowledge of death" and "the thought of death" and who accompany him in his ritual retreat

> Down to the shores of the water, the path by the
> swamp in the dimness,
> To the solemn shadowy cedars and ghostly pines
> so still.

The purpose of this withdrawal is to praise death, the ultimate democracy, which Whitman does in a mood of hushed consecration:

Come lovely and soothing death,
Undulate round the world, serenely arriving, arriving,
In the day, in the night, to all, to each,
Sooner or later delicate death.

And then, although death is called a "dark mother" it is presented more like a bride.

What saves the poem from mere mysticism is of course the symbols: the "powerful western fallen star" standing for the assassinated Lincoln, the lilac signifying rebirth or resurrection, and the hidden bird signifying as in "Out of the Cradle" the poet and the power of poetry. These symbols are brought into a unity which, if not perfect, is adequate to Whitman's purposes.

Reflecting on the mystical invocation to death and the poet's attention to his own emotions, we may well ask: why doesn't the poem say something about Lincoln, especially in view of the fact that Whitman had often seen the President and was later to complain, in *Specimen Days*, that none of the portraits he had seen truly caught Lincoln's real appearance and quality? Not that an elegist is necessarily bound to paint a portrait, but from one's reading of the traditional elegies of Europe, such as Milton's "Lycidas," one would expect to hear more about the fame, honor, and accomplishments of the dead man than the phrase "the sweetest, wisest soul of all my days and lands" that the poet puts in at the last possible moment. Nor, except for the passing vignettes, such as the people mourning at the depots as the coffin journeys westward, is there a coherent sense of the kind of society Lincoln lived in — and this again is at odds with the traditional elegy. The poet who comes to pay tribute to the dead President pays tribute instead to death itself. We have here what may be called (if with some hesitation) an American form of elegy — a kind of lyric melodrama in which everything personal, except the loneliness of the poet, is made abstract and impersonal and in which a mourning society is seen, not as any specific *kind* of society, but only on the one hand as fragmented groups of people and on the other as an abstraction. But this is perhaps to forget what is more important, the rare poetic qualities of Whitman's language:

When lilacs last in the dooryard bloom'd,
And the great star early droop'd in the western sky
    in the night,
I mourn'd, and yet shall mourn with ever-
    returning spring.

Ever-returning spring, trinity sure to me you bring,
Lilac blooming perennial and drooping star in the west,
And thought of him I love.

Although he would recapture it momentarily in brief lyrics, Whitman had made the last great utterance of his elegiac-meditative powers in "When Lilacs Last in the Dooryard Bloom'd." Nor would he again be able to use as successfully as he had in the years between 1855 and 1860 his sense of the tensions and contradictions involved in the drama of the self. These, rather than his "philosophy," are the true sources of his best genius. Readers who overemphasize Whitman's "philosophy" find in later poems like "Passage to India" (1868) an advance over "Song of Myself" because, so the argument goes, the poet has learned to free himself of preoccupation with the merely (merely!) private self and to write on universal philosophic, political, moral, and "cosmic" themes. But Whitman's weakness was not his penchant for writing about the private self and the realities it encounters. On the contrary, that is his source of strength, and his weakness is his penchant for "philosophy" (of which he had none in any precise sense), as we understand when we perceive that it led his mind to become so increasingly prone to rhapsodies celebrating a vague, homogenized, "democratic" universe which could exist nowhere and contain no one.

This does not mean that there aren't many interesting poems in the later editions of *Leaves of Grass* in the sections that Whitman labeled "Whispers of Heavenly Death," "Songs of Parting," "Sands at Seventy," and "Good-Bye My Fancy," nor that there aren't many early poems, not discussed in the present essay, that repay study. Quite apart from the great poems there remain such fine things as "There Was a Child Went Forth," "To a Locomotive in Winter," "A Noiseless Patient Spider," "The Base of All

Metaphysics," "Song of the Redwood Tree," "On the Beach, at
Night," "Sparkles from the Wheel," "Prayer for Columbus," and
"The Dalliance of Eagles."

In 1871, before Whitman left Washington, he published
Democratic Vistas, in which, along with the 1855 Preface and parts
of *Specimen Days* (1882), is to be found much of his best prose (although the thorough reader will want to go on to things like "A
Backward Glance o'er Travel'd Roads," the letters, and, for those
especially interested in Whitman's ideas about the nature and origins of poetic language, "Slang in America" and *An American
Primer*). *Democratic Vistas* is Whitman's most considerable pro-
nouncement on social and cultural issues. In this eloquent work
we see a writer who still clings to his own spiritualized or transcen-
dentalized version of the Jeffersonian-Jacksonian credo and applies
it to the spectacle of the Grant administration days at the outset
of the Gilded Age. Most of what he sees he does not like, and
readers who suppose Whitman to be a mere mindless celebrant of
democracy are always surprised at the vituperation and satire of
some of the passages of *Democratic Vistas*. For example, we find
Whitman attacking the "dry, flat Sahara" of American life. He
thinks that "society, in these States, is canker'd, crude, superstitious, and rotten" and that there is "more hollowness of heart" in
his countrymen than ever before. "The depravity of the business
classes" is matched only by the decadence of "fashionable life," in
which he sees only "flippancy, tepid amours, weak infidelism, small
aims, or no aims at all." Like Howells, Mark Twain, and Henry
Adams, Whitman believed that in the postwar period something
heroic and aspiring, as well as a certain honesty, plainness, and
purposefulness, had been lost from American life.

As was noted above Whitman had long before 1871 given up
his active interest in politics, and in fact the *Vistas* is not, except
indirectly, a political diatribe. It is not in the tradition of Marx-
ism, but follows, in its highly characteristic way, the tradition of
social prophecy that includes Coleridge, Ruskin, Arnold, and Mor-
ris. It seeks to get at political and social realities through observations on culture, on manners and morals, on spiritual qualities,

and on literature and the place of the writer in society. Unlike Tocqueville, who saw forty years earlier that the real danger in a democracy is not too much disunity and rebellion but too much centralization and conformity, Whitman is worried by the chaos and fragmentation of American life (of course one must remember that this would be easy to feel at the time Whitman wrote) and urges that "the quality to-day most needed" is "more compaction and more moral identity." He does not tell us how this is to come about, except by his old formula according to which the freer and more individual the individual is the more identity he will feel with the en-masse. One is moved to ask Whitman precisely what kind of and what degree of institutional mediation is needed between the individual and society so that each may continue to exist but be protected from the other. On this score, we get no answer from Whitman.

We might well expect, however, that the author of "Song of Myself" would have something of value to say about the self in *Democratic Vistas*. And in fact his presentation of "personalism," as he calls it, is very striking. Whitman's intuition of the value of the self he expresses as follows: "There is, in sanest hours, a consciousness, a thought that rises, independent, lifted out from all else, calm, like the stars, shining eternal. This is the thought of identity — yours for you, whoever you are, as mine for me. Miracle of miracles, beyond statement, most spiritual and vaguest of earth's dreams, yet hardest basic fact, and only entrance to all facts." True, Whitman thinks of the self as a moral or perhaps metaphysical entity, without referring it to its own history or, in any concrete way, to its existence in society. And a basic weakness of *Democratic Vistas*, shared by many other nineteenth-century writings of the sort, is its unquestioning belief in progress, its lack of an objective sense of history and of an understanding of society as the locus of evolving institutions. "Society," for Whitman, remains an abstraction or a feeling of "adhesive" love of comrades. History is apparently a benign and maternal process which, now that "feudalism" (that is, everything that happened before 1776) has been transcended, can be counted on not to confront man with tragic or insoluble dilemmas. But although Whitman's optimism and his fundamentally nonhistorical view of things do not accord very well with our twentieth-century realism, we must still agree that in any humane society "personalism" will always be the "hardest basic fact, and only entrance to all facts." To have asserted that this is so is doubtless the main glory of *Democratic Vistas*.

With some accuracy Whitman described *Specimen Days* as perhaps the "most wayward, spontaneous, fragmentary book ever printed." It is an uneven book, much devoted to reminiscence and to random thoughts on nature, men, and ideas. It has three main parts: a short introductory section devoted to memories of the writer's youth and family background; a section of notes and jottings descriptive of his activities during the war; and a third section of nature observation and *pensées* on things in general. The first section is disappointingly sketchy and one wonders anew why so professedly autobiographical a writer should say so little about himself, but there is interest in his memories of his family and in his notes on "My Passion for Ferries," "Broadway Sights," "Omnibus Jaunts and Drivers," "Plays and Operas Too," and one retains the picture of the young Whitman frolicking on the Long Island beaches (Coney Island!) and declaiming "Homer or Shakespeare to the surf and sea-gulls by the hour."

The section on the Civil War days, terse (for Whitman) notations and sketches of the battles and the soldiers he recalls, is perhaps the most valuable part of *Specimen Days* and constitutes one of the most distinguished contributions to the strangely small body of distinguished writing about the war. It takes its place with Stephen Crane's *The Red Badge of Courage*, J. W. De Forest's *Miss Ravenel's Conversion from Secession to Loyalty*, Ambrose Bierce's sketches and tales, and Melville's poems collected in *Battle-Pieces*. In the latter pages of the book the reflections upon Carlyle, Poe, and Emerson stand out vividly, as do some of the less artificial descriptions of nature — these last especially intended, as the author says, "to bring people back from their persistent straying and sickly abstractions, to the costless average, divine, original concrete."

The impulse to get back to nature which we notice in *Specimen Days* was incident to Whitman's gradually failing powers. He had been in uncertain health ever since February of 1873, when, after sitting at his office desk in the Treasury Building (reading a novel by Bulwer-Lytton), he had returned to his room at night and sustained his first paralytic shock. He made a slow recovery from this attack, but after resuming his work for a brief time, he left Washington for good and settled with his brother George in Camden, N.J. Here he lived as a semi-invalid until 1884, when he moved into a small house of his own on Mickle Street. He devoted himself as before to writing poems, to planning new revised editions of *Leaves of Grass*, to ferry and horsecar riding when he was able to make his lamed left leg function well enough so that he could get out. Occasionally he gave lectures (a favorite was one on Lincoln) and readings. During the summers he stayed at Timber Creek with a farming family. In his late years he had become world-famous, and not only did he gather about him a new group of local admirers and disciples (notably Horace Traubel, a young socialist lawyer); he also received eminent visitors from abroad, including Sir Henry Irving, Edmund Gosse, and Oscar Wilde. He was visited by scores of unknown pilgrims, including a Mrs. Gilchrist, a widow with two children, who left the Pre-Raphaelite circles she frequented in England and came to America with the professed intention of marrying the poet whose writings had meant so much to her. But Whitman's main preoccupation as always was with *Leaves of Grass*. A characteristic utterance was (as Traubel quotes him): "There's the book — the dear book — forever waiting — and I seem to be more feeble than ever." Whitman lived on until March 26, 1892.

That Whitman should often have been misunderstood is partly his own fault. For with the zealous aid of his immediate disciples he all but convinced himself that he was the "caresser of life" — the intimate companion of all things and all people, indeed of experience itself. He all but convinced himself too that he was a philosopher and a religious thinker. And he all but convinced himself that he was the national bard of an optimistic, ex-

pansive America. To a certain extent all these images of Whitman
are true, but we cannot be satisfied with these images, since they
do not adequately account for the poet who wrote the poems we
admire.

There is something wrong, then, with the following formulation by Whitman's definitive biographer, echoing, as it does, earlier attributions of "mysticism," "primitivism," and "barbarism"
made by writers as different as Lawrence and Santayana: "this was
the real Walt Whitman, undiscriminating, easily stimulated by
noise, color, and movement, happy to lose himself in the ceaseless
flux of people going and coming." Whitman himself did not necessarily think this was true, for he said, in an important passage
of "Song of Myself," that he was "both in and out of the game and
watching and wondering at it." It will not do to think of "the real
Whitman" as the poet who merges with the flux of experience, because this ignores another Whitman who is just as important: the
Whitman who showed a lifelong capacity for recalcitrance to experience and who opposed to the inchoate flow of life the finished
form of his poems and who made of his personal and public life a
series of significant gestures that culminate in the ideal. For he had
the power of turning his famous poses into exemplary acts and
indestructible ideals which belong to any American's cultural
heritage.

Whitman's idea of himself as a philosopher, religious thinker,
and national bard is to be found in his description of the destiny of
the poet, or, as he is oddly called, the "literatus," in *Democratic
Vistas*. In speaking of the need for a moral and spiritual regenera-
tion in America, Whitman allots to the literatus a highly important
place. His task is to create "archetypal poems" which will give
unity of soul and imagination to his people and to exercise the
offices of moral and spiritual leadership once exercised by organized religion. For, as Whitman writes, "the priest departs, the
divine literatus comes." One is not surprised to learn that the ideal
bards of the future will apparently resemble Walt Whitman. At
least they will not be like the "genteel little creatures" whose "perpetual, pistareen, paste-pot work" is sometimes mistaken for genu-

ine American poetry. The literatus must be moved by "autoch-
thonic lights and shades"; he must be intensely aware of his place,
race, and nationality; he will see that "America demands a poetry
that is bold, modern, all-surrounding, and kosmical, as she is herself"; his poetry must be affirmative, forward-looking, and "ideal";
it must celebrate comradeship and nature; it will be free of "the
idea of the covert, the lurid, the maleficent, the devil, the grim
estimates inherited from the Puritans, hell, natural depravity, and
the like." True, Whitman does say that "in the future of these
States must arise poets immenser far, and make great poems of
death." But we inevitably get the feeling from *Democratic Vistas*,
though not from "Out of the Cradle Endlessly Rocking" or "When
Lilacs Last in the Dooryard Bloom'd," that the thought of death
is easy to entertain and is merely a part of the life process of a
progressive universe.

The reader will see that even if we take this portrait of the literatus as a self-appraisal, it is a description of the poet as prophet
and promulger of a program rather than of the poet as poet, and
that some of Whitman's own best qualities go unmentioned: there
is nothing here about Whitman the comic poet and delineator of
the self. Also it is plain that the most characteristic and important
American literature in modern times has not met Whitman's pre-
scriptions. The "grim estimates" of the Puritans have survived in
one form or another from Henry James to Faulkner. The American writer at his best has not been the affirmative public oracle
Whitman envisioned. He has been a private, often an isolated
writer; he has usually approached social questions, if at all, on the
assumption that moral values do not derive from society or the
nation but are innate in the individual; and he has often been
most convincing when he has taken a dark, even pessimistic and
despairing view of our society. That some of the same things may
be said of Whitman himself is a measure of the distance between
the real Walt Whitman and the self-image of the prophet-poet he
liked to project.

To be sure, there is much about the literatus to remind us of
"the real Walt Whitman," whom everyone discusses but whom no

one can quite discover. Whitman's poetry often apostrophizes an optimistic, "orbic," "kosmical" America, an America devoted to "a strong-fibred joyousness and faith, and the sense of health al fresco." But there is nothing to remind us of that essential Whitman — the divided, covert, musing, "double," furtive man who wrote the poems we have come in recent years especially to prize. The testimony of Leslie Fiedler is relevant here. "Our Whitman," writes Mr. Fiedler, "is the slyest of artificers . . . he is a player with illusion; his center is a pun on the self; his poetry is a continual shimmering on the surfaces of concealment and revelation that is at once pathetic and comical." Mr. Fiedler goes on to say that he was not, or not in essence, the tribal bard: "he was only a man, ridden by impotence and anxiety, by desire and guilt, furtive and stubborn and half-educated. That he became the world's looked-for ridiculous darling is astonishing enough; that he remained a poet through it all is scarcely credible." These words are from Mr. Fiedler's excellent essay called "Images of Walt Whitman." For a further description of the poet who is here being called "our Walt Whitman," one might look into the pages of the first book really to understand this poet, Constance Rourke's *American Humor*. But there is also Randall Jarrell's essay entitled "Some Lines from Whitman" (in his *Poetry and the Age*) and my own book of 1955, *Walt Whitman Reconsidered*.

To be sure, these writings were once thought by many academicians to be, in the word of one of them, "aberrant." Perhaps in some quarters they still are. But if so, "unorthodox" would be a better word than "aberrant." For there has indeed been an orthodoxy among most Whitman scholars. It is not the orthodoxy of the original disciples and of Edgar Lee Masters, which makes Whitman a messiah and tribal bard. It is the orthodoxy of the history-of-ideas approach to literature, which makes Whitman a philosopher or possibly a theologian of the mystic variety (not that vain Walt wouldn't have been pleased by the compliment). This purely intellectualist approach is to be found, for example, in James E. Miller's *A Critical Guide to Leaves of Grass* and in Gay Wilson Allen's useful but misleading *Walt Whitman Handbook,* with its talk of immanence and emanation, acosmism and cosmotheism, pantheism and panpsychism. The *Handbook* never gets around to a discussion of Whitman's real subject, which was the plight and destiny of the self. And it is impossible to sympathize with Mr. Allen's contention that "an exhaustive comparative study needs to be made of the relations of Whitman's thought to the [Great] Chain of Being." Whitman's leading conceptions are the self, equality, and contradiction — appropriate preoccupations for the poet of American democracy. What use had he, in a democratic culture, for the philosophic counterpart of European hierarchies?

Abroad Whitman has always been regarded as the national poet of America, a prophet-bard who spoke with the very voice of his native land. But in his own country his position remains somewhat anomalous. In his essay called "The Poetry of Barbarism" Santayana noticed (and exaggerated) this anomaly. Whitman, wrote Santayana, is "surely not the spokesman of the tendencies of his country, although he describes some aspects of its past and present condition: nor does he appeal to those whom he describes, but rather to the *dilettanti* he despises. He is regarded as representative chiefly by foreigners, who look for some grotesque expression of the genius of so young and prodigious a people." There is no doubt that many more Americans have read Longfellow than have read Whitman, and so far as one can tell, Whitman, though he wished to speak to all Americans, is not nowadays more widely read than the other difficult modern poets — for indeed his poetry is "difficult" compared with that of his contemporaries. But in an important sense Whitman really is "the spokesman for the tendencies of his country." Obviously he celebrates and "promulges" our material progress and our spiritual, moral, and political values (and, as I observed earlier, the feelings of cultural inferiority which used to make Americans apologize for his declamatory style and occasional stridency, bathos, or philistinism have largely been allayed). But more important, Whitman is the representative of his country because he and his poetry mirror in a radical if incomplete way the very contradictions of American civilization. For, as was suggested at the beginning of this essay, to begin to understand

Whitman is to understand him in his contradictions. His inner oppositions, his ambiguities, his wit, like his democratic faith, his optimism, and his belief in the self, are native to the man as they are to America. For these reasons one cherishes Walt Whitman — and takes him to be in a real sense "the spokesman for the tendencies of his country."

SELECTED BIBLIOGRAPHIES

Selected Bibliographies

BENJAMIN FRANKLIN
Collected Works

The Works of Benjamin Franklin, edited by Jared Sparks. 10 vols. Boston: Hilliard, Gray and Co., 1840.

The Writings of Benjamin Franklin, edited by Albert Henry Smyth. 10 vols. New York: Macmillan, 1905–7.

The Papers of Benjamin Franklin, edited by Leonard Labaree and others. 12 vols. to date (January 6, 1706, to December 31, 1765). New Haven, Conn.: Yale University Press, 1959–68. (A joint project of the Yale University Press and the American Philosophical Society, expected to run to 40 vols. when completed.)

Principal Separate Works and Periodical Publications

Franklin wrote only a few books. Many of his best known pieces were circulated in manuscript; others were printed anonymously and without title in newspapers. The following list is selective, with emphasis on items available in modern or facsimile editions. Those marked with an asterisk were originally untitled; a dagger indicates anonymous publication.

*† The Silence Dogood Papers, *New England Courant*, April 2–October 8, 1722.

† *A Dissertation on Liberty and Necessity, Pleasure and Pain*. London: n.p., 1725. Edited in facsimile by Lawrence C. Wroth, New York: Facsimile Text Society, 1930.

† *A Modest Enquiry into the Nature and Necessity of a Paper-Currency*. Philadelphia: n.p., 1729.

Poor Richard, 1733. An Almanack for the Year of Christ 1733. Philadelphia: B. Franklin, [1732]. (First of twenty-five annual issues for which Franklin prepared the literary content. All of this material is now readily available in the *Papers*. There are many selective reprints, such as *Poor Richard's Almanack*, with a Foreword by Phillips Russell (Garden City, N.Y.: Doubleday, Doran, 1928), which prints the 1733, 1749, 1756, 1757, and 1758 issues in facsimile.)

† *Plain Truth: Or, Serious Considerations on the Present State of the City of Philadelphia, and Province of Pennsylvania.* N.p., 1747.

† *Proposals Relating to the Education of Youth in Pensilvania.* N.p., 1749. Edited in facsimile by Randolph G. Adams, Ann Arbor, Mich.: William L. Clements Library, 1927, and by William Pepper, Philadelphia: University of Pennsylvania Press, 1931.

Experiments and Observations on Electricity. London: E. Cave, 1751. (Later editions in 1754, 1760, and 1769. Translations into French (1752 and 1756), German (1758), and Italian (1774).) Edited by I. Bernard Cohen, Cambridge, Mass.: Harvard University Press, 1941.

* Father Abraham's Speech, or "The Way to Wealth," or "Bonhomme Richard," *Poor Richard Improved: Being an Almanack . . . For the Year of Our Lord 1758.* Philadelphia: Franklin and Hall, [1757]. (Separately printed, it is known in more than 150 editions.)

† *The Interest of Great Britain Considered, with Regard to Her Colonies and the Acquisition of Canada and Guadaloupe.* London: T. Becket, 1760. (The best example of a large body of material on British colonial policies; cf. Verner W. Crane, ed., *Benjamin Franklin's Letters to the Press, 1758–1775* (Chapel Hill: University of North Carolina Press, for the Institute of Early American History and Culture, 1950).)

The Examination of Doctor Benjamin Franklin. N.p., n.d. [London: J. Almon, 1766?]

*† The Causes of American Discontents before 1768, *London Chronicle*, January 7, 1768.

† Rules by Which a Great Empire May Be Reduced to a Small One, *Public Advertiser* (London), September 1773.

† An Edict by the King of Prussia, *Public Advertiser*, September 1773.

* Bagatelles. Passy: privately printed, 1779–84? (Most of them are extant in their original form only in a unique volume in the Yale University Library. See Richard E. Amacher, *Franklin's Wit & Folly: The Bagatelles* (New Brunswick, N.J.: Rutgers University Press, 1953).)

Memoires de la vie privée de Benjamin Franklin, écrits par lui-même. Paris: Chez Buisson, 1791. (First printing of the first part of the *Autobiography*. For the intricate history of that work's writing and publication, see *Benjamin Franklin's Memoirs*, Parallel Text Edition edited by Max Farrand (Berkeley and Los Angeles: University of California Press, 1949).)

Bibliographies

Ford, Paul Leicester. *Franklin Bibliography: A List of Books Written by, or Relating to Benjamin Franklin.* Brooklyn, N.Y.: Privately printed, 1889.

Miller, C. William. "Franklin's *Poor Richard Almanacs*: Their Printing and Publication," *Studies in Bibliography*, 14:97–115 (1961).

Spiller, Robert E., and others, eds. *Literary History of the United States*, 3rd ed., revised. 2 vols. New York: Macmillan, 1963. (The selective bibliography, 2:507–15, was originally compiled by Thomas H. Johnson; it has been supplemented by Richard M. Ludwig.)

Biographical Interpretations

Aldridge, Alfred Owen. *Franklin and His French Contemporaries*. New York: New York University Press, 1957.
———. *Benjamin Franklin, Philosopher and Man*. Philadelphia and New York: Lippincott, 1965.
Conner, Paul W. *Poor Richard's Politicks: Benjamin Franklin and His New American Order*. New York: Oxford University Press, 1965.
Crane, Verner W. *Benjamin Franklin and a Rising People*. Boston: Little, Brown, 1954.
Miles, Richard D. "The American Image of Benjamin Franklin," *American Quarterly*, 9:117–43 (Summer 1957).
Van Doren, Carl. *Benjamin Franklin*. New York: Viking, 1938.

Books and Articles Relating to Franklin as a Writer

Amacher, Richard E. *Benjamin Franklin*. New York: Twayne, 1962.
Baender, Paul. "The Basis of Franklin's Duplicative Satires," *American Literature*, 32:267–79 (November 1960).
Cook, Elizabeth Christine. *Literary Influences in Colonial Newspapers, 1704–1750*. Columbia University Studies in English and Comparative Literature. New York, 1912.
Davy, Francis X. "Benjamin Franklin Satirist: The Satire of Franklin and Its Rhetoric," *Dissertation Abstracts*, 19:317 (1958).
Granger, Bruce Insham. *Benjamin Franklin, an American Man of Letters*. Ithaca, N.Y.: Cornell University Press, 1964.
Hall, Max. *Benjamin Franklin & Polly Baker: The History of a Literary Deception*. Chapel Hill: University of North Carolina Press, 1960.
Horner, George F. "Franklin's *Dogood Papers* Reexamined," *Studies in Philology*, 37:501–23 (July 1940).
Lemay, J. A. Leo. "Franklin and the *Autobiography*: An Essay on Recent Scholarship," *Eighteenth-Century Studies*, 1:185–211 (1967).
Lynen, John. *The Design of the Present: Essays on Time and Form in American Literature*. New Haven, Conn., and London: Yale University Press, 1969.
MacLaurin, Lois Margaret. *Franklin's Vocabulary*. Garden City, N.Y.: Doubleday, Doran, 1928.
McMaster, John Bach. *Benjamin Franklin as a Man of Letters*. American Men of Letters Series. Boston: Houghton, 1887.
Meister, Charles W. "Franklin as a Proverb Stylist," *American Literature*, 24:157–66 (May 1952).
Newcomb, Robert. "The Sources of Benjamin Franklin's Sayings of Poor Richard," *Dissertation Abstracts*, 17:2584–85 (1957).
Ross, John F. "The Character of Poor Richard: Its Source and Alteration,"

Publications of the Modern Language Association, 35:785–94 (September 1940).
Sayre, Robert F. *The Examined Self: Benjamin Franklin, Henry Adams, Henry James*. Princeton, N.J.: Princeton University Press, 1964.

WASHINGTON IRVING
Principal Writings

Irving's collected writings have appeared in more than forty editions, one not greatly different from another; most often available is the Author's Uniform Revised Edition: *The Works of Washington Irving* (New York: G. P. Putnam's Sons, 1860–61), in 21 volumes. See Stanley T. Williams and Mary E. Edge, *A Bibliography of the Writings of Washington Irving* (New York: Oxford University Press, 1936). *The Complete Works of Washington Irving*, his journals, letters, and writings, under the general editorship of Henry A. Pochmann, has been announced by the University of Wisconsin Press, which issued the first volume in 1969, another in 1970; see Journals below.

"Letters of Jonathan Oldstyle, Gent." New York *Morning Chronicle*, 1802–3 (reprinted, New York: William H. Clayton, 1824).
Salmagundi; or, The Whim-Whams and Opinions of Launcelot Langstaff, Esq., and Others. New York: David Longworth, 1807–8.
A History of New York, from the Beginning of the World to the End of the Dutch Dynasty. New York: Inskeep and Bradford, 1809.
The Sketch Book of Geoffrey Crayon, Gent. New York: C. S. Van Winkle, 1819–20; London: John Miller, 1820.
Bracebridge Hall; or, The Humorists. A Medley. New York: C. S. Van Winkle, 1822; London: John Murray, 1822.
Tales of a Traveller. Philadelphia: H. C. Carey and I. Lea, 1824; London: John Murray, 1824.
A History of the Life and Voyages of Christopher Columbus. New York: G. and C. Carvill, 1828; London: John Murray, 1828.
Chronicle of the Conquest of Granada. Philadelphia: Carey, Lea, and Carey, 1829; London: John Murray, 1829.
Voyages and Discoveries of the Companions of Columbus. Philadelphia: Carey and Lea, 1831; London: John Murray, 1831.
The Alhambra. Philadelphia: Carey and Lea, 1832; London: Henry Colburn and Richard Bentley, 1832.
The Crayon Miscellany. Philadelphia: Carey and Lea, 1835. As *Miscellanies*, London: John Murray, 1835. (*A Tour on the Prairies*, separately published, London: John Murray, 1835; Paris: Galignani, 1835.)
Astoria; or, Anecdotes of an Enterprise beyond the Rocky Mountains. Philadelphia: Carey, Lea and Blanchard, 1836.
The Rocky Mountains; or, Scenes, Incidents, and Adventures in the Far West; Digested from the Journal of Captain B. L. E. Bonneville, of the Army of the United States, and Illustrated from Various Other Sources. Philadelphia: Lea and Blanchard, 1837. As *Adventures of Captain Bonneville*, London: Richard Bentley, 1837; Paris: Galignani, 1837.

Oliver Goldsmith: A Biography. New York: G. P. Putnam, 1849.
A Book of the Hudson. New York: G. P. Putnam, 1849.
Mahomet and His Successors. New York: G. P. Putnam, 1850.
Wolfert's Roost. New York: G. P. Putnam, 1855.
Life of George Washington. New York: G. P. Putnam, 1855–59.
Spanish Papers and Other Miscellanies. New York: G. P. Putnam, 1866.
The Wild Huntsman. Boston: Bibliophile Society, 1924.
Abu Hassan. Boston: Bibliophile Society, 1924.
Washington Irving's Contributions to "The Corrector," edited by Martin Roth.
Minneapolis: University of Minnesota Press, 1968.

Journals

Journal of Washington Irving, 1803, edited by Stanley T. Williams. New York:
Oxford University Press, 1934.
Washington Irving: Notes and Journal of Travel in Europe, 1804–1805, edited
by William P. Trent. 3 vols. New York: Grolier Club, 1921.
Washington Irving: Journals and Notebooks, Vol. 1, 1803–6, edited by Nathalia
Wright, Vol. III, 1819–27, edited by Walter A. Reichart. Madison: University of Wisconsin Press, 1969, 1970.
"Washington Irving's Notebook of 1810," edited by Barbara D. Simison, *Yale University Library Gazette,* 24:1–16, 74–94 (Winter, Spring 1949).
The Journals of Washington Irving [1815–42], edited by William P. Trent and
George S. Hellman. 3 vols. Boston: Bibliophile Society, 1919.
Tour in Scotland, 1817, and Other Manuscript Notes, edited by Stanley T.
Williams. New Haven, Conn.: Yale University Press, 1927.
Washington Irving: Notes While Preparing a Sketch Book, &c 1817, edited by
Stanley T. Williams. New Haven, Conn.: Yale University Press, 1927.
Journal of Washington Irving (1823–1824), edited by Stanley T. Williams.
Cambridge, Mass.: Harvard University Press, 1931.
"Washington Irving's Madrid Journal, 1827–1828," edited by Andrew B. Myers,
Bulletin of the New York Public Library, 62:217–27, 300–11, 407–19, 463–71
(1958).
Washington Irving Diary, Spain, 1828–1829, edited by Clara Louisa Penney.
New York: Hispanic Society of America, 1930.
The Western Journals of Washington Irving, edited by John Francis McDermott. Norman: University of Oklahoma Press, 1944.

Biographies

Bowers, Claude G. *The Spanish Adventures of Washington Irving.* Boston:
Houghton Mifflin, 1940.
Cater, Harold Dean. *Washington Irving at Sunnyside.* Tarrytown, N.Y.: Sleepy
Hollow Restorations, 1957.
Hellman, George S. *Washington Irving Esquire, Ambassador at Large from
the New World to the Old.* New York: Knopf, 1925.
Irving, Pierre M. *The Life and Letters of Washington Irving.* 4 vols. New
York: G. P. Putnam, 1862–64.

Pochmann, Henry A., ed. *Washington Irving: Representative Selections*. New York: American Book, 1934.
Reichart, Walter A. *Washington Irving and Germany*. Ann Arbor: University of Michigan Press, 1957.
Wagenknecht, Edward. *Washington Irving: Moderation Displayed*. New York: Oxford University Press, 1962.
Williams, Stanley T. *The Life of Washington Irving*. 2 vols. New York: Oxford University Press, 1935.

Critical Studies

Beach, Leonard. "Washington Irving: The Artist in a Changing World," *University of Kansas City Review*, 14:259–66 (Summer 1948).
Brooks, Van Wyck. *The World of Washington Irving*. New York: Doubleday, 1944.
Hedges, William L. "Irving's *Columbus*: The Problem of Romantic Biography," *The Americas*, 13:127–40 (1956).
———. *Washington Irving: An American Study, 1802–1832*. Baltimore: Johns Hopkins Press, 1965.
Hoffman, Daniel G. "Irving's Use of American Folklore in 'The Legend of Sleepy Hollow,' " *PMLA*, 68:425–35 (June 1953).
Hoffman, Louise M. "Irving's Use of Spanish Sources in *The Conquest of Granada*," *Hispania*, 28:483–98 (November 1945).
Laird, C. G. "Tragedy and Irony in *Knickerbocker's History*," *American Literature*, 12:157–72 (May 1940).
LeFevre, Louis. "Paul Bunyan and Rip Van Winkle," *Yale Review*, 36:66–76 (Autumn 1946).
Leisy, E. E. "Irving and the Genteel Tradition," *Southwest Review*, 21:223–27 (January 1936).
Lloyd, F. V. "Irving's *Rip Van Winkle*," *Explicator*, 4:26 (February 1946).
Martin, Terrence. "Rip, Ichabod, and the American Imagination," *American Literature*, 31:137–49 (May 1959).
Pochmann, Henry A. "Irving's German Sources in *The Sketch Book*," *Studies in Philology*, 27:477–507 (July 1930).
Snell, George. "Washington Irving: A Revaluation," *Modern Language Quarterly*, 7:303–10 (September 1946).
Webster, C. M. "Irving's Expurgation of the 1809 *A History of New York*," *American Literature*, 4:293–95 (November 1932).
Wegelin, Christopher. "Dickens and Irving: The Problem of Influence," *Modern Language Quarterly*, 7:83–91 (November 1932).
Young, Philip. "Fallen from Time: The Mythic Rip Van Winkle," *Kenyon Review*, 22:547–73 (Autumn 1960).

RALPH WALDO EMERSON

Principal Works

The standard collected edition is *The Complete Works of Ralph Waldo Emerson*, the Centenary Edition, edited by Edward Waldo Emerson and published

SELECTED BIBLIOGRAPHIES 241

in 12 volumes by Houghton Mifflin in 1903–4. It has been supplemented by the collections listed at the end of this section.

Nature. Boston: James Munroe, 1836.
Essays [First Series]. Boston: James Munroe, 1841.
Essays: Second Series. Boston: James Munroe, 1844.
Poems. Boston: James Munroe, 1847 [1846].
Nature, Addresses, and Lectures. Boston: James Munroe, 1849.
Representative Men. Boston: Phillips, Sampson, 1850.
English Traits. Boston: Phillips, Sampson, 1856.
The Conduct of Life. Boston: Ticknor and Fields, 1860.
May-Day and Other Pieces. Boston: Ticknor and Fields, 1867.
Society and Solitude. Boston: Fields, Osgood, 1870.
Parnassus, edited by Ralph Waldo Emerson. Boston: Osgood, 1875.
Letters and Social Aims. Boston: Osgood, 1876.
Selected Poems. Boston: Osgood, 1876.
Poems. Boston: Houghton, Osgood, 1884.
Miscellanies. Boston: Houghton Mifflin, 1884.
Lectures and Biographical Sketches. Boston: Houghton Mifflin, 1884.
Natural History of Intellect and Other Papers. Boston: Houghton Mifflin, 1893.
Two Unpublished Essays: The Character of Socrates; The Present State of Ethical Philosophy. Boston: Lamson, Wolffe, 1896.
Uncollected Writings: Essays, Addresses, Poems, Reviews and Letters by Ralph Waldo Emerson, edited by Charles C. Bigelow. New York: Lamb, 1912. (Includes especially work from the *Dial.*)
The Journals of Ralph Waldo Emerson, edited by Edward Waldo Emerson and Waldo Emerson Forbes. 10 vols. Boston: Houghton Mifflin, 1909–14. (Not all inclusive.)
Young Emerson Speaks: Unpublished Discourses on Many Subjects, edited by Arthur C. McGiffert, Jr. Boston: Houghton Mifflin, 1938.
The Letters of Ralph Waldo Emerson, edited by Ralph L. Rusk. 6 vols. New York: Columbia University Press, 1939. (There are other major collections of letters to Thomas Carlyle, Arthur Clough, William Furness, Herman Grimm, John Sterling, Henry David Thoreau, and Samuel Ward.)
The Early Lectures of Ralph Waldo Emerson. Cambridge, Mass.: Harvard University Press, 1959.
The Journals and Miscellaneous Notebooks, edited by William H. Gilman and others. Vol. I (1819–22), Cambridge, Mass.: Harvard University Press, 1960; II (1822–26), 1961; III (1826–32), 1963; IV (1832–34), 1964; V (1834–38), 1965; VI (1824–38), 1966; VII (1819–42), 1969.

Bibliographies

The Emerson Society Quarterly (1955–date), edited by Kenneth W. Cameron, provides bibliographical information on a continuing basis.

Carpenter, Frederic I. *Emerson Handbook.* New York: Hendricks House, 1953. (Invaluable for rich biographical and critical material also.)

Hubbell, G. S. *A Concordance to the Poems of Ralph Waldo Emerson.* New York: H. W. Wilson, 1932.
Stovall, Floyd, ed. "Emerson," in *Eight American Authors: A Review of Research and Criticism.* New York: Modern Language Association, 1956.

Biographies

Cabot, James. *A Memoir of Ralph Waldo Emerson.* 2 vols. Boston: Houghton Mifflin, 1887.
Cameron, Kenneth. *Emerson the Essayist.* 2 vols. Raleigh, N.C.: Thistle Press, 1945.
Emerson, Edward Waldo. *Emerson in Concord: A Memoir.* Boston: Houghton Mifflin, 1889.
Firkins, Oscar W. *Ralph Waldo Emerson.* Boston: Houghton Mifflin, 1915.
Hoeltje, Hubert. *Sheltering Tree.* Durham, N.C.: Duke University Press, 1943.
Perry, Bliss. *Emerson Today.* Princeton, N.J.: Princeton University Press, 1931.
Rusk, Ralph L. *The Life of Ralph Waldo Emerson.* New York: Scribner's, 1949.
Sanborn, F. B., ed. *The Genius and Character of Emerson.* Boston: Osgood, 1885. (Selected early views.)

Critical Studies

Adkins, Nelson F. "Emerson and the Bardic Tradition," *PMLA*, 63:662–77 (June 1948).
Berry, Edmund G. *Emerson's Plutarch.* Cambridge, Mass.: Harvard University Press, 1961.
Bishop, Jonathan. *Emerson on the Soul.* Cambridge, Mass.: Harvard University Press, 1964.
Blair, Walter, and Clarence Faust. "Emerson's Literary Method," *Modern Philology*, 42:79–95 (November 1944).
Brown, Percy W. "Emerson's Philosophy of Aesthetics," *Journal of Aesthetics and Art Criticism*, 15:350–54 (March 1957).
Carpenter, Frederic I. *Emerson and Asia.* Cambridge, Mass.: Harvard University Press, 1930.
Cowan, Michael. *City of the West: Emerson, America, and Urban Metaphor.* New Haven, Conn.: Yale University Press, 1967.
Hopkins, Vivian C. *Spires of Form: A Study of Emerson's Aesthetic Theory.* Cambridge, Mass.: Harvard University Press, 1951.
Konvitz, Milton, and Stephen Whicher, eds. *Emerson, A Collection of Critical Essays.* Englewood Cliffs, N.J.: Prentice-Hall, 1962. (Reprints articles by Daniel Aaron, Newton Arvin, John Dewey, Charles Feidelson, Jr., Norman Foerster, Robert Frost, William James, F. O. Matthiessen, Perry Miller, Henry B. Parkes, Sherman Paul, George Santayana, Henry Nash Smith, and Stephen Whicher.)
McEuen, Kathryn A. "Emerson's Rhymes," *American Literature*, 20:31–42 (March 1948).
Nicoloff, Philip L. *Emerson on Race and History: An Examination of English Traits.* New York: Columbia University Press, 1961.

Paul, Sherman. *Emerson's Angle of Vision: Man and Nature in American Experience.* Cambridge, Mass.: Harvard University Press, 1952.
Porte, Joel. *Emerson and Thoreau, Transcendentalists in Conflict.* Middletown, Conn.: Wesleyan University Press, 1966.
Schiller, Andrew. "Gnomic Structure in Emerson's Poetry," in *Papers of the Michigan Academy of Science, Arts and Letters,* Vol. 40 (Ann Arbor: University of Michigan Press, 1955), pp. 313–20.
Silver, Mildred. "Emerson and the Idea of Progress," *American Literature,* 12:1–19 (March 1940).
Smith, Henry Nash. "Emerson's Problem of Vocation: A Note on 'The American Scholar,'" *New England Quarterly,* 12:52–67 (March 1939).
Thompson, Frank T. "Emerson's Theory and Practice of Poetry," *PMLA,* 43:1170–84 (December 1928).
Wellek, René. "Emerson and German Philosophy," *New England Quarterly,* 16:41–62 (March 1943).
Whicher, Stephen. *Freedom and Fate: An Inner Life of Ralph Waldo Emerson.* Philadelphia: University of Pennsylvania Press, 1953.
Yohannan, J. D. "Emerson's Translations of Persian Poetry from German Sources," *American Literature,* 14:407–20 (January 1943).
Young, Charles L. *Emerson's Montaigne.* New York: Macmillan, 1941.

HENRY WADSWORTH LONGFELLOW
Principal Works

Coplas de Don Jorge Manrique, Translated from the Spanish . . . Boston: Allen and Ticknor, 1833.
Outre-Mer: A Pilgrimage beyond the Sea. 2 vols. Boston: Hilliard, Gray (Vol. I), Lilly, Wait (Vol. II), 1833–34.
Hyperion: A Romance. 2 vols. New York: S. Colman, 1839.
Voices of the Night. Cambridge, Mass.: J. Owen, 1839.
Ballads and Other Poems. Cambridge, Mass.: J. Owen, 1841.
Poems on Slavery. Cambridge, Mass.: J. Owen, 1842.
The Spanish Student, A Play in Three Acts. Cambridge, Mass.: J. Owen, 1843.
The Poets and Poetry of Europe, with Introductions and Biographical Notices by Henry Wadsworth Longfellow. Philadelphia: Carey and Hart, 1845.
The Belfry of Bruges and Other Poems. Cambridge, Mass.: J. Owen, 1846.
Evangeline, a Tale of Acadie. Boston: Ticknor, 1847.
Kavanagh, a Tale. Boston: Ticknor, Reed, and Fields, 1849.
The Seaside and the Fireside. Boston: Ticknor, Reed, and Fields, 1850.
The Golden Legend. Boston: Ticknor, Reed, and Fields, 1851.
The Song of Hiawatha. Boston: Ticknor and Fields, 1855.
Drift Wood, A Collection of Essays. Boston: Ticknor and Fields, 1857.
The Courtship of Miles Standish and Other Poems. Boston: Ticknor and Fields, 1858.
Tales of a Wayside Inn. Boston: Ticknor and Fields, 1863.
The Divine Comedy of Dante Alighieri, Translated by Henry Wadsworth Longfellow. 3 vols. Boston: Ticknor and Fields, 1865–67.

Flower-de-Luce. Boston: Ticknor and Fields, 1867.
The New England Tragedies. Boston: Ticknor and Fields, 1868. (Privately printed, 1867.)
The Divine Tragedy. Boston: Osgood, 1871.
Christus: A Mystery. 3 vols. Boston: Osgood, 1872.
Three Books of Song. Boston: Osgood, 1872.
Aftermath. Boston: Osgood, 1873.
The Hanging of the Crane. Boston: Mifflin, 1874.
The Masque of Pandora and Other Poems. Boston: Osgood, 1875.
Kéramos and Other Poems. Boston: Houghton, Osgood, 1878.
Ultima Thule. Boston: Mifflin, 1880.
In the Harbor. Boston: Houghton Mifflin, 1882.
Michael Angelo. London: Houghton Mifflin, 1883.

Selected and Collected Editions

Complete Works, edited by Horace E. Scudder. Riverside Edition. 11 vols. Boston: Houghton Mifflin, 1886. Reprinted in Standard Library Edition, with *Life* by Samuel Longfellow and illustrations. 14 vols. Boston: Houghton Mifflin, 1891. Reprinted also in Craigie Edition, with illustrations. 11 vols. Boston: Houghton Mifflin, 1904.
Complete Poetical Works, edited by Horace E. Scudder. Cambridge Edition. Boston: Houghton Mifflin, 1893. Reprinted in Household Edition, with illustrations. Boston: Houghton Mifflin, 1902.
Longfellow's Boyhood Poems, edited by George T. Little. Saratoga Springs, N.Y.: Ray W. Pettengill, 1925.
Henry Wadsworth Longfellow: Representative Selections, edited by Odell Shepard. American Writers Series. New York: American Book, 1934.

Letters

Letters of Henry Wadsworth Longfellow, edited by Andrew Hilen. Vol. I, 1814–36; Vol. II, 1837–43; other volumes in progress. New York: Oxford University Press, 1966–.

Bibliographies

Dana, H. W. L. "Henry Wadsworth Longfellow," in Vol. II of the *Cambridge History of American Literature.* 4 vols. New York: G. P. Putnam's Sons, 1917.
Livingston, Luther S. *A Bibliography of the First Editions in Book Form of the Writings of Henry Wadsworth Longfellow.* New York: Privately printed, 1908.

Critical and Biographical Studies

Arms, George T. "Longfellow," in *The Fields Were Green.* Stanford, Calif.: Stanford University Press, 1948.
Arvin, Newton. *Longfellow: His Life and Work.* Boston: Little, Brown, 1963.

Austin, George L. *Henry Wadsworth Longfellow: His Life, His Works, His Friendships.* Boston: Lee and Shepard, 1883.

Gorman, Herbert. *A Victorian American, Henry Wadsworth Longfellow.* New York: Doran, 1926.

Hatfield, James T. *New Light on Longfellow, with Special Reference to His Relations with Germany.* Boston: Houghton Mifflin, 1933.

Hawthorne, Manning, and Henry Dana. *The Origin and Development of Longfellow's "Evangeline."* Portland, Maine: Anthoensen Press, 1947.

Higginson, Thomas W. *Henry Wadsworth Longfellow.* American Men of Letters Series. Boston: Houghton Mifflin, 1902.

Hilen, Andrew. *Longfellow and Scandinavia.* New Haven, Conn.: Yale University Press, 1947.

Johnson, Carl L. *Professor Longfellow of Harvard.* Eugene: University of Oregon Press, 1944.

Jones, Howard M. "Longfellow," in *American Writers on American Literature,* edited by John Macy. New York: Liveright, 1931.

Longfellow, Samuel. *Life of Henry Wadsworth Longfellow.* 2 vols. Boston: Ticknor, 1886.

————. *Final Memorials of Henry Wadsworth Longfellow.* Boston: Ticknor, 1887.

Martin, Ernest. *L'Évangeline de Longfellow et la suite merveilleuse d'un poème.* Paris: Librairie Hachette, 1936.

More, Paul Elmer. "The Centenary of Longfellow," in *Shelburne Essays, Fifth Series.* Boston: Houghton Mifflin, 1908.

Morin, Paul. *Les Sources de l'Oeuvre de Henry Wadsworth Longfellow.* Paris: Émile Larose, 1913.

O'Neil, Rev. Joseph E., S.J. "Poet of the Feeling Heart," in *American Classics Reconsidered,* edited by Rev. Harold C. Gardiner, S.J. New York: Scribner's, 1958.

Scudder, Horace E. "Longfellow and His Art," in *Men and Books.* Boston: Houghton Mifflin, 1887.

Thompson, Lawrance. *Young Longfellow, 1807–1843.* New York: Macmillan, 1938.

Van Schaick, John, Jr. *The Characters in "Tales of a Wayside Inn."* Boston: Universalist Publishing House, 1939.

Wagenknecht, Edward. *Longfellow: A Full-Length Portrait.* New York: Longmans, Green, 1955.

————. *Mrs. Longfellow: Selected Letters and Journals of Fanny Appleton.* New York: Longmans, Green, 1956.

————. *Henry Wadsworth Longfellow: Portrait of an American Humanist.* New York: Oxford University Press, 1966.

Whitman, Iris. *Longfellow and Spain.* New York: Instituto de las Españas en los Estados Unidos, 1927.

Williams, Cecil B. *Henry Wadsworth Longfellow.* New York: Twayne, 1964.

Williams, Stanley T. "Longfellow," in Vol. II of *The Spanish Background of American Literature.* 2 vols. New Haven, Conn.: Yale University Press, 1955.

HENRY D. THOREAU
Separate Works Published during Thoreau's Lifetime

A Week on the Concord and Merrimack Rivers. Boston and Cambridge: James Munroe, 1849.
Walden; or, Life in the Woods. Boston: Ticknor and Fields, 1854.

Posthumous Selected Prose Collections

Excursions. Boston: Ticknor and Fields, 1863.
The Maine Woods. Boston: Ticknor and Fields, 1864.
Cape Cod. Boston: Ticknor and Fields, 1865.
A Yankee in Canada, with Anti-Slavery and Reform Papers. Boston: Ticknor and Fields, 1866.
Early Spring in Massachusetts. Boston: Houghton Mifflin, 1881.
Summer: From the Journal of Henry D. Thoreau. Boston: Houghton Mifflin, 1884.
Winter: From the Journal of Henry D. Thoreau. Boston: Houghton Mifflin, 1888.
Autumn: From the Journal of Henry D. Thoreau. Boston: Houghton Mifflin, 1892.
Miscellanies. Boston: Houghton Mifflin, 1894.
The Service. Boston: Charles E. Goodspeed, 1902.
Sir Walter Raleigh. Boston: Bibliophile Society, 1905.

Poetry

Poems of Nature, edited by Henry S. Salt. Boston: Houghton Mifflin, 1895.
Collected Poems, edited by Carl Bode. Baltimore: Johns Hopkins Press, 1964.

Journal

Journal, edited by Bradford Torrey, 14 vols. Boston: Houghton Mifflin, 1906.
Journal, edited by Bradford Torrey and Francis H. Allen. 14 vols. Boston: Houghton Mifflin, 1949.
Consciousness in Concord (lost volume of the *Journal*), edited by Perry Miller. Boston: Houghton Mifflin, 1958.

Collected Editions

The Writings of Henry David Thoreau. Riverside Edition. 10 vols. Boston: Houghton Mifflin, 1894 [1893].
The Writings of Henry David Thoreau. Manuscript and Walden editions. 20 volumes. Boston: Houghton Mifflin, 1906.

Letters

Letters to Various Persons. Boston: Ticknor and Fields, 1865.

Familiar Letters of Henry David Thoreau, edited by F. B. Sanborn. Boston: Houghton Mifflin, 1894.
Correspondence, edited by Walter Harding and Carl Bode. New York: New York University Press, 1958.

Bibliographies

Since 1941 there has been a continuing bibliography in the quarterly of the Thoreau Society, *Thoreau Society Bulletin* (Geneseo, New York).

Allen, Francis H. *A Bibliography of Henry David Thoreau*. Boston: Houghton Mifflin, 1908.

Burnham, Philip E., and Carvel Collins. "Contributions to a Bibliography of Thoreau, 1938–1945," *Bulletin of Bibliography*, 19:16–18, 37–40 (1946).

Harding, Walter. *A Centennial Check-List of the Editions of Henry David Thoreau's "Walden."* Charlottesville: University of Virginia Press, 1954.

Spiller, Robert E., and others, eds. *Literary History of the United States*, Vol. 3. New York: Macmillan, 1948.

Stovall, Floyd, ed. *Eight American Authors: A Review of Research and Criticism*. New York: Modern Language Association, 1956.

Wade, J. S. "A Contribution to a Bibliography from 1909 to 1936," *Journal of the New York Entomological Society*, 47:163–203 (1939).

White, William. *A Henry David Thoreau Bibliography, 1908–1937*. Boston: F. W. Faxon, 1939.

Biographical Studies

Atkinson, Brooks. *Henry Thoreau: The Cosmic Yankee*. New York: Knopf, 1927.

Bazalgette, Léon. *Henry Thoreau: Bachelor of Nature*, translated by Van Wyck Brooks. New York: Harcourt, Brace, 1924.

Brooks, Van Wyck. *The Flowering of New England*. Revised ed. New York: Dutton, 1940. Pp. 286–302, 359–73.

Canby, Henry S. *Thoreau*. Boston: Houghton Mifflin, 1939.

Channing, William Ellery. *Thoreau, the Poet-Naturalist*. Boston: Roberts Brothers, 1873.

Emerson, E. W., and W. E. Forbes, editors. *Journals of Ralph Waldo Emerson*. 10 vols. Boston: Houghton Mifflin, 1900–14.

Harding, Walter. *The Days of Henry Thoreau*. New York: Knopf, 1966.

Krutch, Joseph Wood. *Thoreau*. New York: William Sloane Associates, 1948.

Rusk, Ralph L. *The Letters of Ralph Waldo Emerson*. 6 vols. New York: Columbia University Press, 1939.

Salt, Henry S. *The Life of Henry David Thoreau*. London: R. Bentley, 1890; revised, London: W. Scott, 1896.

Sanborn, F. B. *The Life of Henry David Thoreau*. Boston: Houghton Mifflin, 1882.

Seybold, Ethel. *Thoreau: The Quest and the Classics*. New Haven, Conn.: Yale University Press, 1951.

Shanley, James Lyndon. *The Making of Walden*. Chicago: University of Chicago Press, 1957.
Whicher, George F. *Walden Revisited*. Chicago: Packard, 1945.

Critical Studies

Anderson, Charles R. *The Magic Circle of Walden*. New York: Holt, Rinehart and Winston, 1968.
Cook, Reginald L. *Passage to Walden*. Boston: Houghton Mifflin, 1949.
Harding, Walter. *A Thoreau Handbook*. New York: New York University Press, 1959.
————, editor. *Thoreau: A Century of Criticism*. Dallas: Southern Methodist University Press, 1954. (Contains among other essays Emerson's tribute and the essays by Lowell and Stevenson.)
Matthiessen, F. O. *American Renaissance*. New York: Oxford University Press, 1941.
Meltzer, Milton, and Walter Harding. *A Thoreau Profile*. New York: Crowell, 1962.
Paul, Sherman. *The Shores of America: Thoreau's Inward Exploration*. Urbana: University of Illinois Press, 1958.
Stoller, Leo. *After Walden: Thoreau's Changing Views on Economic Man*. Stanford, Calif.: Stanford University Press, 1957.
Torrey, Bradford. *Friends on the Shelf*. Boston: Houghton Mifflin, 1906.

WALT WHITMAN
Principal Writings

Leaves of Grass. Brooklyn, 1855.
Leaves of Grass. Brooklyn, 1856.
Leaves of Grass. Boston: Thayer and Eldridge, 1860.
Drum-Taps. New York, 1865.
Leaves of Grass. New York, 1867.
Democratic Vistas. Washington, D.C., 1871.
Leaves of Grass. Boston: Osgood, 1882.
Specimen Days and Collect. Philadelphia: Rees Welsh, 1882.
Leaves of Grass. Philadelphia: David McKay, 1891.
Calamus, edited by R. M. Bucke. Boston: Laurens Maynard, 1897.
The Wound Dresser, edited by R. M. Bucke. Boston: Small, Maynard, 1898.
An American Primer, edited by Horace Traubel. Boston: Small, Maynard, 1904.
The Gathering of the Forces, edited by Cleveland Rodgers and John Black. New York: Putnam's, 1920.

Selected and Collected Editions

Complete Poetry and Selected Prose and Letters, edited by Emory Holloway. New York: Random House, 1938.

The Complete Poetry and Prose of Walt Whitman, with an Introduction by Malcolm Cowley. New York: Pellegrini and Cudahy, 1948.
The Poetry and Prose of Walt Whitman, edited by Louis Untermeyer. New York: Simon and Schuster, 1949.
Collected Writings, edited by Gay Wilson Allen and E. Sculley Bradley. New York: New York University Press, 1961.

Bibliographies

Allen, Gay Wilson. *Twenty-Five Years of Walt Whitman Bibliography, 1918–1942.* Boston: F. W. Faxon, 1943.
Miller, Edwin H., and Rosalind S. Miller. *Walt Whitman's Correspondence: A Check List.* New York: New York Public Library, 1957.
Tanner, J. T. F. *Walt Whitman: A Supplementary Bibliography, 1961–1967.* Kent, Ohio: Kent State University Press, 1968.
Wells, Carolyn, and Alfred F. Goldsmith. *A Concise Bibliography of the Works of Walt Whitman.* Boston: Houghton Mifflin, 1922.
White, William. *Walt Whitman's Journalism: A Bibliography.* Detroit: Wayne State University Press, 1969.

Critical and Biographical Studies

Allen, Gay Wilson. *Walt Whitman Handbook.* Chicago: Packard, 1946.
———. *The Solitary Singer.* New York: Macmillan, 1955.
———. *Walt Whitman as Man, Poet, and Legend.* Carbondale: Southern Illinois University Press, 1961.
Asselineau, Roger. *The Evolution of Walt Whitman: The Creation of a Personality.* Cambridge, Mass.: Harvard University Press, 1960.
———. *The Evolution of Walt Whitman: The Creation of a Book.* Cambridge, Mass.: Harvard University Press, 1962.
Canby, Henry Seidel. *Walt Whitman, An American.* Boston: Houghton Mifflin, 1943.
Chari, V. K. *Whitman in the Light of Vedantic Mysticism: An Interpretation.* Lincoln: University of Nebraska Press, 1964.
Chase, Richard. *Walt Whitman Reconsidered.* New York: William Sloane Associates, 1955.
De Selincourt, Basil. *Walt Whitman: A Critical Study.* New York: Kennerly, 1914.
Fausset, Hugh I'Anson. *Walt Whitman: Poet of Democracy.* New Haven, Conn.: Yale University Press, 1942.
Holloway, Emory. *Whitman: An Interpretation in Narrative.* New York: Knopf, 1926.
Miller, Edwin H. *A Century of Whitman Criticism.* Bloomington: Indiana University Press, 1969.
———. *Walt Whitman's Poetry: A Psychological Journey.* New York: New York University Press, 1969.
———, ed. *The Artistic Legacy of Walt Whitman.* New York: New York University Press, 1969.

Miller, James E., Jr. *A Critical Guide to Leaves of Grass.* Chicago: University of Chicago Press, 1957.
———. *Walt Whitman.* New York: Twayne, 1962.
Pearce, Roy H., ed. *Whitman: A Collection of Critical Essays.* Englewood Cliffs, N.J.: Prentice-Hall, 1962.
Perry, Bliss. *Walt Whitman, His Life and Work.* Boston: Houghton Mifflin, 1906.
Schyberg, Frederik. *Walt Whitman,* translated by Evie Allison Allen. New York: Columbia University Press, 1951.
Traubel, Horace. *With Walt Whitman in Camden.* Carbondale: Southern Illinois University Press, 1964.
Waskow, Howard J. *Whitman: Explorations in Form.* Chicago: University of Chicago Press, 1966.

ABOUT THE AUTHORS

About the Authors

THEODORE HORNBERGER, a professor of English at the University of Pennsylvania, is co-editor of *The Literature of the United States* and the author of *Scientific Thought in the American College 1638–1800,* among other books.

LEWIS LEARY is William Rand Kenan Professor of English at the University of North Carolina at Chapel Hill. He has written several books including *Mark Twain's Letters to Mary* and *John Greenleaf Whittier.*

JOSEPHINE MILES, poet and critic, is a professor of English at the University of California, Berkeley. Among her books are *Eras and Modes in English Poetry, Style and Proportion, Poems 1930–1960,* and *Kinds of Affection.*

EDWARD L. HIRSH is a professor of English at Boston College. He taught previously at St. Joseph College, West Hartford, Connecticut.

LEON EDEL is Henry James Professor of English and American Letters at New York University. The author of numerous books, he has won the Pulitzer Prize in biography and the National Book Award for nonfiction.

RICHARD CHASE was a professor of English at Columbia University and a fellow of the Indiana School of Letters. Among his books are *The Democratic Vista, The American Novel and Its Tradition,* and *Walt Whitman Reconsidered.*

INDEX

Index